"Leslie Leyland Fields has done those of us interested in *The Spirit of Food* a great service by collecting thirty-four wonderful essays and recipes. Her careful choices remind us of the many ways God can be present in the human experience of eating. The essays on fasting, feasting, and the Lord's Supper join others which recall the experiences of grace or the call for justice which occur in everyday meals."

—Shannon Jung

author of *Food for Life: The Spirituality and Ethics of Eating*

"I loved reading all these wise, honest, and funny people writing about eating—the conundrums and efforts and delights involved in our relationship to food, and God, and God-as-food. It's a beautiful and inspiring collection of essays. I've been praying and eating better since reading it."

—Debbie Blue

author of *Sensual Orthodoxy*

THE SPIRIT OF FOOD

The Spirit of
FOOD

Thirty-four Writers on
Feasting and Fasting toward God

Edited by
Leslie Leyland Fields

 CASCADE *Books* · Eugene, Oregon

THE SPIRIT OF FOOD
Thirty-four Writers on Feasting and Fasting toward God

Cascade Books
An Imprint of Wipf and Stock Publishers
199 W. 8th Ave., Suite 3
Eugene, OR 97401

www.wipfandstock.com

ISBN 13: 978-1-60899-592-9

Published in partnership with The Other Journal, Seattle, Washington.
www.theotherjournal.com

Cataloging-in-Publication data:

    The spirit of food : thirty-four writers on feasting and fasting toward God /
edited by Leslie Leyland Fields.

    xxvi + 258 p. ; 23 cm.

    ISBN 13: 978-1-60899-592-9

    1. Food—Religious aspects—Christianity. 2. Dinners and dining—Religious
aspects—Christianity. I. Fields, Leslie Leyland. II. Title.

BR115.N87 S7 2010

PERMISSIONS AND CREDITS

To every contributor here, amazing people all, whose work and food life has so deeply fed my own, I can only bow my head and say, *grace*.

Contents

> Patty Kirk takes us into wild berry patches in Oklahoma where she fills her bucket and her soul with God's presence and provision. Back at home, she teaches us to make jelly and preserves from the bounty.
>
> Recipe: Apricot, Chokecherry, and Plum Jams 6

> As he uses his homegrown tomatoes to make a soup, Brian Volck ponders the sensory delights of growing produce in his backyard garden and the many ways that meals knit families together.
>
> Recipe: Spicy Tomato Soup 15

> Jeanne Murray Walker resigns from her faltering church and finds herself frequently visiting Produce Junction, a farmer's market housed in a shack in an inner-city neighborhood; her visits are marked by imperfect vegetables and unexpected grace.
>
> Recipe: Scalloped Potatoes for the Church Potluck 29

In the Kitchen

Denise Frame Harlan lets her curiosity run free and discovers, with help from her friends and a copy of *Supper of the Lamb*, an irrepressible love for the world, for her friends, and for turkey pie.

Recipe: City Slicker's First Pot Pie, Advanced Pot Pie 80

Chef Fred Raynaud gives a chef's-eye view of the making of a perfect Hollandaise sauce, which all depends upon the emulsifier—a larger picture of Christ's own work in our lives.

Recipe: Cilantro Citrus Hollandaise 87

After an earnest fifteen-year abstention from meat, Alissa Herbaly Coons finds a solace in the stockpot, coming to terms with her place in the food chain and the glory to be found in the breaking not only of bread, but of bones as well.

Recipe: One-Pot Paprikás Chicken 96

The Minneapolis bridge collapses just minutes before her son's commute over its span. Life's dangers are assessed and assuaged with the security and tradition of fixing and serving her grandmother's Swedish pancakes.

Recipe: Swedish Pancakes with Lingonberry Sauce 109

The Ways We Eat

Lauren Winner, Jewish by birth and upbringing, takes us into a kosher kitchen where she reflects on her own growing awareness of food and the ways she can better practice faithfulness to God.

Recipe: Lauren's Fresh Cherry Cobbler 117

Fasting

At the Table of the Lord

Feasting

Acknowledgments

When the deadline for the manuscript is finally met (whew!) and the months (years) of work and thought is pulled together, there comes one last task—writing this page. I almost skipped it. In the flurry and crush of essays, all coming in the midst of too much travel and a pressing due date, it felt at first like *just one more thing.* But this book is not complete without it. I cannot send these pages out into the world without some other names attached, names that otherwise might not be seen. First, and most, is Andrew David, who edits for *The Other Journal* as well as the Experiences in Evangelicalism series with Cascade Books. He did nothing less than share the trench with me, taking this project on with an enthusiasm and thoroughness that astonished me. He sacrificed much— including of course, leisure, sleep, real food. (While reading sumptuous essays about the spirituality of food, Andrew confessed to consuming sugary cereals as dinner.) I cheered him on—because I needed his keen eye and sharp yet gracious editor's pen to get us all over the line. I would gladly share a trench with Andrew again.

I want to thank all the good people at Cascade Books of Wipf and Stock Publishers, including Tyler Stewart, Christian Amondson, and especially Jim Tedrick, who believed what I have believed since the conception of this project several years ago: that it's time to speak deeply and beautifully about the sacrament of food. Jim gets special thanks beyond this for letting me interrupt his honeymoon with several panicked emails—all answered kindly.

I must thank my family, who endured my preoccupation and absence the last few months, and who always eat my bread appreciatively, assuring I make more.

One last thing I know: this book has changed me and all who have seen it before you. It is a testament to the force and beauty of the contributors' words that while editing the fasting essays, I was moved to fast. While reading the recipes, I began to gather their ingredients. I will never slice an onion, prepare hollandaise sauce, harvest tomatoes, or serve pecan pie the same way again. I expect every reader will feel the same.

Until the time we can sit down and share a meal (I'll pay!), I thank you all.

Introduction

The season's first salmon hang headless in my daughter's hands, one fish in each, as she walks them up the hill to the house. From the front steps, I can see their heft and length, the shine of their silvered scales, their shimmering backs. I am anxious to hold them myself. It is the first week of the commercial salmon fishery, a profession my children and husband have worked in nearly since birth. For me, it's been thirty-three seasons here on this remote Alaskan island.

I grasp their tails from my daughter on the porch, slide their arm-length bodies onto the counter-sized cutting board. With one hand firm on the skin-thin armor, I begin to steak out the fish with the other. The first cut almost makes me gasp as though I have cut my own finger—the flesh is deep carmine, so bright—is this my own blood? I know this color, can see it, even taste it in the sleep of memory. How many salmon have I gutted and cleaned and portioned on the shore of my island, on this very cutting board these thirty-three years? I keep slicing, the dissection so enlivening my senses I do not measure or make any attempt at uniformity. How shall I cook it, this fish we have been waiting for all winter? Shall I grill it with melted butter, minced garlic, and white wine, my favorite flavors? No, for the first fish, something new, something un-tried and spontaneous, fitting this exact moment and these precise two fish. I begin with melted butter and minced garlic then riffle through my cupboard pulling down brown sugar, a spicy pepper blend, parsley . . . formulating as my hands consider each potential spice, a slow idea of what I would aim for, yes, this time a sweet and spicy crust.

Even now, I couldn't t say how many minutes to grill the fish. I don't follow a clock when grilling. I am not interested in creating a numerical formula for the safe and simplified replication of my attempts at perfec-tion. I stand and watch, testing the juices, whisking each piece off when the flesh begins to turn translucent. Each piece on its own schedule.

I carry the platter of steaks to the kitchen. The mood at the table today is jubilant. Everyone has just come in from a morning on the ocean, picking salmon from the nets. My four older children, who run their own boats, report a good catch. The northeast storm forecast for this morning had mostly passed. Everyone is still fresh in the season, before the long weeks of work drain their strength and anticipation.

I set the salmon on the table, the steaks assembled in a glass dish. Around it, I arrange bowls of steamed broccoli, rice pilaf, fresh fruit salad, ciabatta that I finished making this morning. Meals later in the summer will include wild mushrooms from the pasture, fresh halibut and cod from our front yard waters, deer from our own mountainside, salmonberries from the meadow, leaf lettuce from our garden—if the voles are merciful.

While the food steams on the table, eight faces look at me expectantly, waiting for the signal for prayer. "I'm going to do something a little different today," I say hesitant, knowing that multiple appetites are rumbling under the table and knowing how puny the spirit can feel before such need.

"This is the first salmon of the season. You all know the tradition that fishermen kiss the first fish. Anyone do that today?" My oldest son rolls his eyes, wanting only to eat. I hurry on.

"I'm going to read something before we start."

I pull my Bible onto the table, and before anyone can resist, I begin: "This is from the book of Job:

'But ask the animals and they will teach you,
 Or the birds of the air, and they will tell you;
 Or speak to the earth and it will teach you,
 Or let the fish of the sea inform you.
 Which of all these does not know
That the hand of the Lord has done this?
 In his hand is the life of every creature
 And the breath of all mankind.'"

Everyone listens, watching the food. Then I pray aloud for all of us, that this season we will not forget this. I want to say far more, to deliver a sermon, but I stop, knowing the wafers of fish on our tongues will deliver its own message.

We eat. Faces are too close to the plates, forks are shoveling, heads lift with butter smeared on cheeks and crumbs lodged in beards. Everyone talks with their mouth full; we tease each other; someone will have to yell to get the salad; at least one cup of iced tea will be spilled, and we'll run out of bread. These are our glorious, blessed feasts.

⤙

Like many in our culture today, I am fascinated by food—the whorl of purple cabbage as I slice, each head a distinct pattern as unique as any fingerprint; the crust that forms on a loaf of whole wheat sourdough; the elasticity of a skein of hand-rolled pasta hanging in my hands before the drop into a boiling pot. Not just the handling and preparation of food, but its history, its science, the art of arranging its astonishing colors and textures.

Perhaps I would love food no matter my own life story, but I love it all the more for having discovered it on my own, as an adult. While growing up, food was a grim necessity that I mostly avoided. Breakfast for my entire childhood was leftover twelve-grain cereal, the same pot of cereal heated over and over each day until it was gone. Lunch was a single sandwich in a bag, always the same. For supper, we ate canned mackerel mixed with mayonnaise, lettuce, and raisins, or boiled soybeans, or chicken necks and rice. There was little or no food between meals. We did not cook from recipes—no matter the recipe, we didn't have the ingredients. Cooking was more a matter of assembling whatever we had and heating it, if desired. But we grew massive gardens, and our winter paucity was eased by an overflow of vegetables that assured at least a fresh salad every summer night.

When I left home at seventeen, I did not know how to eat. The whole world became one giant cafeteria filled with new dishes and foods (real spaghetti sauce!). I saw that food could be beautiful and sensual and spiritual. I wanted to eat everything, and nearly did, trying to fill that long, deep hunger. Overeating was followed by starvation, beginning years of struggle to find a way to approach food without fear, lust, or guilt.

I have been healthy for a long time now, and I have found that the food that once threatened me contained its own seeds of healing. I feed myself and many people every day, and I labor joyfully and passionately to feed them well with homemade jellies, grass-fed beef and deer, whole-grain hand-made breads.

I am hardly alone in my various food pursuits. We've become a nation of foodies, whether the food is junk and fast or organic and slow, whether boutique fare or diner fare, comfort food or haute cuisine, whether we're gaining weight or losing it.

Eating out is a national pastime. Cooking in and hosting supper clubs and dinner parties is popular entertainment. Culinary schools are full. And food isn't just for eating anymore—we are watching more cooking shows than ever. At least one network is devoted entirely to food. Even radio shows bring us tales from the kitchen. A widening array of books on food stacks the best-seller lists and the shelves of local bookstores: cookbooks, food memoirs, exposés, histories, biographies.

This national attention to all things food-related is needed and overdue. Perhaps we are revolting against the age of information that harnesses us to desks and computers for most of the day, our bodies forgotten in this bodiless realm. Many writers, growers, nutritionists, and theologians are calling us back from a kind of forgetfulness and inattention to our physicality, our appetites and our food, a neglect that quite literally threatens our health. We eat far too many meals one-handed, the other on a steering wheel. So many of us eat too much of the wrong foods too fast. Family dinners are threatened by our all-consuming schedules. We all know the consequences: rising rates of obesity and diabetes, the pandemic backlash of eating disorders, the projected costs to our national health, the growing toxicity of our soil and food supply.

In the midst of plenty, we have forgotten how to eat, it seems. Our kids have grown up in a world where ketchup and French fries are counted as vegetables, where soda is the beverage of choice, and where meat and a gooey dessert is expected at every meal. I see schoolchildren eating diced hot dogs and slurping salted, fried noodles from Styrofoam cups for lunch everyday. Meal bars are increasingly replacing plates of steaming dinners and hot breakfasts. We are in the midst of a "national eating disorder" pronounces the *New Yorker* magazine.

There's a lot at stake besides our personal health, though that is serious enough. Increasingly, we are understanding the wider costs of our food choices: the impact on our God-created environment as we have shifted from family farms and ranches to Agri-businesses, where efficiency overrules integrity and environmental stewardship. Genetically modified foods raise a number of biological and ethical questions. The inhumane treatment of animals that provide us with meat, dairy, and eggs cause us to question our compassion and responsibility. With frequent breakouts of food-borne illnesses, we wonder about the safety of our food supply.

If we follow the news, the best-selling books, the latest diet trend, the debates and exposés of our national food practices and production, we can feel overwhelmed. Guilty. The table we stand before is no longer a banquet table offering sustenance; it's a minefield threatening our own destruction or the destruction of the planet. With our plate in hand, our stomachs rumbling, and our well-informed minds on alert, we survey the offerings as we walk the length of the table: that appetizer is full of trans fat; that plate of fruit is bathed in pesticides; that salad exploits migrant workers; that noodle casserole is nutritionally bankrupt; that stroganoff comes from abused animals. We are paralyzed. What do we choose? How do we eat? How do we respond as people of faith? And if we make all the right choices, will good food rightly procured and produced then save us?

Even as I ask these questions, I know something is missing. Something our grandmothers and mothers knew at their church potlucks, as they carried to the communal tables Velveeta broccoli casseroles and Jell-O salads greener than any fruit dared to grow. In our zeal for purity and right living, we may have forgotten something other generations and cultures knew. That food is more than politics; food is more than economics; food is more than culture, entertainment, nutrition, even justice. As important as each of these is, none of them singly identifies or describes all that food is and does and is meant to be.

Food is nothing less than sacrament. All food is given by God and is given as a means to sustain not just our bodies, but also our minds and our spirits. In all of its aspects—growth, harvest, preparation, and presentation—food is given as a primary means of drawing us into right relationship toward God, toward his creation and his people. Even its intentional absence, through fasting, pulls us toward a deeper dependence on God and one another.

As I turn to the Scriptures now, I am amazed at the centrality of food in its pages. God's redemption story opens in a garden, where some of God's first words to the first man and woman were words about eating: "Behold, I have given you every herb bearing seed . . . and every tree

... to you it shall be for meat." The whole world is presented to them as their table. "Every bite of food, given by God himself, is to make God known to man, to make man's life communion with God," Alexander Schmemman writes in *For the Life of the World* (14). But the world fell into sin soon after those loving provisions. Our dependence on food, air, and water became a tightly enclosed circle, where these elements became an end in themselves, the source of both life and fulfillment.

Into the midst of this lifeless cycle, Jesus came. He came as "living water," as the "bread of life," and he spent much of his time feeding the hungry both truth and loaves of barley bread. He taught us to pray for "our daily bread." He ate and drank so freely with friends and sinners he was accused of gluttony and drunkenness. He fasted as well, demonstrating his physical and spiritual dependence upon his heavenly father. He chose to spend his last hours on earth at a dinner with his disciples, where he chose homely bread and local wine to mark his death and ongoing life within us. When he returned, after death, he proved his physical presence among his friends by sharing a meal with them. While we sup on the bread and wine of the Eucharist, we wait hungrily for the marriage supper of the Lamb, when we will drink and feast to the *now*ness of the kingdom of God, its presence made real and present to us through its wondrous food.

In that feast and after that feast, we will do far more than simply sit at a banquet table, eating food God has made holy. Zechariah, my new favorite Minor Prophet, who surely loved food, tells us that at the end of time, when heaven comes down to earth, a throng will gather on a pilgrimage to the new Jerusalem, to worship God and celebrate the Feast of Tabernacles, an eight-day festival of eating and worship. Zechariah ends his entire book with this image of heaven:

> On that day HOLY TO THE LORD will be inscribed on the bells
> of the horses, and the cooking pots in the LORD's house will be
> like the sacred bowls in front of the altar. Every pot in Jerusalem
> and Judah will be holy to the LORD Almighty, and all who come
> to sacrifice will take some of the pots and cook in them.

Every pot will be holy to the Lord. Mine. Yours. And every soup and vegetable and grain and fish and casserole and soufflé and crepe prepared within them will be holy to all who partake, and holy to the God to whom it all belongs.

Perhaps we're not to wait for this day. Perhaps we are to begin now, growing, harvesting, cooking, serving from pots made holy by our work, our love, our worship. I don't pretend to understand or even to practice all of this now. I am only beginning to implement ways to better attend to the spirit of food in my life. But I have found lots of help. I have gathered around myself a company of adventurous and inspiring writers and cooks who have opened their gardens, their kitchens, and their tables. With theology as enriching as their food, they illuminate the many ways that food has drawn them toward God, toward his creation, toward his church, and toward their neighbors. In a time of great interest and equal confusion over the place of food in our lives, this rich collection will delight the senses, feed the spirit, enlarge our understanding, and deepen our ability to "eat and drink to the glory of God." Take, eat, and be blessed!

Patty Kirk is the author of *Confessions of an Amateur Believer.* She is Writer in Residence and associate professor of English at John Brown University. She has an MFA in creative writing from the University of Arkansas and has taught and studied in Berlin, Beijing, Hong Kong, Boston, New Orleans, and Irvine, California. She and her family live on a farm in eastern Oklahoma. This essay is an excerpt from *Starting from Scratch: Memoirs of a Wandering Cook.*

1

Wild Fruit

It is late summer in eastern Oklahoma: ninety-one degrees. Sixty-five percent humidity. Forty percent chance of rain.

As usual during this season, I am in the middle of preserving a batch of wild fruit. Not because I am starving. Or because I am some sort of homemaking weirdo, eager to impress my friends with my culinary prowess. Or because I have nothing to do. I struggle mightily to fit the time-consuming tasks of picking and washing and preserving seasonal fruits between writing and teaching, getting my family ready for school and work, starting loads of clothes and dishes, making my romantic daughter Charlotte the bread that she told me she had dreamed about this morning, cooking dinner, and getting us all into bed by ten o'clock so that my husband can get me up at five thirty the next morning and start the whole process all over again.

I am not complaining. I do most of what I do—write, grade papers, bake my daughter's fantasies, wash the clothes, cook the dinner, and even wash up afterward—because I like to. And, although these responsibilities often pile up and become onerous, gathering and preserving fruit is not just another chore. It is my reward.

We are surrounded by fruit in this part of Oklahoma, and I pick and preserve whenever I can, all summer long and on into the fall. First the sour dewberries that grow in the ditch out by the road. Then domesticated blueberries from a farm across the state-line in Arkansas, where you pay less if you pick your own. Then blackberries from the overgrown former racetrack behind our house. Then wild plums from outside my neighbors' chicken houses. Then elderberries that I steal from a neighbor's neglected field out by the highway. Then crab apples from the ornamental trees at the university where I work. And so on as the weather turns colder and black walnuts fall from the trees in our woods and the bitter wild persimmons freeze and darken and become as sweet and soft as dates. All of these fruits accumulate in my consciousness throughout the summer and fall and winter, and it is no more of a chore to acquire them than to desire them in the first place. I gather and preserve fruit because it is the best thing I do all year long.

Berry-picking is my year's retreat—my "thin place," to use a Celtic Christian term from a book I'm reading for a place where one feels unusually aware of God's nearness. Every aspect of berry-picking has spiritual relevance for me. Nothing proves God's abundant love like the provision of huge blackberries among the brambles, arriving in such profusion that the birds and deer and June bugs and my family and friends and I combined can't begin to deplete them. Even our dogs—who, though not normally fruit-eaters, always accompany me berry-picking if they are around—hunger for the sweet black nuggets among the thorns, and paw at the brambles for their share.

Nothing shows God's foresight like the shade of a tree that I share with nearby cows when I think I will faint from heat in the armor I am wearing against ticks and chiggers and thorns and sun: my jeans tucked into thick socks and boots, a long-sleeved turtleneck under a more thorn-resistant button-down shirt, tight rubber gloves, sweatband, hat. Nothing makes me as aware of the curse of toiling, or the threat of serpents at my heel, as thrusting my arm through the prickly branches for the same prize that the skinny green tree snake seeks, the same glistening berry, taut with sweetness. When I am picking berries, I am in communion with all creation and with God as at no other time. My daughters call me from the yard, their voices so far off and faint that they sound like birds, and I can't tell if it is the phone or their hunger or a visitor that is so urgent that I must be called away. Often I feign deafness and pick on until the bowl is too heavy and full to carry back home without leaving a black trail for any little animals that might scamper in my wake.

Today it is the elderberries, from which I will make jelly. I picked them yesterday evening. The birds had gotten almost all the berries on the few bushes on our place, and I knew my neighbor wouldn't want the berries for himself. No one does. In his overgrown pasture, the elderberries hang in heavy, flat-bottomed bunches, bending down the slender branches to the tops of the tall grasses and thistle beneath. I waded through the high weeds, awkward in my husband's rubber boots, now and then popping a puffy, green apricot underfoot. They're not really apricots, despite the name, but a local species of *Passiflora*, passion fruit—also called maypops—that grow on spiny vines and have a heady, passion-fruit flavor and smell when ripe. There are masses of wild apricots this year, more than I have ever noticed before. They, too, will go uneaten by my neighbor and anyone else who comes this way—except me, perhaps. I may try jam from them this year, since there are so many. They will be ready for harvest when they go soft and begin to shrivel up on the outside, probably in a few weeks, judging from the already powerful smell of the squashed ones.

Last night, after I got home from picking the elderberries, I rinsed them, clump by clump, in cold water and laid them out on an old sheet to dry. And this morning I spent an hour pulling the tiny black balls from their stems. If you have never seen elderberries, you need to know that they are among the most beautiful berries on earth and the most satisfying to collect. The bushes have no thorns, and each time you reach up to pick yields a satisfyingly heavy clump. Imagine a flat plate of small, black berries, each one lifted up on a tiny stem. Imagine Queen Anne's lace with dark berries instead of little white blossoms. You will want to eat them, they are so beautiful, and you may do so, but their flavor is alarming. Not so much sour or even bitter, as they are often described, but bland and vaguely herbal. Like medicine of some sort—which, in fact, they have been used for, in times past throughout the centuries and around the world for treating everything from colds to burns and acne.

The berries are cooking now. Cooking, they gain a weirdly appealing smell of dirt and air and winey fruit, which is also how they taste if you spoon up a bit of the hot juice. And the black-purple jelly I will make—once the juice has dripped through a piece of cloth in which I will suspend the cooked berries from my pot rack and once I have added almost a whole bag of sugar and a lemon or two and cooked the mixture down until it drips in a sheet from a spoon—will taste like that too: like earth and air and wine, only sweeter and more delectable. Like the outdoors. Like Oklahoma in late summer. Like the rain that is predicted and hangs in the air this moment and is visible in the sagging clouds but still hasn't come down.

Last week I attended a summer workshop for interested faculty at my nondenominational Christian university. We were learning about the shared doctrine of the various brands of Christianity we practice and believe in, the fundamentals our students learn in more detail in a required course called Essentials of Evangelical Christianity. As a relatively recent convert to Christianity, I take advantage of any available opportunities to learn more about my faith. Plus, we get paid to attend such faculty development workshops, which is nice. It's like being paid to gather blackberries.

Nevertheless, in class I was struggling to stay rapt. A friend's husband had dropped off a big bucket of goose plums: thumb-sized, bright red, startlingly sour fruits that make the best jelly in the world, better even than the red currant jelly the French make, if that's possible. And the elderberries, I knew, were coming ripe. What we were discussing in the workshop seemed obvious. The Trinity. Creation. Redemption. And what we *didn't* discuss increasingly annoyed me. What exactly did we mean by "evangelical," I wanted to know, but no one had a clear answer. And if everything was all so obvious from the Bible or creation or any other source reputed to testify authoritatively to one benevolent God and an existence beyond the one we know now, why couldn't even those who called themselves Christians agree on what any of it meant for us in our day-to-day lives?

I have always struggled with the problem of denominational differences. We are, after all, supposed to have been created in God's own image. Shouldn't that mean we know what we're about?

The workshop leader read from Genesis:

> God made the wild animals according to their kinds, the livestock according to their kinds, and all the creatures that move along the ground according to their kinds. And God saw that it was good.

Then God said, "Let us make man in our image, in our likeness, and let them rule over the fish of the sea and the birds of the air, over the livestock, over all the earth, and over all the creatures that move along the ground."

So God created man in his own image,

in the image of God

he created him;

male and female

he created them. (Gen 1:25–27)

Then the workshop leader listed on the whiteboard some ways in which we are like God and unlike other animals and solicited more examples.

"We like order," someone said. "We love," someone else added. Everyone had something to say. We steward. We work. We rest. We tell stories.

We ran out of room on the whiteboard before I could offer my revelation. Here it is. Just as God combined parts of his creation—lights and dark sky, dirt and breath—to make other things, we also combine things—berries and sugar and lemons and heat—to make other things and pronounce them good. We don't just graze, like cattle. We plant and till and fertilize and harvest the plants we eat, and then sort and grind and prepare them further, often in mixtures or using heat to make them taste different. We don't simply kill and devour the animals we eat, as my dogs do. We slaughter them, remove their skin or feathers, and roast or boil or sauté them. We make sauces for them from grains and liquids and combine them with vegetables. In short, we cook.

From the earliest chapters of human history, we have not only gathered and hunted but combined what we amassed of God's creation with other wonderful creations—salt, honey, fragrant greens, clean dry air, fire—and made our own, admittedly lesser, creations. We cooked before cookbooks. And before civilization as we know it now. Before we knew we were cooking but were only mindlessly mimicking the divine impulse to create something new and good. Cooking, for me, is the emulation of the deity's most essential habit: to create. As such, to cook is to worship.

Most of the cooking we do these days begins in medias res. Recipes don't start with raising and slaughtering animals or with harvesting and grinding our flour but with packaged meat, prepared grains, and fruits and vegetables that have been grown and picked and often partially or entirely cooked or preserved before we ever see them. The only part left of the creative act is the combining and pronouncing good, and more and more people leave even those opportunities for worship to restaurants and underpaid factory workers they will never meet.

Gathering and preserving wild fruit, for me, is to share, in the most elemental way, in what it means to be human, made in the image of God, guardians of earth and sea and sky, male and female, alive. God's creation—the berries themselves, the creatures that I share them with, the shade, the minute breeze I wouldn't have noticed if I were not picking berries—humbles me in comparison to my own, however heavenly the smell that wafts through the house as my elderberry jelly cooks down in its pan. To participate in the created world in this way, and to give the little jars of sweetness to the people I love, seems to me the greatest blessing I can expect in this world or the next.

Apricot, Chokecherry, and Plum Jams

INGREDIENTS

Fruit (apricots, chokecherries, or plums)
Water
Sugar

RECIPE

Jam is the same as jelly but contains not just the juice but particles of the fruit itself. It will require that you core and slice or chop larger fruits. For berries, just rinse them lightly, put them in a pot, and crush a few to get the juice running. If you want to remove tiny seeds from fruit such as blackberries, cook them first as you would for jelly, then use a food mill of some sort or a spoon against a heavy-duty sieve. You lose the shape of the berry doing this, which my daughter Lulu objects to, but some people, especially people with dentures, are really bothered by little seeds.

When you have prepared the fruit the way you want it, bring it to a boil in a covered pot—adding the tiniest bit of water if the fruit is rather dry at first—and cook till soft.

Add the same amount (measure what your pot holds and then eyeball it) of sugar, all at once. Jelling is not as critical with jam as it is with jelly, since the fruit itself provides some bulk.

Dropping the jam off a spoon also won't work as well as it does for jelly, so use a thermometer and go for a lower jelling temperature of 217° to 219°F. Again, you want a soft, smearable jam. Jar the jam as for jelly.

You can make any fruit into jam. A New Orleans friend recently told me there was a small fruit that grew on neighborhood trees there that the kids all eat, and when I lived there, I collected it and made it into jam. I don't remember this fruit or this jam in particular, but it seems to me I have done this everywhere I have lived—if the fruit can be eaten, it can be preserved. Here are some jams I especially like.

Apricot Jam

My favorite jam. Include some hard, barely ripe apricots. Quarter or halve the fruit. Some people would call this recipe "preserves" because the fruit is left relatively large.

For an interesting, almondy back-flavor, add two or three kernels from the apricot seeds per jar as you fill them. Use a hammer or a big rock on a concrete surface, such as a porch, to get the kernels out. This recipe also works for peach jam, but you'll want to slice the fruit.

Chokecherry jam

Chokecherries are wild tree fruits that grow all over the United States. They are bitter and mostly seed but make an intriguingly herbaceous-tasting black jam. Cook them first and use a sturdy food mill to get the little pits out. Or make jelly and forget about the pits. This recipe also works well for grapes.

Plum jam

Most store-bought plums make luscious jam. Coarsely cut up the fruit or crush it as it cooks. Plums—both wild and domesticated—have plenty of pectin, so don't even think about adding any. So pretty. Plum jam must be eaten with biscuits.

Brian Volck is a pediatrician at Cincinnati Children's Hospital Medical Center. Through the University of Cincinnati College of Medicine, he founded an elective in literature and medicine and helped design a curriculum on poverty, justice, and health. He regularly travels to rural Honduras and the Navajo Nation to provide medical service. He is the coauthor of *Reclaiming the Body: Christians and the Faithful Use of Modern Medicine*. His essays have appeared in *Doubletake*, *Image*, and other literary and medical journals, and he is currently researching a book on the intersection of history, culture, and health among the Navajo people.

2

Late October Tomatoes

After a long summer of exceptional heat and drought, autumn has arrived, a late but welcome guest. In my backyard, the tulip tree leaves tremble, yellow against a cloudless blue. There will be frost tonight. Not a killing frost; just enough of a dusting to remind us what's coming. The last of the vine-ripened tomatoes sit on a wooden frame above the kitchen sink, red globes between the hand soap and honey jar. Soon—perhaps tomorrow—I'll pull up what tomato vines remain in the garden, tossing the ropy strands in the compost for next year's planting, individually wrapping the larger green fruits in newspaper and placing them in a paper bag to ripen. By New Year's, I'll have forgotten what a fresh-from-the-vine tomato tastes like. Much-traveled Chilean imports miss the mark, as do local hothouse produce with the texture of Styrofoam.

The tomatoes above my sink are imperfect. One has a small soft spot and dark blemishes. A spider web of deep, black crevices spreads from the stem end of another. October tomatoes are never as sublime as August's, but they are no less beautiful, despite their flaws. Beautiful in part because they are miraculous, in part because I planted them, staked

8

them, watered and pruned them, and finally picked them. A tomato's progress from seed to fruit is familiar to me, as is the sweaty stewardship it requires. The manual labor of gardening reminds me to bless the many hands through which my food has passed on its way from field to plate. These tomatoes passed through mine, but even that is a practice handed down to me from another.

I learned to keep a garden from my father. Behind the house where I grew up, in the far corner of the yard, he raised tomatoes, asparagus, cabbages, and peppers. For years, he grew apples, too: pale yellow fruits we plucked from gnarled branches. At the honored center of the rectangular garden plot stood the compost heap, a round wire enclosure which resembled, in my memory at least, the baptismal pool of a small parish church. In it, old plants, leaves, and kitchen waste transformed into rich earth.

My father, a city man all his life, taught me the value of farm-grown food. During the Depression, he and his father sold vegetables off a wooden cart. My father made clear from the way he lived that growing food or bringing it home was a serious joy. On early June weekends, when summer's heat settled in before the solstice, I was often with him out back, cultivating between rows or turning compost. These were chores to me then; I had yet to learn my father's joy. I might begin with gusto, but soon I'd shrug and sputter, calculating how little I could do and call my work done. At such times, my father would stand up from shoveling hard garden earth and catch his breath, his sweat-soaked, sleeveless white undershirt clinging to his chest, a finger's width of dirt above his right eyebrow. Turning, he'd flash me a look halfway between stern and smiling, wordlessly reminding me that this work was worth doing well.

On Saturday mornings the year round, he chatted with vendors at Findlay Market, where we shopped for meat and produce. Everyone there, so it seemed, knew Art Volck by name. He might bring home a box of lettuce that Jim, whose produce stand stood on the corner, saved just for him, knowing my father's taste for salads. Another day he'd receive a surprise discount from Mr. Wassler, the butcher, for a cut of beef. For my father, good food became so through friendship, connection. In the months between my mother's death and his own, nothing made him visibly happier than to share a meal with his children and grandchildren.

His grateful smile could turn macaroni and cheese from the box into a feast.

My father-in-law, a lifelong gardener, too, built the first compost bins at my current house. Sturdy cubicles made of scrap lumber, they were well built but poorly placed, too far back along the garage, where dappled sunlight and my inconsistent attention slowed the change from trash to treasure. I have since torn them down, building instead a longer, partitioned structure of posts and wire placed where sun, water, and I reach them more frequently.

I've made many things by hand before. Some I've made with my father-in-law. Together, we built a curved retaining wall, the two of us crouching alongside the trench, repeatedly checking our lines, meticulously leveling sand and stone. The compost bin, though, was the first construction he complimented me on. At least it was his first compliment I took to heart. He grew up on Chesapeake Bay, where vibrant life ubiquitously and conspicuously springs from silent decay. He labored many years to protect the bay, restoring underwater habitat and teaching children how to fish, how to recycle and reuse, how to live. Both of us, I think, find the humble habit of composting the nearest thing to resurrection this side of the grave.

Standing in the kitchen this October, I look out on the backyard, rehearsing my garden to-do list. I've already brought in the potted herbs and placed them by their usual sunny windowsills. The pole beans are gone and the basil is harvested. Jars of pesto fill a refrigerator shelf. After I pull up the tomato and pepper plants, leaving behind kale, sorrel, and what remains of the parsley, I'll extend the garden and the raspberry beds a few more feet. I'll mix some finished compost with topsoil I saved last spring to fill the new borders. Soon, there will be leaves to rake and pile in the compost. Later still, I'll push my hand deep into the pile to feel the transforming warmth, fruit of a billion microbial furnaces. Then come seed catalogs read by the fire or under a wool comforter, talking with friends about what worked well and what didn't, followed by potting soil, peat pots, and grow lights.

Holding this year's tomatoes in my hand, I already imagine standing in next May's warm and welcome sunshine. Stooping low, I'll space holes in the tilled garden earth not far from the potato row, setting tomato plants deep enough to cover the first set of true leaves with compost and dirt.

But I'm getting ahead of myself.

My wife tells me she wouldn't mind all my yard work if it gave me visible pleasure. What she can't see is my daydreaming, my silent delight. Most of my time in the garden is spent, by choice and temperament, alone. What she sees is my dismay at not having enough time, my conviction that with more attention and hard work things would come close to what I imagined in the pages of those seed catalogs. It's the same frustration I feel looking at a shelf of books I long to read, wondering when, if ever, I'll find the time. But there's more to it than that. Some part of me clings to the mistaken belief that the whole miraculous enterprise depends on me, that the garden won't grow unless I make everything happen just right and on time.

Such egotism is silly, of course, a kind of works righteousness I could do without. Except, perhaps, for fishing, no fruitful work depends more on chance or grace than farming. Nature is never mastered. I know this from doctoring, but it's my patients, not professors, who tutor me. In the garden, plants are my teachers. I till, enrich, and water the soil; plant, fertilize, and protect my seedlings; trellis, prune, and harvest my crop, but all my work really amounts to is this: I cooperate with the usual miracles and witness the outward signs of a mysterious, inward grace.

"Human," "humble," and "humus" all spring from the same root word, meaning "earth" or "ground." An afternoon in the garden grounds me. Kneeling in the dirt between the tomatoes, basil, and peppers, pruning shears in my hand, I relearn what ought not be taken for granted. The worm's-eye view offers necessary perspective. Precious little in the garden is my doing. All the rest is gift and grace, including the opportunity to receive these gifts with gratitude and use them well.

⌣

What my father brought home from market or in from the garden, my mother cooked. She was a schoolteacher by profession, but the kitchen was her studio; knives and cutting boards, bowls and spoons, pots and skillets, her tools. Only when I began cooking myself did I recognize her skill. When I moved to an apartment after graduating from college, she wrote down my favorite recipes on index cards. Each one had a title written above the red line near the top, with ingredients and explicit instructions recorded below in her careful schoolteacher's cursive. By that time she, who had fed us for years on organ meats—beef tongue, liver, heart—and simply prepared vegetables, embraced what seemed dizzy-ingly exotic cuisine. She included several of these—sweet and sour fish, Lebanese kibbe, Indian bangan burtha—in that small recipe library. She also gave me my first copy of her favorite cookbook, *The Joy of Cooking*, introducing me not only to hundreds of new recipes, but also to the Rombauers' writerly meditations on "The Foods We Heat," or "The Foods We Eat," and short lyric essays on ingredients, with no-nonsense titles like "About Asparagus." That gift has long since disappeared, its cover torn away by hard use, whole pages unreadable beneath a dozen stains. I've owned many cookbooks since, including newer versions of *Joy*, but none so meaningful as the one my mother gave me.

What remains in my kitchen is something of her presence, some of the joy of the cookbook's title and the pleasure taken in good things well made. Like my father, my mother's relationship to food was formed, for good and ill, by her times. She knew how to stretch ingredients. She understood that sauerbraten was one way the shrewd hausfrau rendered cheap cuts of meat not only edible, but also delicious. Wasted food was, for her, a sacrilege. On the other hand, she fell for that twentieth-century modernist canard that, if science equals progress, processing only made food better. A child of the Depression herself, she found packaged, ready-to-cook foods too attractive to pass up. I've learned to live quite happily without reconstituted powdered milk or spreadable "cheese food" in a jar. Knowing how such things go, I look forward to discovering which of my dietary quirks my children deem atrocities.

What my family remembers best, though, are those things my mother did the old, slow way. My cousins still talk about "Aunt Mary's Thanksgiving Dressing": giblets, pork sausage, and plenty of sage, for which there was no substitute. They would ask a month ahead of time if she was making the dressing for that year's feast, and agitate if she said anything but "yes." My mother-in-law's mashed potatoes now fill that niche in my children's life. Dinner with Grandma is unthinkable without them. I don't know if my children will clamor for their parents' recipes. I'm content they can and do cook for themselves. Will grills the meat we otherwise wouldn't have; Peter specializes in late-night desserts; and Maria is princess of pasta. But I still treasure the opportunity to cook for them. Better still, they eat the food I make.

It's getting late. Soon it will be time for dinner. I place some onions, late October's tomatoes, and a cutting board on the kitchen table. Pulling my favorite serrated knife from the drawer, I take a seat. The knife handle fits easily in my hand. There is a gouged-out burn at the butt end, a casualty from some run-in with the stove. I use this knife often.

I lay an onion on the cutting board, slice off the stem and bud ends, and peel away the papery brown skin. Standing the onion on one of its flattened ends, I cut a deep latticework into its flesh, then turn the bulb on its side and slice through longitudinally. Pieces of onion fall away in small, slightly curved rectangles. Using the flat end of the knife, I scrape the chopped onion into a pot of melted butter and place it on the stove to sizzle at low heat.

Turning to the tomatoes, I slice away the stem end. Some still have a parasol of leaves attached. These go, along with the onion scraps, into the compost bucket. Mucinous seeds burst from tightly packed locules as the knife cuts through tomato flesh. I keep slicing into smaller and smaller pieces for soup. Many recipes call for parboiling tomatoes first to peel away the skins, but I don't take the time. Skins rarely bother me.

When the onions in the pot have turned translucent, I add four cups of stock and the tomato pieces. In, too, go chopped flat parsley and some sorry-looking basil leaves from the chilly garden, as well as two leaves from the bay laurel at the front window. From the spice cupboard, I pull paprika, cloves, nutmeg, sugar, salt, and pepper. While I'm measuring and stirring these in, my son, Peter, enters the kitchen. He's taking another break from homework.

"What's for dinner?" he asks.

"Spicy tomato soup."

Peter grimaces and mutters something under his breath.

"There'll be grilled cheese sandwiches to go with it," I say.

He smiles. "That's better, then."

I'm confident I didn't appreciate my father's relationship to food when I was Peter's age. I doubt I fully appreciate it now. It's taken years for me to grasp what little I actually understand. For now, I but faintly echo my father's hard and joyful work.

When I take the time to cook attentively, observing the rituals my mother taught me, there's a way in which my parents and benefactors, living and dead, are present. The meals we share as a family are different—more peopled, perhaps—than the sandwich and coffee I grab for lunch at work. At work, I can still mentally thank the worker who spread the tuna on my bread, the campesino who picked the coffee beans, but at home, the links are tighter, the connections more visible. At table, my family is reconstituted.

⌇

The soup pot simmers. The house walls barely contain the scent of tomatoes and cloves. Darkness settles outside while a few wispy clouds redden far in the west, above the horizon of trees. My wife comes home from work, greets the children, the dog, and me. We kiss and talk briefly of the day, of what must be accomplished before bed. She asks what she can do to help, and I tell her about the grilled cheese sandwiches I promised Peter. She and my daughter, who has come downstairs to announce she's starving, set to work, gathering the griddle, butter, slices of bread and cheese. The kitchen is filled with busy people, the smell of good food, the sizzle of a hot griddle. I call Peter several times before he leaves the computer screen and hurriedly sets the table.

Grumbling or famished, we come at last to the table and take our places. We learned this from those who loved us, who labored to shower us with graces they, too, received as grace. At my or my wife's reminder, we join hands and give thanks, blessing the Lord of the Universe for these gifts, fruit of the garden and work of human hands. Then, when all is ready, we fill our bowls together and eat.

Spicy Tomato Soup

Adapted from Helen Crafton and Dorothy Lindgren, *Elsah Landing Restaurant Cookbook* (Elsah, IL: Chicago Review, 1981).

INGREDIENTS

2 tablespoons butter or olive oil

1 to 2 large onions

4 cups stock (preferably chicken stock)

6 cups chopped fresh tomatoes, or 2 (28-ounce) cans crushed tomatoes

1/4 cup chopped fresh parsley

2 bay leaves

Several leaves chopped, fresh basil, or 1 teaspoon dried basil

1 teaspoon paprika

1 teaspoon sugar

1/4 teaspoon cloves

1/4 teaspoon nutmeg

Several turns of the pepper grinder

Salt (optional)

Sour cream or unsweetened whipped, heavy cream (optional)

Crusty bread or grilled cheese sandwiches (optional)

Serves 6 to 8

RECIPE

Melt butter over low heat in a large, heavy soup pot or saucepan. Dice onions and sauté for 5 minutes in the butter until translucent.

Add to the sautéed onions the stock, tomatoes, parsley, bay leaves, basil, paprika, sugar, cloves, nutmeg, and pepper.

Cover and simmer for at least 30 minutes. From time to time, find an excuse to stir the pot and sample the aroma closely.

Add salt as desired. Taste and adjust spices accordingly.

Fill bowls. If desired, top each bowl with a dollop of sour cream or unsweetened whipped, heavy cream. Serve with crusty bread or grilled cheese sandwiches.

JEANNE MURRAY WALKER is the author of seven collections of poetry, the latest is *New Tracks, Night Falling*. Her poems and essays have appeared in *Poetry*, the *Georgia Review*, *Image*, the *Atlantic Monthly*, and many other journals. Among her awards are an NEA Fellowship, an Atlantic Monthly Fellowship, and a Pew Fellowship in the Arts. In 2007, she was given the Glenna Luschei Prairie Schooner Prize. She recently hosted a public television documentary on poetry in the Commonwealth of Pennsylvania. A professor of English at the University of Delaware, Jeanne also teaches in the Seattle Pacific Low Residency MFA Program.

3

The Communion of Saints

One day in the fall I wake up alone. It's dark. There is an empty spot in the bed next to me and I remember, my husband is working in another state. Through the window I see a black shape tossing its leaves like the mane of a great tethered horse, as though it were trying to get away. The wind hisses. I smell wet earth. Seconds later, just after seven a.m., our clock radio erupts with the news that there's a tornado watch. The storm might hit any time until two this afternoon. Feeling a smattering of rain blowing sideways into the open window, I get up, pull a hoodie over my nightgown, and tug at the window until it slams shut.

Rain is swilling down outside, splattering fatly into pools of standing water. I imagine the brown rabbit who lives in our backyard must be huddling under the rhododendrons. I envision my mother's grave, how she is lying in a tiny room underground with rain pounding down, knocking, knocking. The untrustworthy body, the body that breaks down. I pray that is not the final, final end, and I try to imagine her in heaven, maybe sauntering with my father down a golden street or strolling by the river of life with her own mother. But I'm still here in our cold bedroom, which feels as lonely and primal as a cave.

Last night I made a list of chores I need to do today, but I can't remember where I put it. I do remember that my husband is coming home this afternoon, and there's nothing in the house to eat, so I have to buy vegetables before I go to school to teach. Vegetables, I think, know about dark, cold rain. They come from the earth.

Soon I am parking and walking toward Produce Junction. The rain has thinned to mist. The wind turns my umbrella inside out. Out of the corner of my eye, I notice a cardboard box flying through the air. Turning, I spot a semi filled with boxes of mushrooms. The man unloading his truck has stumbled and lost his footing, so hundreds and hundreds of button mushrooms are raining down all over the driveway and sidewalk. He curses vibrantly. Shoppers stop briefly to watch, snickering, then hurry on through the mist. He surveys the soggy mess, kneels to pick up the mushrooms, peers around at us, his audience, and grins. Some of us stop to help him. Hands of all sizes and shades, and ages, mine among them, drop wet mushrooms into his box.

Produce Junction is a simple one-story shack slathered in dirty beige stucco. On its left stands an abandoned, rickety garage, and to the right, an expanse of cracked sidewalk. As I juggle slippery mushrooms, I realize I've come here every day this week, and I can't remember why. Not because I needed to buy food, I know. Although I can't afford the time to keep coming back, when I feel the call of the place, I come.

Inside the shack, a bank of dusty windows filters light, revealing how the main part of the building stretches back several hundred feet, thinning to a dim cave where workers drag and unload boxes. Above us, crude rafters are hung with light bulbs dangling from bare wires. I stand looking around until my eyes adjust to the dimness. There are about a dozen people cruising the fruit and vegetables.

A woman holds up a papaya. "What's this-here thang called?"

"You don't want them. They're overripe," a worker yells.

The place is filled with bins, and every bin is piled to tumbling with hunks and colors. The air in here smells like the earth and rocks and moss. None of the produce is labeled; there are no names or price tags.

"These rutabagas is ugly as carp today!" an old Chinese lady complains to her husband.

A young mother barely misses me, sprinting for her toddler, who has dumped raspberries on the floor. She calls to her older daughter, "Samantha, will you get over here? And tell your sister to stop playing with the raspberries!"

Meanwhile, a tanned diva in dark glasses and toreador pants drifts from strawberries to the cantaloupe. She collides with a thin blond man in a postal uniform who's just barreled in the front door. Outside someone blasts a horn, and I see the postman has double-parked his truck. As he brushes past Toreador Pants, he cheerfully calls back an apology. Then he seizes two cantaloupes from the bin, one in each hand like barbells, and goes to stand in line.

People are streaming around me, as if I were a statue of a woman, and I realize that I'm meditating in the doorway, that I need to move. When a worker walks by, carrying a cardboard box filled to the top with bright green dill, I follow him, or rather, I follow the smell of the dill, which he is dumping into one of the bins. Running my hand over the wet, soft, ferny fronds, I pick up a bunch that's light as a handful of air. I take it over to the checkout line.

While we are standing in line, a worker in tall olive rubber boots appears from the back and orders us all to move to the left so he can hose down the floor. Someone has just dropped a bunch of tomatoes and they've been smashed to a bloody pulp by our feet. Like a chorus line, we obediently step to the left.

I didn't come for herbs. But for the rest of the day, my car is filled with the aroma of dill.

What I didn't understand at the time, what lay buried beneath a year of escalating visits to Produce Junction, was the fact that six months earlier, I had lost my church.

We were gathering in the shabby, comfortable parish house, where a dozen of us vestry members had spent hundreds of hours considering furnace problems, worrying about our leaky nineteenth-century roof, poring over revisions in the liturgy, thinking of ways to get the Eucharist to shut-ins. I took pleasure in working through these problems because they brought us together, my friends, a group of warm, funny, smart parishioners.

That spring Thursday evening, one of them, still wearing her pea jacket, was passing around pictures of her gorgeous dark-haired children, and then another showed up with a big plate of brownies. I slipped out of my coat, draped it around a chair, and pulled up at the large table. Warmed by the smell of chocolate and surrounded by the sweet harmony of chatter, I studied the parish balance sheet, formidable tables and columns of numbers. The e-mail announcing this meeting had told us that we would be voting on a big budget question.

The meeting started with prayer. Then our priest explained that she felt we needed to hire an assistant. Unfortunately, however, the day-to-day expense of lighting and heat and salaries and shoveling the sidewalks was taking up our whole parish budget. And still, she said, she desperately needed someone to help her with her duties.

Our Finance Warden took over then, saying that the main budget question was this: could we violate a trust agreement that had been set up fifty years ago? The trust, he said, had been made by an elderly couple who attended and supported the church for many years. In the 1950s, they gave a large bequest in exchange for a written and signed promise that none of the principal would ever be used to pay for day-to-day operating expenses. For over fifty years, the church had paid operating expenses from the trust's interest, but it had respected the terms of the agreement and never touched the principal.

Impatient with his long explanation, our priest stepped in and emphasized that she needed an assistant. She needed one badly, she said, and she wanted us to break the trust agreement.

The vestry sitting around the table became very quiet. We stared at our hands. After a few minutes of heavy silence, the priest told us she would go around the circle, one vestry member at a time, and each of us had to tell her how we would vote.

I felt panicked to be put on the spot in this way. Fear and resentment rose in my chest as one friend after another spoke, and the focus moved closer to me. I worried about some of my friends, too, who were more diffident than I.

The first three or four vestry members, one by one, agreed with our priest that she had a lot to do. And after all, none of us knew the couple who had bequeathed the money. And it was a long time ago. The first four members of the vestry said they felt it would be OK to violate the trust.

About the time our priest got to me, the anger inside me reached flood stage and was filling up my throat, so I spoke faintly. I didn't think we needed an assistant, I said, since we averaged less than a hundred people in church on Sunday mornings, though I confess I was also thinking of the fact that our priest had just enrolled in a graduate program that was sapping her time. I said, "I think before we hire an assistant, we should work on attracting more members, and then maybe we will be able to afford an assistant without breaking the trust."

Our priest fixed her eyes on me, her face reddening. She asked, "Don't you think you should have more faith?"

I didn't know what to say. I found myself looking at her awkwardly while the silence accumulated.

"God's just testing us to see whether we have faith," she explained. "The point is not some legal document. We need the funds now, and we *have* the funds. This trust belongs to us. God is faithful," she said. "And he'll replenish whatever we take out."

I said, "If we made a promise to the old couple, God will honor us for keeping our promise."

"It wasn't *us* who made the promise. That was fifty years ago. And when they signed that contract, they didn't realize we'd need the money now."

"The people who signed the contract," I said, "were the church then. And we're the church now. The *church* promised."

My friends on the vestry looked out the window. The smell of the hyacinths in the vase on the table suddenly seemed to stain the air with overbearing scent. A door slammed loudly in the hall.

"This is a dark time," the priest went on, "like Good Friday. A dark time. Dark times are precisely when we need to trust God." She looked pointedly at me and asked whether I trusted God.

This time she didn't leave space for me to answer. It was several weeks after Easter. She was wearing her collar and revving up the decibels. She slipped into a sermonizing cadence and went on while I looked around the room at the bright water-color paintings by Sunday school children.

"What *you* need is Good Friday faith," she concluded, looking directly at me. "If you don't have Good Friday faith, you shouldn't be on the vestry."

The priest paused, waiting for me to answer, but I felt claustrophobic and puny and powerless to reply. I felt so mortified by the way she had singled me out that I couldn't think of a way to respond. Maybe she's right, I thought. Maybe I shouldn't be on the vestry.

"I vote against breaking the trust" was all I could think of to say.

Her piercing black gaze fell on me briefly and then traveled on to the next vestry member. Five of us voted against breaking the trust, but there were a dozen of us altogether, so we went ahead and broke the couple's trust and took funds from their principal to place an ad for an assistant rector. Then we paid him every month with the money the donors said we were legally barred from using.

Because our priest had told me so publicly that I didn't belong on the vestry, for several weeks I wrestled over whether I should resign, but that seemed unfair to the people who had elected me. So I finished my term.

After that, I didn't go back to church.

⌒

As I am walking toward Produce Junction, a man driving an eighteen-wheeler leans out his window and bellows at me to get out of the way. He swings his rig onto the sidewalk, jumps down from his cab, and at the rear of the truck, leans his upper body on the lever to raise the heavy door. Then he begins unloading wooden crates marked EGGPLANT.

I can't remember what I came for. I don't even recall the drive over. I must have been listening to NPR, letting the car drive itself. I warn myself about how unsafe that is, and a cold wind blows through my heart. I plunge my hands into my jeans pocket to feel for my grocery list. Light bulbs, it says. Freezer bags. Cereal. Half and half. Nothing I can buy here.

I think about leaving, but instead I stand and watch.

"You know anything about this vegetable?" a young woman asks the clerk at the checkout counter.

"Kohlrabi."

"What do you do with kohlrabies?"

"You cook it, ma'am. Did you want these peppers?" The clerk holds up a plastic bag of red peppers. Sassy, glossy, exquisite.

I find myself stopping by the market regularly four or five times a week now. It's almost winter. The workers are bundled in coats and brown cloth gloves, and some of them wear earmuffs as they dump boxes of carrots into tubs and sweep the cement floor. I shiver in the freezing draughts blowing through the windows and walls. Today the apple bins are full of fruit hardly bigger than golf balls. *That's what nature can do to you*, the management seems to be saying, so that's what I pick up.

There are no shopping carts or baskets, so we hug the dirty produce in our arms. Stuff topples to the floor. I lose a bunch of grapes, squat gracefully, sidesaddle, and swipe at the floor, just missing them. My bag of apples tumbles to the ground. When I lean over to pick up my apples, the bananas and broccoli fall.

An Asian teenager with tattoos, long black hair, and an earflap hat stops, bends down, picks up my produce, and plunks things back in my arms. His tattooed hand sweeps against my hand.

"Thank you," I say in surprise.

"Hey, no problem," he replies, trotting off toward the flowers.

I cradle my fruit and vegetables, walking over to stand in line.

The lady in front of me turns. She's African American with ample hips and she is wearing dark blue jeans with rolled-up cuffs and boots. Over this ensemble she has thrown a fake tiger cape.

"I'll never use all this zucchini," she says. "Take a few."

I'm a million miles away, thinking about something else. I can't remember a stranger asking me to split an order. I don't need zucchini, or I'd have picked some up. I want to help her out, but I'm worried that so many vegetables will rot in my refrigerator. Besides, I don't know the etiquette for transactions with other shoppers.

So I balance my stuff, manage to pull a dollar out of my pocket, and offer it to the lady with the zucchini. She waves me off with long, graceful red fingernails. I ask her whether she'd like some yellow squash. She says thank you, but she doesn't need any. She lays three big zucchinis atop the produce in my arms, lifts her bags with poise, and walks out.

I stand holding my produce with her zucchini on top. I realize with a pang that I might not see her again, that I have accepted vegetables from her and will not have a chance to pay her back. I don't know whether I've won or lost, and then I am taken aback by my way of measuring the exchange. It feels so limited and competitive.

That night I think about the zucchini woman, and again the next morning I remember her. I believe I've seen her at Produce Junction before, maybe more than once. I decide to look for her next time I'm there. Sometime after that, the truth dawns on me: it was when I stopped going to church that I started driving to Produce Junction almost every day.

⤳

My first reason for loving Produce Junction was because it's full of bargains; five eggplants for a dollar, a box of raspberries for two dollars. Finding the place felt like discovering that Aladdin's lamp is really a garden and we'll never go hungry. Like many children of Depression parents, I adore bargains. I come from a grandfather who once bought a thousand trailer hitches because he could get them for a nickel apiece. No wonder I was thrilled to get three bags of celery for a dollar. The fact that I had to buy three, if I bought any at all, didn't worry me. I took them home and stashed them in our refrigerator.

In a month or so I had to carry two soft, blackening bunches of celery to the trash, because we just don't eat that much celery. One of the main differences between celery and trailer hitches, I realized, is that celery goes bad and trailer hitches don't. For five years my grandfather sold trailer hitches, one by one, to filling station attendants across the state of Minnesota, and eventually he made a profit. But I began to live on fairly close terms with death. There was nearly always a vegetable or fruit in my refrigerator that was in some stage of decomposition—softening, molding, rotting into black liquid. This didn't represent a waste of money, because they had been so cheap, but every time I had to clean a corrupting bunch of asparagus from our vegetable cooler, I felt a little sick.

I decided to take responsibility for the surplus. So I started to give vegetables and fruit to neighbors and to our grown children. I still do, feeling slightly apologetic as I hand the stuff over, but my victims bear my gifts of peaches or arugula or scallions with patience. They thank me and assure me it will be useful. Still, forcing vegetables on them feels slightly un-American, because America is about choice, and my friends don't get to choose what I give them. The fact is, what I bring home isn't exactly my choice either.

One day I walk into Produce Junction looking for russets. Not only is the market out of russets, they have two bins of brussels sprouts instead of any broccoli. The beets are scaly and misshapen and clotted with a little mud. It makes me a bit irritable. I think of driving to Super Fresh. But I've already figured out that one of the reasons I return to this shack is that I rather like working around the seasons. I don't mind if some things aren't available. At least, I say that I *like* craving what's not there, looking forward to the first whiff of asparagus in the spring, anticipating the way it resists a fork, imagining its buttered taste. If I have to improvise meals around what's available, I feel in partnership with the earth. If I have to think about collaborating with nature, I remember I am not the creator; I am a creature.

⌒

After the vestry meeting where we voted to violate the elderly couple's trust, I didn't leave one church for another. I went on strike. One year with no church stretched to two. Sometimes I tried other churches, but just showing up and sitting in the pew would turn me into a lump of self-righteous, critical protoplasm without grace or charm or a sense of humor. When I am thinking of someone I can't forgive, I become the sort of person I hate. Many members of my old church scattered to other parishes and we sometimes brooded together on the various offenses of the spirit that had occurred there. We felt excluded and violated. I had enough sense to know that after sharing the Eucharist with friends every week for decades, I'd feel lonely if I gave it up, but every time I got close to any church, misery shut me down.

Following the mushroom incident, as I drove to school through the rain, I thought, maybe gathering mushrooms in that storm was so crucial to me because in my suburb there isn't much street life. The summer my husband and I first moved here from the city, I remember, we ate breakfast on the front porch, thinking we would get to know our neighbors that way. After three weeks, I realized the reason there are no people on the street is because when we leave our houses, we get into our cars in our backyards. And coming home, I pull into the back, as we all do. It's no wonder we don't see one another. True, we do have block parties and we meet over lawn mowers in the summer. We share an amiable mailman and ask our neighbors to feed our cat when we're on vacation, but we don't see one another frequently.

And beyond that, I realized there are very few places where Americans get to talk to people of other ages and races. Supermarkets are amphitheaters with nervous music and garish lights. When I'm there I don't talk to neighbors; I feel mesmerized. I've read that the aisles are specifically designed to move us along, because the store has only so many shopping carts, only so much space. Since I've been shopping at Produce

Junction, I've noticed that the food in supermarkets is trimmed, injected with color, waxed, and sealed under plastic—supermarkets aren't about human connection or about a connection with nature. I don't remember ever having an opportunity for either insight or moral behavior in the supermarket.

A couple of days later I am driving to Produce Junction, imagining the pungent aroma of fresh lemons, which are the *sine qua non* for our evening's dessert. We don't usually have dessert, but tonight we are celebrating the successful end of a big project. I walk directly to the fruit and discover the lemons are almost gone. I'm vaguely aware that an older woman with a soft, powdered face is circling the herbs. She's dressed as if for church or a concert, in a good quality, loopy black wool coat and a big, flowered scarf tied at her neck. I lunge toward the last bag of lemons just as she floats to a stop in front of the bin. Our hands meet. We both withdraw. I'm moving faster, with more certainty, and I got there first. But she is older.

She gives me an appraising look.

"Go ahead," she says. "You were here before me."

Her expression is that of someone pleasant and eager to please. Maybe this trip is her outing for the day. Maybe she has gotten dressed just to come here. Maybe she is determined to have a good time, whatever happens.

But her voice conveys disapproval. I consider what to do. There's no time for another stop. It's these lemons or no lemons. Nevertheless, I think I ought to let her have them. That will show her she's not a victim, which might be good for her, I think, with entirely too much self-righteousness.

The woman and I each politely urge the other to go first until the exchange feels embarrassing. I give in and grab the lemons. I take them home and we have a splendid dinner. But I don't eat any of the lemon torte, because I'm realizing what I could have done that might have made me happier than dessert. I should have picked the lemons up and put them in her hands.

That evening it dawns on me that what happens at Produce Junction is not unlike what happens at the Eucharist table. Maybe that sounds blasphemous. But for me buying produce was by then tangled up with the mystery of being fed. Those of us who regularly come to Produce Junction come for food and for fellowship.

⌒

The first time I left a church, I was twenty. I'd been sitting in a pew in our Baptist church like a ventriloquist's dummy for months, no, for years, so many years that my mind and soul were full of sawdust. I no longer believed I would find anything holy there, so I didn't. The truth is, instead of encountering God, I tended to spend the time cataloging everything that was wrong with the place. During one Sunday evening service I found myself holding a list that I had scribbled in pencil on the bulletin. It was numbered. It was a grudge list. When I realized that, the penny dropped.

I needed to be sorry so I could be forgiven. But I wasn't sorry. I felt I was right. It was a terrible, terrible church. But at least I realized that criticizing the church was getting me nowhere. Maybe it would be better to stop going to church at all than to go to a place where my main activity was to feel superior. Slumping there in the pew under the fluorescent lights, I decided that the next Sunday I would try St. Mark's Episcopal in the neighboring suburb. I had friends who loved that place.

Sitting in my Baptist church for the last time, I thought with irony that no one knew what I had just decided. The last time you perform certain actions, it is marked and celebrated. There are little ceremonies, for instance, marking the last day of school, marking the day you stop being forty-nine years old. But leaving church doesn't get commemorated. It's unremarked, like the last time you see your mother. As I plotted to leave my fundamentalist people, they stood around me singing, *Let the Lower Lights Be Burning.* No one guessed my spot would be empty next week, and the next and the next.

That week I felt like a weedy, vacant lot with the wind whistling through it. But I didn't go back on my decision. I just hedged a little. I would try St. Mark's, yes, fair enough, but I reserved the right to go back to my fundamentalist people if I couldn't deal with the new, strange religion I might find in the Episcopal church.

From the minute I passed though its red door, St. Mark's electrified me. At the end of the service, the priest yelled, *Thanks be to God!* and everyone shouted, *Thanks be to God. Alleluia. Allelujah!* I felt off balance and out of place and humble. I couldn't find the right pages in the prayer book. When I sipped the real alcoholic wine from the chalice, teetotaler that I had been to this point, a disconcerting buzz filled my head, and I worried about catching a cold from the shared germs. During the entire first week afterward, I feared punishment from God, which my fundamentalist people said he visited on people who turned to false religion. But astonishingly, as I kept returning to St. Mark's, the spare language of the prayer book seemed to express exactly what I felt. I realized it was becoming *my* prayer book. I would catch my breath, close my eyes, and grip the back of the pew in front of me.

This is what I gave up when I gave up my church after the terrible vestry meeting. This is what I gave up: worshipping with friends I think of as the communion of saints.

⌣

I keep driving back to Produce Junction three or four times a week, even though I think my attraction to this place is preposterous. I have shopped at produce markets on the streets of Bogota and Paris and London and Barcelona. I have shopped at street markets in small Maine villages, in California, in Vancouver, and in Minnesota towns. Unlike many of them, Produce Junction isn't outdoors, and it isn't run by the people who grow the food, and it's not organic, and I don't have any idea what the place pays its workers.

I have begun to think about the workers there the way I used to think about our neighborhood filling station attendants, not as friends, exactly, but as minor stars, revolving within my galaxy. Some look Eastern European. One Saturday two of them listened sympathetically to my inquiries about whether one of the plants was an annual or a perennial, then shrugged, meaning they'd answer if only they could understand the question. Some of the workers are teenagers who, I suspect, might more profitably be in school. Several of the women laugh and comment to one another in Spanish, probably about us shoppers. Or is it paranoid to imagine that?

I want to think the faces of the workers at Produce Junction are full of character, but I know I might be partly inventing that. One late middle-aged man with a theatrical, expressive face and springy curls said, each time he gave me change, "Make this a good day." I never took this lightly, but then, suddenly, he disappeared and where he's gone, I don't know.

I don't recognize many shoppers at Produce Junction, and that doesn't matter. I don't mind coming and going as a stranger. When I'm there, I don't have to pretend to be more patient or reliable or smarter than I am. What I do will not affect my status or job. It will not shape the ongoing persona other people know as me. It's enough, I think, that the choices I make there frequently reveal me to myself. Sometimes I am decent, sometimes truly awful.

So I'm standing in the vegetable market, coming to terms with the fact that we aren't going to have russets for dinner tonight. Then I notice broccoli on the floor, stoop down, retrieve it, and replace it in the arms of the woman who dropped it. She's wearing a Chanel-style jacket and a black hat with a black veil. It was the slender, tattooed Asian teenager who taught me to pick vegetables up from the floor and return them to their owner. As I put the broccoli into the woman's hands, the warmth of her hand reminds me of passing the peace.

The word *peace* passes through me like a radio wave.

And I know, suddenly I *know* that I am no longer holding a grudge, that I can return to church. I stand for a minute in the middle of the people and vegetables, while foolish tears swim in my eyes. The bins blur until they shimmer like jewels.

The next Sunday I wait outside a simple old brick church in Philadelphia under a canopy of maples, surrounded by graves that date back to the sixteen hundreds, and listen to the congregation sing *All Hail the Power of Jesus' Name*. I walk by a big maroon sandwich board welcoming visitors to enter through the large white doors, which are propped wide open. I'm feeling nervous, slightly nauseated. I don't know exactly why I am so afraid. When the last notes of the hymn fade, I gather my courage and step onto the stone floor of the church, feeling the air shift slightly to coolness. A man in a suit hands me a bulletin. I find a pew, pick up the prayer book, which feels in my hands like my own prayer book, and begin reciting the confession with the rest of the congregation.

Scalloped Potatoes for the Church Potluck

INGREDIENTS

4 to 5 pounds peeled red potatoes

3 tablespoons butter

3 tablespoons bleached white flour or Red Mill gluten-free flour

1 teaspoon salt

3 1/2 cups milk

2 1/2 cheddar cheese, grated

RECIPE

Preheat the oven to 425˚ F.

Slice the red potatoes into thin pieces.

Place the potatoes in a pot, add water to an inch above the potato slices, add salt to taste, and boil for 3 minutes.

Drain the potatoes and arrange them in a greased casserole dish.

Melt the butter in a saucepan and then add the flour and salt.

Blend in the milk, whisking to make a roux.

Add the cheddar cheese.

Pour this mixture over the potatoes.

Cover and bake in oven for 1 hour.

Then uncover and bake until lightly browned on top.

ANN VOSKAMP is the daughter of a fifth-generation farmer, is married to a seventh-generation farmer, and is raising six children of the next generation of farmers. A monthly columnist for DaySpring (a division of Hallmark), a global advocate travelling for Compassion, and the author of *One Thousand Gifts: A Dare to Fully Live Right Where You Are* (Zondervan, 2011), Ann writes daily of her farming family's dirt-common lives at her award-winning Web site journal, www.aholyexperience.com.

4

The Land that Is Us

"You heard that there's a for sale sign on the farm across the road?"

Sunday morning light slides in through glass, pools in my pot. Phone cradled to my ear, I stir porridge.

"You've got your offer in, I hope."

How could Dad say anything but that? The sign went up two days ago.

I smile, shake a bit of salt into boiling oats, a handful of ground flax, and stir.

"Oh, we'd like to. 200 acres, 150 workable. But there's no way. In these kinds of markets, we simply don't have the money to buy another farm."

"It's land, Ann."

What else is there to say?

I look out the corner kitchen window. Autumn weds countryside. Maples down the lane blush, silently disrobe. Fields roll east, the land gold. Our field of corn witnesses.

"How often in your lifetime will the farm right next to yours come up for sale? Not more than once or twice." I can see him shaking his head, him sitting there eating breakfast, looking out on his own fields of corn, land he raised me on. "It's an investment for your children . . . in your children. The banks will lend it to you. *It's land!*"

Like he can shake sense into me with those two words.

Sun lays out long on the farm across the road, across its honeyed wheat stubble, and this feeling barbs, burns.

It's land.

Coming home from wheat fields one afternoon, just before lightning had forked across the western sky, my daughter Hope said the same. One hand on the steering wheel, I turned and caught the tilt of her head, the tone of her words. She had brushed the tangled hair out of her face, smudged her cheek with dirt from the back of her hand. She'd glanced at her tired, grimy brothers pressed in around her, looked up at the mirror, and then turned toward me.

"*After combining wheat with Dad, we'll need to go home for baths, won't we? We are all like . . . dust.*"

I couldn't speak. My fingers fumbled to slip through Hope's dirty hand. Dirt met; we squeezed tight. Heavy raindrops pelted the windshield. We drove home from fields, dust in a rainstorm.

That dirt is what I sweep off floors, wash from jeans, scrub off hands; the same dirt that frames up the soul; the same dirt that grows our food to sustain our limbs, that nourishes our bodies.

When asked what we do for a living I always hesitate; there's no grand title and I can read their eyes. Farming requires no specialized degree, no impressive wage for menial labor, the primitive work of any civilization. We're farmers. We just grow food. We just raise pigs. It doesn't get more rudimentary.

The children read it aloud once from their history text, how the most denigrated class of people in ancient Egypt was the swine herders. They'd looked at each other, at their dad and I, we pig farmers.

I had held the book in my hand, smoothed the page out flat, and the words had come slowly, like bent backs rising, but they had come and we all stood taller because of them. *How can growing nourishment for temples wherein Christ dwells be dirty, base work? If it isn't fish at the end of a fork, it ultimately came from dirt, from the bowed back of a farmer. And this dirt-tilling, isn't it engaging in Genesis work, stewarding and cultivating his creation? Some say that there are only two kinds of people who brush very God. The priest in the sacraments. The farmer in the soil. We've known it, standing at the end of a field, the wagons filling with yield: working earth touches God. Working humus feeds humanity. We are dust farming dust, preparing food for men planting food, living this circular dance: from dirt, through dirt, until the return to the dirt; for from him and through him and to him, all things. Need we be ashamed?*

The children had all nodded.

It's land. The land, she's kin.

I hang up the phone with Dad, stand long in the kitchen, looking out across to that section of earth with the for sale sign. Across my chest, this unexpected kindling, a yearning. I want her. She's of my lineage, kin I know. I want to walk her dirt, open her up, spend the seasons with her.

The wind rustles corn; the field whispers.

The back door closes softly and I can hear the water running. Farmer Husband always washes his hands in the mudroom sink, washing away the smell of his stock and his work. I glance at the clock. He and our six kids have made good time this morning. Six hundred and fifty sows fed and watered, afterbirth from newborn litters collected and laid back out on the land, nearly a thousand piglets carefully tended to, the mothers' milk-full udders checked, the heavy sows prepared for the birthing—all while the moon still lingered. Now the sun begins her arc across the lid. They're in for breakfast, to wash up for church.

"Dad thinks we should put an offer in." I ladle bowls.

Farmer Husband, with hands that grew a couple hundred acres of wheat this year, cuts bread. I ground those kernels yesterday. Weeks ago, those kernels waved in the wind. I am cooking sausage from our own pigs. We are not eating commodities for breakfast, packaged food yanked from its context and source. We know the paths of this food: we picked stones off the land in May, the rain came in June, hail pelted the wheat in late July. We speak of the frost that browned the squash vines, the corn we raised in the field then fed to the pigs in our barn. We tend the hens in the coop that puts meat and eggs on our plates. Six children sit at the table and a son grins at the food, the colors, the tastes. We eat of the earth and chew summer's sun and swallow down the late August rain. We live and know the circle intimately, from death and a seed, to earth and a bed, to stalk and a yield, to table and a meal.

"An offer?" Farmer Husband nods, lays the bread in for toasting. "You think we should take out a loan and buy another two hundred acres?"

I carefully count out eight spoons, eight cups, set them slow around the table while I think. Isn't it always a question of numbers, a question of sustainability? That though we own the hundred acres we live and raise these pigs on, and rent my mother's four hundred acres and the hundred acres that backs our farm, working six hundred acres is a pittance in an era of industrial farms. How many times do we sit down to eat the food we've grown and ask: do we buy more land, fall deeper into debt? Do we invest in bigger equipment, more hired help? Do we grow genetically modified seeds? How many times have we laid in bed and talked late, the vast black night hushed low over fields? And we've wrestled hard: do we apply fertilizers, herbicides, insecticides? Do we plant the conventional rotation of corn, wheat, soybeans? Or do we plow a new path, grow kidney beans, flax, strawberries, and cucumbers?

Though we farmers are producers, the consumers determine how and what we produce. It is the consumer's lifestyle, nutritional interests, and ethical values that determine how a farmer produces food. And it's their hunger that determines the value of a bushel of wheat, a ton of beans, a pound of ham, the price the middleman will pay us at our farm gate. We farmers have always been beggars of sorts, taking whatever the middleman will give us for the nights we didn't sleep, the holidays we worked, the prayers we begged for rain, to bring a crop in, to feed our stock. I ask myself constantly: do our children want to live as we have lived, at the whim of markets and middlemen?

The Farmer and I, we've laced the fingers together in the night and made prayerful, considered decisions for our farm individually, but there is only so much that farmers, less than three percent of the North American population, can do to effect real change in the way food is produced, the way agriculture and the land shapes itself.

"When farmers are going broke, it's wrong to expect them to reform the system," asserts the poet-farmer Wendell Berry. "In fact, there are too few actual farmers left to reform anything. . . . Reform is going to have to come from consumers. Industrial agriculture is an urban invention, and if agriculture is going to be reinvented, it's going to have to be reinvented by urban people."

How can handfuls of farmers alter monolithic agricultural infra-structures, change the way whole nations of consumers eat?

"Oh. I didn't say I wanted another loan." I pour milk. Children and chatter stream in from the barn. A million dollars for two hundred acres of crop dirt? A lifetime of toiling under sun, of praying to heavens to favorably wield skies? And we'd never see the end of the payments. These kids, piling in for breakfast, they'd inherit the dirt and the debt—and in their lifetime, after a lifetime of our work, they might tear up the mort-gage. But does this matter? What if working the land is a calling?

Farmer Husband carries toast to the table. Our four boys, two girls, they talk, stir their bowls while they wait for us to pray. He and I butter toast. We say nothing. We're thinking of the value of land. I think of Thoreau who said, "You must love the crust of the earth on which you dwell more than the sweet crust of any bread or cake . . . . You must have so good an appetite for this, else you will live in vain."

Do I live in vain?

How much do I love land?

We lay down our butter knives, take hands, and pray over bowls and bread. We eat the fat of the land. We've an appetite and we eat and live, and we pray this living is with purpose, intent, rooted to earth, looking to heaven. Yet even as I eat, eating to live, there is this inextricable sense of death, of Alexander Schmemann's startling suggestion that "eating is the communion with the dying world, it is communion with death. Food itself is dead, it is life that has died and it must be kept in refrigerators like a corpse." I often think of this, sitting at the table before food.

Eating is a miracle of transformation—from seed to soil to food—but there's no denying it: what we eat from our tables, succulent and sweet, this is food of a dying world. Though we may carefully select each piece of fruit for its perfect firmness, food never satisfies. It rots, it molds, and we hunger again. We who combine wheat, beans, corn, when the plant has lived its entire life cycle, when it ripens and dies, we too who eat the meat on our table, we will die. Tilling land may be hallowed and essential work, but we make no idol of it. There is Bread who gives real Life, Flesh that asks to be eaten who will eternally satisfy the crav-ings of the spirit.

Joshua asks me to pass the jar of honey. I watch him drizzle it on his toast. I can sense it, taste it—this food is sacramental. Though what we raise may be dying food, it too is symbolic of the Christ who chose agricultural elements such as a kernel of wheat, bread and wine, vine and lamb, to name and speak of himself, the Living Food. Did Christ choose to identify himself with food, because in the process of eating the dying, entering into dying, there too is renewal?

In his poem "The Man Born to Farm," Wendell Berry poignantly, precisely, writes of our lives as farmers, "He enters into death yearly and comes back rejoicing." The agricultural act of eating food, like eating Christ, is no different: we eat, entering into death, and come back rejoicing. The daily eating of food is but a way of remembering death, a way of experiencing resurrection.

The living dead, we eat of the dead, and the miracle happens again: we revive.

～

It's after the Sunday services. When we leave our little country church surrounded by hay fields, pasturing cattle, fields of corn, we drive past the land for sale. We see how she lies. If she calls our names.

"What do you think?" I ask Farmer Husband, his eyes scanning the gentle rolls, the acres laid out. The children are quiet, surveying too. They know this is about them.

"She sure needs some tender love and care." The fences are overgrown, the ditch neglected.

"Could we clean her up, Dad?" My oldest son asks from the back seat. He must feel it too, in the veins like a pulse.

"We could . . ." He's driving slow, scrutinizing, figuring. "Clover's growing up through the wheat stubble. "You'd need to drain her right away so you wouldn't have compaction getting the crop off in the fall." He's talking more to himself than me, already making a list. He's listening to her. "I think you could make a real farm of that piece of property." He's smiling. Grandchildren with that same glint could work this dirt.

Two crows cackle on hydro wires. I read the sign on the hydro pole in the field's far corner. He misses it and I wish I had too.

"She's sold."

The words leave my mouth involuntary, punched from the gut.

Oldest son grabs the back of my seat. "Sold? Really? It only went up last week!"

I can only manage to point to the sign. Crows take wing. Who can speak?

Silence falls, a sadness, like watching kin drive down the lane and away. We turn around, down our gravel road, turn up our lane.

"We don't need to buy anymore work anyways." Farmer Husband cuts the engine. No one moves for a door. All eight of us sit still, looking out at our land, our corn. She's gold in light.

"More land would just be for the kids." His voice is soft, wistful. "And who says any of the kids want to farm?"

"I do!" At least one child jumps in, adamant. The others only watch corn.

Now I'm the one speaking. Head leaning against the cool of the passenger window, these are words to myself, words murmured, words nearly soundless in the quiet, us all quiet.

"I guess I had thought I wanted them to go on. For the kids to go and get degrees, be pastors, doctors, engineers." The waking to what I have done, what I have inadvertently done, to us, to them, to our collective future—it stuns. My eyes sting. I can hardly whisper, "That's how I've made all their priorities, their education, their plans. About them all going, to be power changers, culture makers, in marbled halls. All somewhere else."

That barb, that burn again in my throat.

I turn to face Farmer Husband. He was born on a farm, was smart enough to go but wise enough to stay.

"Why have I thought a good education was about sending our children away?" My voice is gravelly now. Every word squeezed past the lump in my throat hurts. "Why do we teach that dirt doesn't matter and growing food is menial?" Haven't I, farmer's daughter and farmer's wife and mother to the next hope of farmers—*haven't I done just this*? The words choke out, "Why do we think success is measured in the distance we travel away from the land and its crops that our very stomach craves three times a day?"

And I remember it then, how my dad once stood in his farmyard, my childhood farm, and read to me the words on the back cover of a book about farmers, "'No race can prosper till it learns that there is as much dignity in tilling a field as in writing a poem.' Booker T. Washington."

I'd smiled. I'd told Dad how our fourth child, third son, had had to copy out that same quote a few weeks earlier for penmanship. Levi had been disgusted, called us all to come listen to this quote he was sure was all wrong.

"With his brow furrowed," so I tell Dad, "Levi had clarified. 'Don't you see what's wrong? Anybody who is smart at *all* knows there's a lot *more* dignity in working a field than in writing a poem!'"

Dad had slapped his leg, howled laughter ringing off barn and shed. His grandson had dirt in the blood. Then the laughter had dammed up into a swell of sentiment.

He'd pointed his gnarled finger. "You tell Levi." He shook his finger to punctuate every word. "You tell that Levi . . ." He struggles to grab the words in this flood of feelings, "that for real farmers . . . that for me . . . . tilling a field *is* poetry."

Dad had turned away from me looking straight into him.

He had looked to his land.

The farmer's daughter is the farmer's wife who looks to the land on a Sunday morning home from church, before she goes to her pots and her pantry. I look out to that poem of wind and light and humus waiting for weathered hands and prayer-worn knees and my chin trembles. The corn blurs in rain of my own making.

And the words spill, water for hardened earth.

"Who will stay and dwell in the land?"

Tangy Glazed Pork Roast
(Our Sunday Company Recipe)

INGREDIENTS

Meat

2 teaspoons rubbed sage

1 teaspoon salt

1/2 teaspoon pepper

2 cloves crushed garlic

1 (5 pound) boneless pork loin or pork roast of choice

Sauce

1 cup sugar

2 tablespoons cornstarch

1/2 cup vinegar

1/2 cup water

4 tablespoons soy sauce

Serves 8

RECIPE

Preheat oven to 325° F.

In a bowl, mix sage, salt, pepper, and garlic thoroughly and then rub all over the pork roast. Cook in an uncovered roasting pan on the middle oven rack for approximately 3 hours or until a meat thermometer reads at least 150° F.

For the sauce, combine sugar, cornstarch, vinegar, water, and soy sauce in a small saucepan and place on low heat. Stir occasionally until the sauce begins to bubble and slightly thicken.

Then remove from heat and brush the roast with glaze 3 or 4 times during the last 1/2 hour of cooking. Pour remaining sauce over the roast and serve.

MARGARET HATHAWAY, a self-described foodie, was the manager of Manhattan's famed Magnolia Bakery when she and her husband, burned out with urban life, imagined a more spirit-filled life in the country, with a pasture full of goats. They quit their jobs and embarked on a yearlong odyssey to discover all things goat-related. Out of that year came a book, *The Year of the Goat: 40,000 Miles and the Quest for the Perfect Cheese*, a move to a rural farm in Maine, and a new livelihood centered around organic produce and goats. Margaret is at work on completing another book, *Living with Goats*, and a memoir about her spiritual and food pilgrimage.

5

For a Sweet New Year

It is the weekend before Rosh Hashanah, the Jewish New Year, and the maples in our woods have begun to shimmer scarlet and golden. The day is blustery, and through the kitchen window I watch the trees bend and sway under clear turquoise skies. In the orchard, past our garden, apples drop in cascades with each gust, bouncing in the deep grass, red and ochre spheres finding their places in the wild, tufted tapestry of autumn.

As we do every Friday in anticipation of the Sabbath, my daughters and I are making challah. Charlotte, age two, stands on her helping stool while I work the dough. Balancing precariously in her patent-leather shoes as she pushes her little fists in, she is ostensibly helping me knead but truly grabbing illicit handfuls, which she eats raw. I try to trust that she won't fall (we're doing God's work, aren't we?) as she rakes her fingers across the counter, furrowing the flour, delighting, as I do, in the gift of grain. Beatrice, at five months, is strapped to my chest in the baby carrier and opens her arms wide, as if to welcome the bread. We have punched the dough and waited, punched it again and waited some more. We knead it one last time, saying a little prayer for everyone in our family, adding a name at each quarter turn until finally, beneath a floured towel, a mass of pillowy dough rises. We rest as it does, coordinating nap time with the middle rise, the long one. Charlotte, who always needs convincing, is coaxed to sleep with the promise of the dough's dramatic puff.

For the New Year, we make round loaves rather than braided, circular to symbolize the continuity of life. When they are up again, the girls and I roll out long snakes, then wind them around themselves, tucking their tails demurely beneath the final coil. The bread is studded with plump raisins, made rich with eggs from our hens. It will rise for a final time in shape, the yeast breathing in levity, the dough ready for a last glossy wash.

It is Jewish tradition, on Rosh Hashanah, to dip bread and sliced apples in honey for a sweet new year. When my husband and I bought our old farmhouse in central Maine, moving from the chaos of New York City to the relative calm of the country, our goal was to live as close to the land as possible, to close the circle of our consumption by making and raising as much as we could and returning our waste to the earth. Our kitchen scraps go to the compost pile and, in winter, to the bin of worms in our family room; leftover milk from our goats fattens the chickens and ducks; animal bedding is tilled into the garden.

My husband Karl and I became engaged on *erev* Rosh Hashanah, the evening that begins the holiday. We dreamt then of beginning the new year—and, more expansively, our new life as a family—with the fruits of our land, and to a large degree, we do. For Rosh Hashanah supper, we will slice apples from our orchard and loaves of our own bread. We will roast one of our chickens, which Karl slaughtered and I cleaned and stuffed with herbs from the pots on our front porch. The tzimmes, a dish of sweet stewed root vegetables whose name has also come to mean "to fuss" because it takes so much time to prepare, will contain potatoes that our little peasant daughter helped us dig, and bright fuchsia heirloom carrots from the garden, sliced into coins that, according to Ashkenazi custom, will foreshadow prosperity and good fortune in the new year. The extra row of leeks that we planted for the holiday will be stewed with the last of our tomatoes, leeks that the Talmud tells us signify a fresh start, since their name in Aramaic, *karti*, is the same as the Hebrew word "to cut off." We eat the word, the Word, consuming our faith literally and figuratively, and teaching our children to do the same.

The majority of what makes it to our table has been raised on our farm, but our attempts at harvesting our own honey, insurance for a sweet new year, have been a failure. On Charlotte's first Hanukkah, Karl bought two empty hives and signed me up for a class with a master bee-keeper. Once a week, I gave the baby a long nursing session and left her home with Papa as I drove an hour north to the extension office. These nights were as much about my evolving motherhood as they were about the bees; they were the only hours I was away from Charlotte that first year, and I often cried for a few miles. I missed my girl and couldn't wait for that moment, pulling back into our driveway, when I could see my little warm family through the lit windows and knew the soup I'd left for Karl would be simmering for me on the woodstove. But bees would make our farm flower, and learning to be their steward was parenthood of a different kind.

On the second floor of the extension office, in a dusty classroom that had once held the town jail but was now papered with posters of in-digenous pests and various tree fungi, I listened and took notes, marking down the equipment I would need, tips for keeping my smoker alight and cleaning my honey extruder, characteristics of mites and blight. Charlotte's first spring, we ordered two packages of bees and, wearing my helmet and veil and pacifying the bees with mists of sugar water and puffs of sumac smoke, I pried open the queen cages and shook my buzzing boxes into the opened hives.

We checked the bees periodically throughout the spring and sum-mer, watching in amazement as they coated the wax frames I'd assembled with comb, as the queen lay eggs in each tiny hexagonal box, as the ba-bies nibbled their way out and joined the colony. Our orchard bloomed a dazzling, snowy white; our garden flourished with the trumpets of squash flowers. Dangling jewels of clustered tomatoes adorned thirty plants, a profusion of ripe wild blackberries and blueberries scattered through our woods. The bees blessed our land, dancing their fertile way across the property and leaving bounty in their wake. Even before their honey, they sweetened our summer.

By the fall, I was newly pregnant. The anticipation of our second baby was, of course, sweet, but the reality of daily life that Rosh Hashanah was not. Overwhelmed by the farm, by the abundance that our bees had wrought, I let tomatoes rot on the vine, and I ruined the pickle brine in my nausea. I did not collect honey, could not even touch the prophylactic antibiotic I should have dusted over the hives, so finally, I sent Karl down to the orchard to administer heavy syrup and wrap the hives in tar paper for the winter. In the spring, when I finally fired up the smoker and pulled the bee suit around my swollen middle, the hives were empty.

⌒

In many ways, Rosh Hashanah is a holiday of parenthood. Androgynous, it is both the commemoration of the birth of the world and a celebration of submission to its Father and King. Its Torah portion is one of the most horrific stories of parenthood I know: the binding of Isaac by Abraham, the near sacrifice of a son by his father. But the New Year's imagery is of fecundity and sweetness, its round *challot*, like so many pregnant bellies, delivering us with each bite into the ten Days of Awe and, finally, the renewal of a fresh year. Much will be asked of us in this new year, but much, much more will be given.

Just as we are children of God, we are parents of our children and we are guardians of the land and its creatures. In our family's agrarian practice of our faith, that is the circularity we celebrate at this holiday. As we do so often in Judaism, at Rosh Hashanah we say a *Shehechiyanu* to thank God for sustaining us and enabling us to reach the holiday. Implicit in the prayer is gratitude for the responsibilities of our lives, for the sweetness that comes with the ties that bind us. We do our best, and we are thankful.

The girls and I poke one final raisin into the top of each challah and slide the loaves into the oven. Karl is home early for the holiday and we set a timer on the bread, then take baskets down to the orchard to pick apples for our Rosh Hashanah meal. Charlotte runs ahead, scampering through the bramble at the edge of the orchard to pick low-hanging fruit. When we catch up, Bea, her baby fingers grasping at everything, pulls at leaves, twigs, finally an apple.

Had we introduced more honey bees this year, we would have installed them in the hives last April. Instead, I gave birth. We welcomed our baby Bea during the week that we should have put in a new colony; the abandoned hives were left in their corner of the orchard, tar paper torn and flapping, an empty can of sugar syrup rusting between the boxes. Binding weeds, vibrant in their autumn cloaks, now creep forward to pull the hives into the underbrush. Ignored and camouflaged, they are forgotten, nearly invisible.

It is Charlotte who notices the bees, fearless in their striped armor, zipping past us to the fallen apples beneath our trees. The closer we look at the fruit, the more astonished we are. Wrinkled, rotten, fermenting sweetly in the sun, the apples teem with bees. They fly by the hundreds on this warm day, buzzing in the trees as they do in spring, alighting briefly on the edge of our baskets. I brush them from the girls' sleeves and, gazing at the sky, try to follow the bee-line back to its origin. The hives. Repopulated with wild bees, the neglected hives are humming once more.

$\backsim$

Karl and I are not perfect parents. We know that we are fallen, but we struggle and juggle and try each day to nurture our family and its small corner of this earth. Sometimes we succeed and sometimes we don't. At our best, we know and accept that ultimately, we are not the ones in control.

The bees came back. Untamed, unexpected: a new, terrifying sweetness to begin the year. We bless the honey:

Y'hi ratzon mil'fanekha Adonai eloheinu vei'lohei avoteinu sh't'chadeish aleinu shanah tovah um'tukah.

May it be your will, Adonai our God and God of our ancestors, that you renew for us a good and sweet year.

Sweet Raisin Challah

A traditional bread of Rosh Hashanah.

INGREDIENTS

1 tablespoon active dry yeast
1/2 cup sugar
1/4 cup honey
2 cups warm water
1/2 cup plus 2 tablespoons canola oil
A few threads of saffron, crushed
1 tablespoon kosher salt
3 large eggs
2 cups whole wheat flour
3 to 5 cups all purpose flour
3/4 cup raisins (optional)
1 egg yolk mixed with 1 tablespoon cold water for glaze

Makes 2 large loaves

RECIPE

In a large mixing bowl, combine the yeast, sugar, honey, and warm water and let proof.

When it has turned creamy and begun to foam (after about 5 minutes), add the oil, saffron, salt, eggs, and whole wheat flour.

Beat with a wooden spoon until all the ingredients are incorporated.

Gradually add the all purpose flour, beating in a 1/2 cup at a time.

When the dough becomes too stiff to beat with a spoon, begin to knead in the flour with your hands until you have a smooth, supple dough.

If using raisins, knead them in.

Then cover with a clean, damp dish towel and let rest for 10 minutes.

Turn out the dough onto a floured surface and knead until the dough is elastic, adding more flour as you go, if necessary.

Put a few drops of oil into a large bowl and roll the dough around, so that its surface is lightly oiled.

Cover with a clean, damp dish towel and let rise in a warm place until doubled in bulk, about 1 1/2 hours.

Punch down, cover again, and let rise for another hour.

Divide dough in half and cut each piece into thirds.

Roll out the dough into long snakes and braid into 2 loaves, placing on a baking sheet and tucking the ends under so that the loaves stay together. Alternatively, for Rosh Hashanah, divide the dough in half and roll each piece into one long snake and then coil it into a round loaf; it will look like a turban. If making round loaves, place one raisin in the center on top.

Preheat the oven to 325° F. Cover the loaves with a clean, damp dish towel and let rise for another 45 minutes.

Uncover and brush with egg wash. For a shinier loaf, wait 5 minutes and brush with egg again before baking.

Bake for about 1 hour, until the loaf is lightly browned and sounds hollow when its underside is rapped with a knuckle.

FR. ROBERT FARRAR CAPON, a lifelong New Yorker, was a full-time parish priest in Port Jefferson, New York, for almost thirty years. In 1965, he published his first book, *Bed and Board*, and in 1977, he left full-time ministry to devote more time to his writing. Seventeen books followed, including *The Supper of the Lamb*, *The Parables of the Kingdom*, and his newest book, *The Mystery of Christ*. He has also taught cooking classes, written as a food columnist for *Newsday* and the *New York Times*, and authored several cookbooks. He is currently an assisting priest at St. Luke's Church in East Hampton, New York, and Canon Theologian to the Bishop of Long Island. This is perhaps the most famous passage from the enduring classic *The Supper of the Lamb*.

6

The Heavenly Onion

Select three or four medium-size onions—I have in mind the common, or yellow, onion normally available in the supermarket. The first movement I(A) of my recipe is simply a stew; small white onions, while more delicate as a vegetable in their own right, are a nuisance to cut up for inclusion in something else. The labor of peeling is enlarged beyond reason, and the attempt to slice up the small slippery balls you are left with can be painful.

Next take one of the onions (preferably the best-looking), a paring knife, and a cutting board and sit down at the kitchen table. Do not attempt to stand at a counter through these opening measures. In fact, to do it justice, you should arrange to have sixty minutes or so free for this part of the exercise. Admittedly, spending an hour in the society of an onion may be something you have never done before. You feel, perhaps, a certain resistance to the project. Please don't. As I shall show later, a number of highly profitable members of the race have undertaken it before *you. Onions* are excellent company.

Once you are seated, the first order of business is to address yourself to the onion at hand. (You must firmly resist the temptation to feel silly. If necessary, close the doors so no one will see you; but do not give up out of embarrassment.) You will note, to begin with, that the onion is a *thing*, a being, just as you are. Savor that for a moment. The two of you sit here in mutual confrontation. Together with knife, board, table, and chair, you are the constituents of a *place* in the highest sense of the word. This is a *Session*, a meeting, a society of things.

You have, you see, already discovered something: The uniqueness, the *placiness*, of places derives not from abstractions like *location*, but from confrontations like man–onion. Erring theologians have strayed to their graves without learning what you have come upon. They have insisted, for example, that heaven is no place because it could not be defined in terms of spatial coordinate. They have written off man's eternal habitation as a "state of mind." But look what your onion has done for you: It has given you back the possibility of heaven as a place without encumbering you with the irrelevancy of location.

This meeting between the two of you could be moved to a thousand different latitudes and longitudes and still remain the *session* it started out to be. Indeed, by the motions of the earth, the solar system, the galaxy, and the universe (if that can be defined), every place—every meeting of matter . . . becomes a kind of cosmic floating crap game: Location is accidental to its deepest meaning. What really matters is not where we are, but who—what real beings . . . are with us. In that sense, heaven where we see God face to face through the risen flesh of Jesus, may well be the placiest of all places, as it is the most *gloriously* material of all meetings. Here, perhaps, we do indeed see only through a glass darkly; we mistake one of the earthly husks of place for the heart of its mattering.

But back to the onion itself. As nearly as possible now, try to look at it as if you had never seen an onion before. Try, in other words, to meet it on its own terms, not to dictate yours to it. You are convinced, of course, that you know what an onion is. You think perhaps that it is a brownish yellow vegetable, basically spherical in shape, composed of fundamentally similar layers. All such prejudices should be abandoned. It is what it is, and your work here is to find it out.

For a start, therefore, notice that your onion has two ends: a lower, now marked only by the blackish gray spot from which the root filaments descended into the earth; and an upper, which terminates (unless your onions are over the hill, or have begun to sprout because you store them under a leaky sink trap) in a withered peak of onion paper. Note once again what you have discovered: an onion is not a sphere in repose. It is a linear thing, a bloom of vectors thrusting upward from base to tip. Stand your onion, therefore, root end down upon the board and see it as the paradigm of life that it is—as one member of the vast living, gravity-defying troop that, across the face of the earth, moves light and airward as long as the world lasts.

Only now have you the perspective needed to enter the onion itself. Begin with the outermost layer of paper, or onion skin. Be careful. In the ordinary processes of cooking, the outer skin of a sound onion is removed by peeling away the immediately underlying layers of flesh with it. It is a legitimate short cut; the working cook cannot afford the time it takes to loosen only the paper. Here, however, it is not time that matters, but the onion. Work gently then, lifting the skin with the point of your knife so as not to cut or puncture the flesh beneath. It is harder than you may have thought. Old onion skins give up easily, but new ones can be stubborn.

Look now at the fall of stripped and flaked skin before you. It is dry. It is, all things considered, one of the driest things in the world. Not dusty dry like potatoes, but smoothly and thinly dry, suggesting not accidental desiccation, not the withering due to age or external circumstance, but a fresh and essential dryness. Dryness as an achievement, not as a failure. Elegant dryness. Deliberate dryness. More than that, onion paper is, like the onion itself, directional, vectored, ribbed. (It will, oddly, split as easily across its striations as with them: Its grain has been reduced by dryness to a merely visual quality.) Best of all, though, it is of two colors: the outside, a brownish yellow of no particular brightness; but the inside a soft, burnished, coppery gold, ribbed—especially near the upper end—with an exquisiteness only hinted at on the outside. Accordingly, when you have removed all the paper, turn the fragments inside-up on the board. They are elegant company.

For with their understated display of wealth, they bring you to one of the oldest and most secret things of the world: the sight of what no one but you has ever seen. This quiet gold, and the subtly flattened sheen of greenish yellow white onion that now stands exposed, are virgin land. Like the incredible fit of twin almonds in a shell, they present themselves to you as the animals to Adam: as nameless till seen by man, to be met, known, and christened into the city of being. They come as deputies of all the hiddennesses of the world, of all the silent competencies endlessly at work deep down things. And they come to you—to you as their priest and voice, for oblation by your heart's astonishment at their great glory.

Only now are you ready for the first cut. Holding the onion vertically, slice it cleanly in half right down the center line, and look at what you have done. You have opened the floodgates of being. First, as to the innards. The mental diagram of sphere within sphere is abolished immediately. *Structurally*, the onion is not a ball, but a nested set of fingers within fingers, each thrust up from the base through the center of the one before it. The outer digits are indeed swollen to roundness by the pressure of the inner, but their sphericity is incidental to the linear motion of flame inthrusting flame.

Next, the colors. The cross section of each several flame follows a rule: On its inner edge it is white, on its outer, pigmented; the color varying from the palest greenish yellow in the middle flames, to more recognizably onion shades as you proceed outward. The centermost flames are frankly and startlingly green; it is they which will finally thrust upward into light. Thus the spectrum of the onion: green through white to green again, and ending all in the brown skin you have peeled away. Life inside death. The forces of being storming the walls of the void. Freshness in the face of the burning, oxidizing world which maderizes all life at last to the color of cut apples and old Sherry.

Next pressure, look at the cut surface: moisture. The incredible, utter wetness of onions, of course, you cannot know yet: This is only the first hinted pressing of juice. But the sea within all life has tipped its hand. You have cut open no inanimate thing, but a living tumescent being—a whole that is, as all life is, smaller, simpler than its parts; which holds, as all life does, the pieces of its being in compression. To prove it, try to fit the two halves of the onion back together. It cannot be done. The faces which began as two plane surfaces drawn by a straight blade are now mutually convex, and rock against each other. Put them together on one side and the opposite shows a gap of more than two minutes on a clock face.

Again, pressure. But now pressure toward you. The smell of onion, released by the flowing of its juices. Hardly a discovery, of course—even the boor knows his onions to that degree. But pause still. Reflect how little smell there is to a whole onion—how well the noble reek was contained till now by the encompassing dryness. Reflect, too, how it is the humors and sauces of being that give the world flavor, how all life came from the sea, and how, without water, nothing can hold a soul. Reflect finally what a soul the onion must have, it boasts such juices. Your eyes will not yet have begun to water, nor the membranes of your nose to recoil. The onion has only, if you will, *whispered* to you. Yet you have not mistaken a syllable of its voice, not strained after a single word. How will you stop your senses when it raises this stage whisper to a shout?

Now, however, the two halves of the onion lie, cut face up, before you. With the point of your paring knife, carefully remove the base, or bottom (or heart) much as you would do to free the leaves of an artichoke or of a head of lettuce. Take away only as much as will make it possible to lift out, one by one, the several layers. Then gently pry them out in order, working from the center to the outside. Arrange them in a line as you do, with matching parts from the separate halves laid next to each other, making them ascend thus by twos from the smallest green fingers, through white flames, up to the outer shells which sit like paired Russian church spires.

Then look. The myth of sphericity is finally dead. The onion, as now displayed, is plainly all vectors, risers, and thrusts. *Tongues of fire.* But the Pentecost they mark is that of nature, not grace: the Spirit's first brooding on the face of the waters. Lift one of the flames; feel its lightness and rigidity, its crispness and strength. Make proof of its membranes. The inner: thin, translucent, easily removed; the outer, however, thinner, almost transparent—and so tightly bonded to the flesh that it protests audibly again separation. (You will probably have to break the flesh to free even a small piece.) The membranes, when in place, give the onion its fire, its sheen, soft within and brighter without. But when they are removed, the flesh is revealed in a new light. Given a minute to dry, it acquires a pale crystalline flatness like nothing on earth. Eggshell is the only word for it; but by comparison to the stripped flesh of an onion, an eggshell is only as delicate as poured concrete.

Set aside your broken flame now and pick up a fresh one. Clear a little space on the board. Lay it down on its cut face and slice it lengthwise into several strips. (You will want to tap it lightly with the edge of the knife first. There is a hollow crisp sound to be gotten that ways—something between a *tock* and a *tunk*. It is the sound of health and youth, the audible response of cellularity when it is properly addressed. Neither solid nor soft, it is the voice of life itself.)

Next take one of the slivers and press it. Here you will need firmness. If you have strong nails, use the back of the one on you middle finger; if not, steamroller the slice with a round pencil. Press and roll it until it yields all the water it will. You have reached the deepest revelation of all.

First, and obviously, the onion is now part of you. It will be for days. For the next two mornings at least, when you wash your hands and face, your meeting with it will be reconvened in more than a memory. It has spoken a word with power, and even the echo is not in vain.

But, second, the onion itself is all but gone. The flesh, so crisp and solid, turns out to have been an aqueous house of cards. If you have done your pressing well, the little scraps of membrane and cell wall are nearly nonexistent. The whole infolded nest of flames was a blaze of water, a burning bush grown from the soil of the primeval oceans. All life is from the sea.

And God said, Let the waters bring forth abundantly. . . . And God saw that it was good. This juice, this liquor, this rough-and-ready cordial, runs freely now on board and hands and knife. Salt, sweet, and yet so much itself as to speak for no other, it enters the city of being. What you have seen, to be sure, is only the smallest part of its singularity, the merest hint of the stunning act of being that it is, but it is enough perhaps to enable you to proceed, if not with safety, then with caution.

For somehow, beneath this gorgeous paradigm of unnecessary being, lies the Act by which it exists. You have just now reduced it to its parts, shivered it into echoes, and pressed it to a memory, but you have also caught the hint that a thing is more than the sum of all the insubstantialities that comprise it. Hopefully, you will never again argue that the solidities of the world are mere matters of accident, creatures of air and darkness, temporary and meaningless shapes out of nothing. Perhaps now you have seen at least dimly that the uniqueness of creation are the result of continuous creative support, of effective regard by no mean lover. He likes onions, therefore they are. The fit, the colors, the smell, the tensions, the tastes, the textures, the lines, the shapes are a response, not to some forgotten decree that there may as well be onions as turnips, but to his present delight—his intimate and immediate joy in all you have seen, and in the thousand other wonders you do not even suspect. With Peter, the onion says, Lord, it is good for us to be here. Yes, says God. Tov. Very good.

Fair enough then. All life is from the sea. It takes water to hold a soul. Living beings are full of juices.

But watch out.

I once gave a dinner party at which I conned my wife (then hardly more than a bride) into garnishing a main dish (I think it was a mixed grill) with fried parsley. *Persil frit* is one of the traps that is laid to teach humility to men beset by culinary presumption. I had spent the better part of a morning off devising a way of making attractive bunches of parsley for frying, and I had finally come up with what I still consider (apart from the disaster that followed) the perfect presentation of persil frit. I took bread sticks and, with a coping saw, carefully cut them into three-quarter-inch length. Then, ever so gently, I bored out the centers with a small twist drill. This provided me with a number of neckerchief slides, as it were, into each of which I thrust a sufficient number of parsley sprigs to make a snug fit. Since my wife had bought excellent parsley, they made magnificent little sheaves of green.

Unfortunately, however, I neglected to tell my wife that, in spite of all this artsy-crafty ingenuity, I had never prepared, cooked, eaten, or even seen fried parsley before. What she trustingly accepted from me as a manageable fact was nothing but a conceit. We sow, on bright, clear days, the seed of our own destruction.

For a young thing she had done more than well. Hors d'oeuvres, soup, and fish had come off beautifully—but at an expense of spirit to which I was blind. The working cook of a major meal operates under pressure, and the ivory tower gourmet should never forget it. The mixed grill was in the broiler, the French fryer was heating on the stove, and my wife, tense but still game, picked up my little parsley masterpieces and dropped them into the fat.

What followed was the nearest thing we have ever had to a kitchen fire, and one of the nearest to a marital disaster. Parsley: freshness: water. All life is from the sea. Water: heat: steam. When the bouquets hit the fat, the whole business blew up. Steam: sound: fury. And grease all over the kitchen. Fury: wife: tears. All waters return to the sea.

I spent the fish course in the kitchen mending my fences, trying to bluff my way out. To this day, I remember nothing about the rest of the meal. Except one thing. The parsley was glorious. It fries in ten seconds or so and turns the most stunning green you can imagine. It was parsley transfigured, and I shall never forget it. It is just as well. My wife has never cooked it again.

Between the onion and the parsley, therefore, I shall give the summation of my case for paying attention. Man's real work is to look at the things of the world and to love them for what they are. That is, after all, what God does, and man was not made in God's image for nothing. The fruits of his attention can be seen in all the arts, crafts, and sciences. It can cost him time and effort, but it pays handsomely. If an hour can be spent on one onion, think how much regarding it took on the part of that old Russian who looked at onions and church spires long enough to come up with St. Basil's Cathedral. Or how much curious and loving attention was expended by the first man who looked hard enough at the inside of trees, the entrails of cats, the hind ends of horses, and the juice of pine trees to realize he could turn them all into the first fiddle. No doubt his wife urged him to get up and do something useful. I am sure that he was a stalwart enough lover of things to pay no attention at all to her nagging; but how wonderful it would have been if he had known what we know now about his dawdling. He could have silenced her with the greatest riposte of all time; Don't bother me; I am creating the possibility of the Bach unaccompanied sonatas.

But if a man's attention is so repaid so handsomely, his inattention costs him dearly. Every time he diagrams something instead of looking at it, every time he regards not what a thing *is* but what it can be made to *mean* to *him*—every time he substitutes a conceit for a fact—he gets grease all over the kitchen of the world. Reality slips away from him; and he is left with nothing but the oldest monstrosity in the world: an idol. Things must be met for themselves. To take them only for their meaning is to convert them into gods—to make them too important, and therefore to make *them* unimportant altogether. Idolatry has two faults. It is not only a slur on the true God; it is also an insult to true things.

They made a calf in Horeb; thus they turned their Glory into the similitude of a calf that eateth hay. Bad enough, you say. Ah, but it was worse than that. Whatever good may have resided in the Golden Calf—whatever loveliness of gold or beauty of line—went begging the minute the Israelites got the idea that *it* was their savior out of the bondage of Egypt. In making the statue a matter of the greatest *point*, they missed the point of its *matter* altogether.

Berate me not therefore for carrying on about slicing onions in a world under the sentence of nuclear overkill. The heaviest weight on the shoulders of the earth is still the age-old idolatry by which man has cheated himself of both Creator and creation. And this age is no exception. If you prefer to address yourself to graver matters, well and good: Idolatry needs all the enemies it can get. But if I choose to break images in the kitchen, I cannot be faulted. We are both good men, in a day when good men are hard to find. Let us join hands and get on with our iconoclasm.

There is a Russian story about an old woman whose vices were so numerous that no one could name even one of her virtues. She was slothful, spiteful, envious, deceitful, greedy, foul-mouthed, and proud. She lived by herself and in herself; she loved no one and no thing. One day a beggar came to her door. She upbraided him, abused him, and sent him away. As he left, however, she unaccountably threw an onion after him. He picked it up and ran away. In time the woman died and was dragged down to her due reward in hell. But just as she was about to slip over the edge of the bottomless pit, she looked up. Above her, descending from the infinite distances of heaven, was a great archangel, and in his hand was an onion. "Grasp this," he said. "If you hold it, it will lift you up to heaven."

One real thing is closer to God than all the diagrams in the world.

Scrap Soups and White Stock[1]

Delicious off-the-cuff soups can be made from vegetable and meat leavings that would ordinarily be thrown away. Just keep your eyes open for opportunities.

INGREDIENTS

Vegetable trimmings (mushrooms, asparagus, or celery)
Small amount of minced onion

1. Italics indicate editorial additions for this book.

Butter

Weak stock, or water plus chicken-wing tips or necks (*store-purchased broth might do*)

Sherry or Madeira

Flour

Cream or top milk (optional)

RECIPES

Mushroom Soup

Sauté chopped mushroom stems, skins, or trimmings in butter with a little minced onion until the onion is transparent.

Add a modest amount of stock and boil for 20 minutes. Add a few drops of Sherry or Madeira at the end.

You now have an infusion. Remove chicken parts, if any, and put the rest through the blender. Alternately, simply strain out all the solids.

Make a roux of flour and butter (*1 tablespoon of butter, melted, and 1 tablespoon flour, simmered together and stirred until inseparable, about 1 minute*) and thicken this infusion judiciously.

Taste it, and add as much cream or milk as you like, just so you do not wash out the flavor. Correct seasoning.

Asparagus Soup

Save the tough, lower ends of the asparagus spears. Chop them into small pieces and sauté in butter with a little minced onion until the onion is transparent.

Proceed as above, but omit the sherry. If you blend, strain out the fibers afterward.

Garnish the finished soup with leftover cooked asparagus tips, if you have any.

Celery Soup

Proceed as before, using celery ends, light leaves, and odd stalks, but keep the quantity of onion very discreet and omit the Sherry. Don't bother to blend at all.

Garnish the finished soup with finely diced raw celery.

Stephen and Karen Baldwin live and cook together in Saint Louis, Missouri, where they offer hospitality to guests of Covenant Seminary and serve as Pastoral Couple in Residence among theological students. They have been involved in pastoral ministry in the Washington, DC, area and planting churches in Ireland, Colorado, and most recently, North Carolina, with the aim of restoring worship to all aspects of life, including food.

7

A Way of Loving

When our three children were in their mid to late teens, we were living in Colorado in modernist-style home that was often full of their friends. One afternoon the family room was alive with laughter, music, and the passionate voices of high school students rising through the stairway into the kitchen. I was beginning to think about dinner. It was late summer, so school had just started and homework was easy to put off—of course everyone would stay for dinner.

To satisfy the hungry crowd, I decided on pasta for twelve, a big salad, and lots of garlic bread. As I was making the bread dough and my husband Stephen was arranging the ingredients for the pasta, some of my daughter Rachel's friends wandered into the kitchen. When they saw that the bread, the pasta, and the pasta sauce were not coming out of prepackaged boxes and bottles, but were all being made from raw ingredients, they seemed disoriented. At the same time, they were enticed by the sharp-sweet scent of garlic, tomatoes, and herbs in hot extra-virgin olive oil.

A mound of flour sat on the countertop, ready to be transformed into pasta dough, and with his usual enthusiasm, Stephen invited the spectators to help, showing them how to mix up that dough. David, our son, stepped in to take over rolling out and cutting the dough into fettuccine, passing it through the hand-cranked pasta machine. He was eager to show his friends how fun and easy it was—making pasta is simple but artistically impressive. In a few short minutes one goes from having a pile of flour, eggs, and olive oil to long smooth strands of fresh pasta hanging on drying racks to keep them from sticking together. And the pasta is ready for the pot of boiling water. From the reactions of Rachel and David's friends, you would have thought we were performing magic.

Before long, the bread was baking in the oven, releasing its warm, yeasty aroma. The sauce was simmering on the stove top, and the lettuce was washed, drained, and torn into bite-sized pieces. All that remained was to whisk up a fresh salad dressing and set the table. I never hesitate to put everyone to work, so I asked a couple of the girls to take on the table-setting. We gathered up the cutlery, plates, napkins, and glasses, and we headed to the dining room where I left them to it. After a few minutes, I went back to check on the girls' progress and discovered neither had a clue how to set a table properly. All the cutlery was in the wrong place, and the napkins were on the wrong side.

Using the occasion to teach the basics of table setting in a friendly way, I spoke up, "The plate goes in front of the chair. The napkin goes on the left of the plate, folded; the salad and dinner forks go on top of the napkin. The salad fork goes on the outside, since salad is eaten first, and then nearest the plate is the dinner fork. On the other side of the plate, the spoon goes on the outside, since the soup or pasta course come before the main course, so nearest to the plate goes your knife. The water glass goes on the person's right-hand side, and the salad plate goes on their left." I told them that how a table is set not only communicates aesthetically, it also tells a story. If you know the signals, a spoon or fork at the top of the plate says, "There's dessert!" They got it right and seemed happy to learn how to set the stage for an act in which they would soon be among the players.

Over the next several years, similar scenes often played out in our home. I marveled at how little these kids knew about preparing food, creating an inviting table setting, or using knives, forks, and spoons. It is sad how foreign it is to sit unhurriedly, to eat lovingly crafted food attentively, and to have meaningful, personal conversations during meals. We found that what we considered to be the usual way for families to connect was exceedingly rare. Many of our younger friends ate alone, at no particular time, and they usually did so in front of the television. Whereas when we offer food thoughtfully and with respect, caring for and honoring those present at our table, it creates an atmosphere where sharing, laughing, and relating happens naturally. Offering our hospitality is a medium of grace that opens hearts to deeper things. It is a simple way of loving.

So how can you begin to develop the confidence to plan and prepare a meal for the people God brings into your life? Start simply. If the weather is cold, make a simple soup. Add a grilled cheese sandwich or put together two or three cheeses on a cutting board with crackers or sliced baguette. Plan ahead how to serve your soup and sandwich or cheese. Clear the clutter from the table and set it with the necessary cutlery and napkins. Use a casual tablecloth. Don't try to be fancy or presumptuous—that is not what you are looking for. You are creating a space that is warm and inviting, a place that feels secure for a person who needs safety in relationship. Warm the soup bowls and plates if you are serving something hot. Place the cheese, unwrapped, around the cutting board with knives for cutting the cheeses, and let the cheese come to room temperature. Put your bread or crackers on a platter or in a basket lined with a napkin. Perhaps cut up an apple or a pear, or place some grapes on another plate. This is so simple and yet so appealing.

At the table, set a tone that says, "This is a place to linger." Ask those at your table if they have seen any good films lately or what they are reading. Listen for clues about what makes them laugh or what makes them angry or frustrated. Nothing gets a conversation going like showing interest in someone and being willing to listen. If you have a friend who won't open up, you can talk about your day and what you are reading or growing in your garden. As you talk, you will be demonstrating how to have a meaningful conversation around a table without the distractions that usually hold our attention and keep us from touching each other's lives. Obviously (or maybe not in our day) in place of the television, turn on pleasant music (at a non-intrusive volume).

Stephen and I have hosted friends, family, and new acquaintances at our table. On nights like that night in Colorado, we've orchestrated dinner for a crowd of our children's friends, and on other nights we've eaten a quiet meal with just the two of us. And in that same spirit of openness, invitation, and hospitality we like to begin each meal by thanking God and lifting our friends up before the one who invites us to come and eat of the bread of life that he gives. Our friends may not share our deepest convictions, they may not understand the great significance we place in this time at the table, but we can't recall any expectant mothers or anxious students declining our request to pray for them. So we never feel timid about raising a glass of wine or a plate heaped with fragrant food, and then, with simple gratitude and joy, extolling the Creator who celebrated his creative power and genius by resting and blessing his handiwork. And as we say amen, we recognize that in our Creator's image, we have also completed a work of preparation, and so we enter into a celebration-rest together at the table where there is both food to nourish our bodies and fellowship to revive our souls.

In this way, every meal is a still life, in real time and space, of the convergence of God's creative and redemptive acts, even if this is not overtly explained with words in a blessing or a conversation. The complex array of tastes, colors, textures, and smells in which we participate around the table rise out of the wisdom, wonder, and variety of God's creative acts. The table fellowship is a foretaste of full redemption when Christ's finished work culminates in the wedding feast of the Lamb, at which we will sit and enjoy the finest of friends, good aged wine, and the best of foods. Friends of food recognize Isaiah 25 as a notable description of the feast of redemption, where, as in *Babette's Feast*, earthly scruples will be swallowed up, utterly outstripped by God's lavish display of love and artistry for his children.

As we have cooked together, learned about food, and shared meals, we have experienced an increasing sense of awe and wonder in the Creator. The nearly infinite diversity of his gifts of taste and smell, of color and texture, have moved our hearts and caused us to take delight in the simple sharing of food and table fellowship. We have seen how these savory pleasures draw our friends into the kitchen and then into community with one another, how preparing food from scratch and then dining purposefully together can graciously suspend the busyness of our culture and illuminate God's love.

Stephen has a stirring memory (pun intended) of me cooking one day, entirely absorbed in my medium. All of my senses were engaged— the sight of food browning, the sound as its moisture content changed, the smelling, tasting, and touching of the food. This day he heard me muse quietly, unconsciously perhaps, yet oh so rightly, "When I cook, it is worship."

Basic Pasta

DOUGH INGREDIENTS

2 1/2 to 3 cups all-purpose flour
3 large eggs
1/2 teaspoon extra-virgin olive oil
Salt

TOMATO SAUCE INGREDIENTS

1/4 cup extra-virgin olive oil
2 cloves garlic, peeled and sliced thin
2-inch sprig of fresh basil stem and leaves
2 (28-ounce) cans peeled whole tomatoes
Salt and fresh ground pepper
Splash of balsamic vinegar
1 pat (1/2 tablespoon) butter
Freshly grated Parmesan cheese (optional)

RECIPE

Dough

Mound the flour in the center of a large wooden cutting board. Make a well in the middle of the flour and add the eggs and the olive oil.

Using a fork, gently beat together the eggs and oil and begin to incorporate the flour, starting with the inner rim of the flour well.

As you expand the well, keep pushing the flour up from the base of the mound to retain the well shape. The dough will come together when half of the flour is incorporated.

Start kneading the dough with both hands, using the palms of your hands.

Once you have a cohesive mass, remove the dough from the board, scraping up and discarding any leftover bits.

Lightly flour the board and continue kneading for 6 more minutes, until the dough feels elastic and a little sticky.

Wrap the dough in plastic and allow it to rest for 30 minutes at room temperature.

Then roll and shape the dough as desired. Your pasta machine will have instructions, but here is the way we do it:

Once your pasta dough has rested, you are ready to begin making noodles. Dust your flat surface again, with all-purpose flour, so that it doesn't stick.

Using your fingers, flatten and shape the dough into a rough rectangle about 1/2 inch thick; then further flatten the end that you will feed into the pasta machine.

With the pasta machine set on the highest (widest) setting, place the thin end of the dough in between the two main rollers. While turning the handle, pass the dough through the rollers.

Dust this lengthened piece of pasta with more flour, fold in it thirds, and then press together and repeat this action several more times until the pasta has a smooth, consistent, slightly moist and silky feel. Now you are ready to decrease the thickness of your pasta by stepping down the machine setting one notch at a time.

When the pasta is too long to work with, cut it in half and lay one half aside while you work with the other half.

Cover the resting pieces with plastic wrap to keep them from drying out. As you work with each piece, the result should be long, smooth ribbons without cracks or blemishes.

For *tagliatelle*, just take these strips and cut them in inch-wide strips of 8 to 10 inches in length with a pizza cutter.

For *fettuccine*, cut the sheets about every 12 to 18 inches. Attach the cutter to the pasta machine and feed one end of the pasta sheet into the spinning rollers. The pasta will emerge as beautiful fettuccine. After a several inches of the pasta emerges, lift it along with your open hand and then drape it over a clean wooden dowel (even a clean broom handle between two chairs will work) and gently separate any pasta that is sticking together. This will become a little easier as it gets drier. Alternatively, you can dust the noodles with a light coating of flour and loosely pile them on your work surface.

Bring a large pot of water to a boil and add salt. The water should taste like the sea. Drop the fresh pasta into the boiling water and cook until it is tender, 1 to 2 minutes. Drain the pasta and toss with the sauce.

Sauce

In a 3-quart saucepan, heat the olive oil over medium heat. Add the garlic and cook until soft; then add most of the basil.

Next, add the tomatoes and their juice, leaving the tomatoes whole for now. Season the mixture with salt and pepper. Let simmer for about 30 minutes.

Break up the tomatoes with a wooden spoon, add the balsamic vinegar, and cook for 5 more minutes.

Remove from the heat and check to see if there is the right amount of salt and pepper.

Now add the butter and a few fresh basil leaves over the top of your sauce, just as the Italians love to do, adding different versions of the same herb to layer the flavors. Serve over fresh pasta with freshly grated Parmesan cheese.

R. Gary LeBlanc lives and works in the Tidewater region of Virginia as managing director of a small hotel company and devotes his free time to family and Mercy Chefs. Gary founded Mercy Chefs in the wake of Hurricane Katrina to feed people as evidence of Christ's love. Gary is ordained as a minster at New Life Providence Church and has won many local and state accolades for his volunteer efforts. Mercy Chefs is currently managing two field kitchen sites in the relief and rebuilding efforts in Haiti and expanding its disaster relief reach to the entire continental United States.

8

Go Feed People

I always wanted out of the kitchen. I've tried my whole career to work my way out, but God had other plans.

It began on a beautiful late summer day in 2005. My wife and I had recently purchased a house in Virginia and were finishing some renovation. The TV was on. We watched the latest report of Katrina, a storm that had crossed the southern most part of Florida and was heading in the general direction of my hometown, New Orleans. My grown daughter was there. So were my grandmother, all my cousins, and my aunt. My home church and my dearest friends were there. I watched with growing concern.

On Saturday, I called to see if my cousins had set up my grandmother for the storm. Much to my surprise, they told me they were preparing to evacuate in a convoy with Nanny in her Cadillac leading the way. I was stunned.

We had been in New Orleans in '65 for Betsy and in '69 for Camille. We always hunkered down and did what we needed to be safe, and we took care of each other. But in all my life, no one in my family even *considered* leaving. It was ominous, then, that they had chosen to leave for this storm.

In just a day, our worst fears were realized. Most of New Orleans, including my daughter's home, was under seven feet of water. Along with the rest of the nation, I watched the shocking televised images of people stranded on roofs, left on overpasses, and abandoned in public buildings. I watched as bodies floated in the floodwaters. *If a television crew could get there to film these images,* I wondered, *why couldn't the government and relief organizations mobilize help for these desperate, needy people?* I was embarrassed as an American and devastated as a New Orleanian.

But I was also moved to action as a believer in Jesus Christ. I had to do something. Over and over I thought, *there must be something I can do.*

I knew that Operation Blessing International, an organization that mobilized relief in stricken areas, had acquired a mobile kitchen just a week or two before Katrina. On Tuesday, the day after Katrina hit the Gulf states, I contacted them to volunteer. To my disappointment, they told me that like everyone else, the ferocity and magnitude of this late season storm caught them by surprise. OBI was moving all the resources they could into the affected area, but the kitchen was bare, without even a can opener or cutting board. They couldn't stop their other relief efforts to fix the kitchen, they told me, but I was free to take a stab at it.

God had flung the door wide open. But I knew that no matter what I did, he'd have to show up too if anything was going to happen. I needed a chef, a crew, a health permit, a truck full of equipment, food, cooking supplies, and a lot more. But—it all happened. Our local health department in Virginia did the impossible and got us a health permit for New Orleans in one day—nothing short of a miracle. I blasted an e-mail to my colleagues at Hilton Garden Inns, my friends, and whoever else I could think of, and I had a kitchen crew assembled in no time. I set up a meeting with a Sysco equipment specialist and made a list of supplies and equipment for the mobile kitchen that was nearly five hundred items long. Two to four weeks was the usual delivery time, four to six days for the critically urgent. The guys at Sysco did it in two days. For the items they couldn't find, they tracked down who had last purchased the kitchen supplies, then borrowed them back, promising the customers we would replace it the next week. By the weekend, we had a loaded, honest-to-goodness, fifty-three–foot, tractor-trailer mobile kitchen ready to go.

My first night on the Gulf Coast was in Biloxi, Mississippi, at a staging area for volunteers. I had picked up a rental car in Mobile, Alabama. Gas was in short supply, so I chose the car by checking which one had the most gas in the tank. There was no guarantee I'd find more if I ran out.

The Gulf Coast is usually a place of good food and friendly people, a place to come for relaxation and an almost Caribbean-like ambience. But now there was little left. Buildings were destroyed or just gone. Boats and barges were pushed several blocks inland. And all of it was shrouded in an eerie silence. Other than the occasional hum of a generator, there was no sound at all—no AC units, no traffic, no children playing, no birds singing, not even the usual buzz of flies, mosquitoes, and gnats.

That night I slept in the rental car outside the football stadium that served as our staging area. I lay on the car seat with the windows down. A clean, sweet-smelling breeze blew in off the Gulf. I was thankful: the debris was already beginning to stink. Around 2:00 a.m., I reached back to get a chef coat to keep the chill away. That's when I heard something. The sound was faint, and I could barely make it out at first. But it seemed to grow in volume as I began to make out its source. Then my blood ran cold, and I shivered—not from the chill in the air, but from the sounds of brokenness.

I heard people crying inside the damaged homes that ringed the stadium. But they weren't crying out in fear or pain: it was the weeping of hopelessness, a weeping that asked, *How will we cope? What will we do? What will become of us?* I thought, *It sounds like the hopeless wailing of someone condemned to live apart from God.* I was broken by their cries. And I realized that the Lord was taking me apart to put me back together in a whole new way. He was calling me to help comfort these people who had lost so much—to bring compassion and hope in some way. I felt so small and so unequipped to do this. But I heard him say to me, "If you can let go of yourself, I can use you." I fell back to sleep, my tears now joined with theirs.

Our group moved further west toward New Orleans and could get only as far as Slidell, Louisiana. The folks there were hit hard. We set up our mobile kitchen and started to do what we could. I remembered as a child seeing my grandmother work so hard to feed friends, family, and strangers. She prepared authentic food in abundance, but more importantly, she served joy, comfort, love, and support. I hoped to do the same.

I thought of her that first morning as I rose hours early to prep for breakfast. As a little boy, I would get up early to make breakfast with her. Everyone would still be asleep but us. I learned to make coffee, to break eggs, to mix dough, to cut biscuits. This morning's menu was nearly the same: simple scrambled eggs and a biscuit. That's all I had to serve that first morning in Slidell.

Working in the narrow mobile kitchen for hours with my crew, I had no idea what to expect once we started serving. When we were ready, I opened the service window to an ocean of people waiting in line, more than two thousand souls. The young, the old, the scared, the lost, every face full of emotion and hurt, all standing in line for this food. I was overwhelmed. But as they came together that morning for a meal, I saw something happen. I saw crying and heard appalling stories of loss, but smiles appeared over the Styrofoam containers of food. I could even hear laughter. Over the simplest of meals, I saw God's grace and the beginning of healing, just as I had seen in my grandmother's kitchen.

We went on to cook many meals, but we had so little to work with. I tried to make something close to a jambalaya using the famine packs of rice, canned ham, and salsa. Another day I made a pasta Bolognese with canned dried beef in marinara and pizza sauce. It also brought new meaning to the phrase "Tonight's secret ingredient is . . ." (Try doing Iron Chef with a pack of famine rice sometime!). Neither of these dishes would have won me a prize in a chef's competition, but to the thousands we fed every day, it was miraculous food.

It was there in Slidell that I got the news: Nanny, who was always up before everyone else, tripped and fell in the dark, breaking her hip and leg. She was in a good hospital, though, which was more than most people could find after Katrina. I got to see her on my way home. I was driving from Slidell to Jackson, Mississippi, and I planned to stop at her rehabilitation home for a visit.

I visited with Nanny for as many hours as I could before I caught my plane home. We napped holding hands, told stories, and prayed together for her and for others who had lost so much. She was worried about my cousins, about how my wife Annie was doing without me, about the new house, and about the kids going back to school. I told her about the mobile kitchen and feeding the hungry and needy. What did we cook? What did they say? Did I try this and that? She was full of questions. When she got well, she said, she wanted to go with me and help the next time the mobile kitchen was needed.

We lost my sweet grandmother a few months later. I miss her still and always. Even today, when I get inside a field kitchen, I look at what we have to work with and think, *What would Nanny do with this?*

Back home in Virginia, I relished long showers and soft sheets as if I had been gone decades. That's when the call began to grow even stronger. In the quiet of the night, I would wake up full of ideas. How could I do this better, easier, and more efficiently? How can we do more with less? In no time, I had notebooks full of notes and designs. Somehow, I envisioned solutions and inventions as if they were already done.

Equipped with these God-given ideas, I continued to think of people I knew who could help—professional chefs, church volunteers, non-government agencies—and how they could be brought together to multiply resources and energy. It all became so clear. Then I began to dream about doing it. I was being called. I was being sent. Then one day, I clearly heard these words from God: "Go feed people. Just go feed people." Now, five years later, I run two state-of-the-art mobile kitchens of my own, and they do look like the ones I saw in my dreams. So here I am back in a kitchen, but not any man's kitchen. I'm serving in the Lord's kitchen, feeding people God loves.

Jacmel Jambalaya

The last time I was in Jacmel, Haiti, I was cooking for an advance team doing relief work in the aftermath of the earthquake. All we had was a small canned ham, some famine-relief rice, an onion, and some salsa. I pulled this recipe from memory and took a chance. They ate it all and loved it. This recipe is much better, but it still reminds me how simple foods can so deeply satisfy.

INGREDIENTS

4 cups finely chopped onion

2 cups finely chopped green pepper

2 cups chopped celery

10 cloves garlic, minced

1/2 stick butter

6 cups diced chicken

4 cups diced ham

3 pounds smoked sausage, cut in 1/4 inch slices

2 quarts fresh salsa

4 quarts canned chopped tomatoes, untrained

5 cups raw white rice

7 cups chicken broth

2 teaspoons dried thyme

1/3 cup chopped fresh parsley

Chili powder (to taste)

2 tablespoons salt or less to taste

1 tablespoon white pepper

1 teaspoon cayenne pepper

1 tablespoon black pepper

Serves 20 to 30

RECIPE

Preheat oven to 350° F.

Slowly sauté the onion, green pepper, celery, and garlic in butter. After the veggies are tender, add the chicken, ham, and sausage. Stir for 5 minutes. Then stir salsa and tomatoes with their liquid, the rice, broth, thyme, parsley, chili powder, salt, and pepper. Transfer to a roasting pan, cover, and bake for 70 to 80 minutes or until rice is tender. Immediately fluff and serve.

DENISE FRAME HARLAN writes, teaches, and crafts wool into toys and garments by day. By night she is a lover of everyday home cooking, including hand-crafted noodles that may sometimes surpass her own grandmother's. Denise writes for several publications, and she recently completed an MFA in creative nonfiction. She lives in Gloucester, Massachusetts, with her husband, Scott, and her two children.

9

And She Took Flour: Cooking Lessons from Supper of the Lamb

Hank phones to say he's crossed the Massachusetts state line and is headed for our coast, and I say good, you are two hours away. I begin to pull bowls and containers from the refrigerator, to bring them to room temperature. He asks if he can take my family out for dinner and I say no, we are making a home-cooked meal just for you, and it's a surprise. He likes surprises, he says, and I can hear the slow smile in his voice.

To tell you how Hank and I are friends would be like showing you an acorn while we stand in front of an oak tree, the size of our friendship now, a friendship that began from nearly nothing. Twenty years ago I lived with Hank and thirty other people in a big beach house for the summer. I suffered a terrible crush on the man, with his dark curls and merry eyes, and eight years later, I married his roommate, Scott—who has merry eyes, too, but no curls. When I say Hank is my best friend, Scott answers, "No, Hank is my best friend," and my children argue, "No, Hank is *our* best friend!"

No matter whose best friend he is, Hank is driving north to spend a few days with us, and that is what matters. We will all claim him, we will all be sorry that he needs sleep and time alone, though we would devour him whole, if we could. We will all goad him because he moves slower than cold molasses on snow, and he takes naps at inopportune times, and he loves each of us with such stubbornness that it's hard to hurry him along, ever. His company reminds us how funny and charming we are. When he drives away, we are better people than when he arrived. Hank's only real fault, besides his slowness, is that he lives so far from us.

We will cook for him. Hank likes home-cooking better than anything he could buy. But because he lives alone and hates to waste food, he doesn't cook much. So we will make him a rare and amazing dish: leftovers. But leftovers transformed.

⤳

I warm the cider gravy on a low burner. I turn the oven to 350 degrees. And I smooth a generous handful of flour onto the cool countertop with the flat of my hand. I close my eyes, just for a moment, and try to remember every silken-floured countertop or wooden board I've ever known. I push back my sleeves.

I pull my grandmother's wooden rolling pin from its perch above the cookbooks—the working cookbooks, not the Sunday cookbooks. Another generous handful of flour for the pin and we are ready for the chilled dough to come out of the refrigerator. The oven is already warm. Bowls of odds and ends rest on the counter. The filling will be assembled from Thanksgiving leftovers, meat and a fruited wild rice stuffing, peas, carrots, potatoes. On the stove, cider gravy waits, thinned with more turkey broth; it is ready to carry the leftovers into another plane of existence. Today the scraps will be a feast.

I split the round lump of dough without handling it too much: two-thirds for the bottom crust. The remainder goes back into the refrigerator. Assembly could take a few minutes, and cold is everything when rolling out crust. I roll from my belly toward the back of the counter, lift the dough and turn it one quarter turn, then roll another stroke.

⤳

My grandmother crafted famous fruit pies and filled pies and desserts of all kinds, but her opinion of her own pies was as stern as a contest judge. "Do you think the crust on this one is a little tough?" she would ask. No. No, never could you make a crust that is tough. "Maybe I should add an egg wash next time." Unwilling to pick an argument, I'd simply eat as much pie as could be spared from my ravenous brothers, not knowing when the next pie might be baked. My younger brother insisted on birthday pie instead of cake. After my grandmother's death, my mother searched local shops until she found a bakery whose pies were nearly as good. The drive to the bakery was an hour, round-trip, but the quality of the pie was close to my grandmother's perfection. And close is good enough, for a non-cook. My aunt tried her hand at piecrust, too, but her inner contest judge proved too harsh.

Lucky me, I have no inner contest judge. I can't recall a homemade piecrust I didn't like. I've made a hundred bad ones, I am certain, and I've eaten the filling from the middle of more than one middling restaurant pie, but I've never complained over honest effort. After numerous less-than-fabulous attempts at pie, I found Julia Child's notes on crust-making and food processors, and I've never turned back. All I need is a proper filling.

⤳

My recipe directions read: "Place the deep dish pie pan onto the crust and draw a wide circle around the pan with a sharp knife."

My grandmother let me watch her work with piecrust—she folded the flattened crust in half, and then into quarters, and lifted the entire circle of crust off the counter. She would not let me touch the dough. A tear in the crust is too hard to repair when your aim is to be perfect. Some cooks roll the crust onto the rolling pin to lift it, but folding gives the crust a definite center point, a guideline for placing this crust in the pan. And that's how my grandmother did it. I nestle the crust gently into the pan. Then the vegetables form a bottom layer, then rice stuffing with its bits of apricots and cranberries, then the turkey meat.

⤳

To be fair I should've learned the art of cooking from my grandmother, like my brothers did. They learned to make things themselves; I remained a happy spectator, half-believing she was magic. Juanita Edwards was widely known to be The Finest Cook in Randolph County, Indiana, and likely several adjoining counties might've claimed her as well. She started a restaurant in Farmland, Indiana, as a newlywed in 1922, serving lunches for the workmen who were constructing the railroad. For thirty-nine cents, a man could get a meal better than his own family could make. John Dillinger's gang cleared the restaurant and filled their bellies in 1933. When they called to meet the cook, she handed the pistol in her apron pocket to one of her dishwashers and walked through the swinging doors. The men were real polite, she said, and they tipped well, too. It's possible she was pregnant with my mother at the time. Dillinger's gang robbed their first bank in Daleville, Indiana, the next town over, within a few days.

My grandmother headed her own restaurant for twenty years, then the trains no longer stopped in our town. She managed a restaurant for a large department store for the next twenty years, and when she retired she catered a meal at my father's Lion's Club once or twice a month.

Like my brothers, I'd bicycle across town to my grandmother's house just to see what was on the stove or cooling on the counter. When my older brother graduated to paid restaurant work, I inherited his job as catering assistant when my grandmother cooked for special events. Even as a distractible teenager, I could see event catering was an act of organizational genius, mathematics, graciousness, and patience. Every minute, my grandmother held heaven and earth in balance, and charmed away any cooking disaster.

My grandmother tolerated me in her kitchen because I clean well and I eat with deep appreciation. As a catering assistant, my job was first to comment glowingly over every bite (this was not a hardship) of my potatoes, swimming with butter, and peach pie, eaten on a barstool in the Lion's Club kitchen after all the men had been served. And my second job was to wash dishes, which I could do endlessly while singing to myself, daydreaming. Perhaps I'd be thinking of the tall stack of dollar bills my grandmother would pile in my hand at the end of the evening. But more likely, I'd let myself be lost in the scent of dish soap and steam.

She loved the praise. She loved the men returning for seconds and thirds, groaning with satisfaction. She loved making her own income. But I can't say she enjoyed herself. It was a job. It was a job I did not believe I could ever perform myself.

So I did not learn to cook from my grandmother or my mother, who cooked largely from boxes and bags, or from home economics class. Nor did I wish to emulate any of the cooks I knew. They worked too hard. They seemed to be magicians and scientists, mathematicians and economists, all the things I was not.

⌒

Out of the refrigerator comes the remaining bit of dough that will become the top crust. I roll it flat, too, and fold it just the same as the bottom crust. I pour gravy over the filling and place that top crust over everything. My crimping of the crust is uneven, distinctively homemade. With the knife, I carve a quick vent in the center—two curved slashes form a rough heart.

The phone rings and I wipe flour streaks down the front of my apron. Hank is an hour away.

⌒

I learned to feed myself a few years before I met Hank, after years at the mercy of college cafeterias. I took a summer job in the Rocky Mountains, far away from Midwestern cooking and boxes and packages. My roommate worked in the kitchen, and as an act of kindness, she brought me a vegetarian Dagwood sandwich. I promptly disassembled the sandwich layer by layer, asking carefully about each food. Exactly what is an avocado? Where do sprouts come from? To tell me hummus comes from chickpeas would help me only if I'd seen a chickpea. I'd never eaten cheese that wasn't bright yellow and square, and I hated bright yellow squares of all kinds, but this oval of provolone was entirely different. I loved all of it.

I took my food exploration outdoors, where I learned about wild edibles on a guided hike, and I fell in love with the staff naturalist, who spent the rest of the summer showing me where to find wild greens and blueberries, as well as bats and hummingbirds. As a new student of wonder, I proved to be the perfect disciple. My roommate showed me a recipe for wheat crackers and for the first time I thought perhaps crackers existed before cardboard boxes. I began to wonder about the origins of every sort of food. I stumbled into a passion for freshness, for flavors. I hungered for the company of people who knew where to find goodness in the world.

I returned to my Indiana college dorm in the fall, where I grew alfalfa sprouts in an old peanut butter jar, on the windowsill of my room, proud of my miraculous food for nearly free. In the height of the Reagan-preppie era of conspicuous consumption, I treated my friends to sprout-and-peanut-butter sandwiches, served with tea purchased from an exotic café in Boulder, Colorado. I'd gained inside knowledge about how to live. I didn't mind being a bit odd at my conservative Christian college, because I'd tasted, and now I wanted to share my wealth. Somehow the thought of "making do"—living cheaper, lovelier, better—seemed magical. I was delighted with the world, yes, but I was also delighted (for the first time) with myself.

Eating and cooking are two different things, though, and I was still a long, long way from making pie. My full conversion began the summer I turned twenty-two. I had moved from Indiana to Pennsylvania for six weeks of seminary training for college ministry.

For the whole summer I'd share a kitchen, deck, and large living room/dining room with four apartment-mates. We would trade off cooking duties, Ruth, the college ministry mentor who lived with me, announced the first day. We would each cook one night a week. I stifled a laugh. I knew how to eat and how to make cookies but not how to cook meals.

"Which kind of canned soup do you like?" I asked.

"Soup is a good place to start," she said, and she pulled down her cookbooks. One fell open to Cream of Broccoli.

"People make this?" I asked.

She wrote "broccoli" on the grocery list, along with onions, garlic, and cheddar cheese. Then she wrote "French bread," laughing that she wouldn't ask me to bake bread yet. I remembered an old boyfriend had walked me through a simple recipe for crustless cheesecake. Cream cheese, sugar, eggs, berries, sour cream went onto the grocery list. I thought the good bread and cheesecake might make up the difference if I scorched the soup.

I cooked. The soup scorched. We ate it anyway, with bread. The cheesecake was spectacular with its browned filling of raspberries and sour cream. I began to worry about the second week.

That same week marked the beginning of another richer conversion in a theology classroom in the basement of a church near Penn State University. After a forgettable introduction, a balding professor walked to the lectern and began, predictably, examining the opening passages of Genesis. God pronounced all created things good, he intoned. Half of the seminary classes I've ever attended started the very same way. Then he wondered aloud whether God's act of creation might be ongoing, and he suggested we close class with a reading from a cookbook. We yawned and nodded. He pulled out a stained yellow copy of Robert Farrar Capon's *The Supper of the Lamb*, opened the book, settled his glasses on his nose, and began to read.

"For all its greatness," Capon says, "the created order cries out for further greatness still. The most splendid dinner, the most exquisite food, the most gratifying company, arouse more appetites than they satisfy. They do not slake man's thirst for being; they whet it beyond all bounds."

I listened, stunned. Are Christians supposed to have appetites and thirst? To whet is to sharpen—are we to sharpen our appetites for the things of earth? The professor's face flushed and flushed again, and tears streamed from his eyes as he read about "The Inconsolable Heartburn . . . by which the heart looks out astonished at the world and in its loving, wakes and breaks at once." This heartburn, Capon, says, this sadness for what is not yet here is ultimately a longing for God's final feast, the supper of the Lamb, when the Host of Creation will set all things right and will do so more beautifully than we can imagine.

The created order cries out—I knew that from Romans. Creation groans for further greatness still. Greatness in the kitchen? Greatness as a supper?

I knew intellectually that God was not about souls but about all things, just as I'd memorized from the book of Colossians—above all things, working through all things. But literally all things? Less than ideal things? Gritty things? Risky things? Beautiful, sensual things?

As if it were a near-death experience, my life flashed before me while the balding professor read scenes of wild blueberries eaten on a sunny mountainside, of riding a bicycle with hands raised to the sky, of watermelon rind pickles eaten at Thanksgiving, and of fingers tipped with green olives. I remembered my first taste of Communion wine at midnight Mass in the Colorado Rockies, my favorite sugar cream pie, and my grandmother's homemade noodles with chicken.

I glanced to my side to see my classmates as astonished as me by this professor weeping for joy over onions and flour, sausages and cigars, over a God who lavishes the whole universe with his affection, a God who holds us all in a state of dearness. The pen fell from my hand without my notice. I was more openhearted in that moment than I had ever been.

I'd never known what to do with all the love in my heart for this beautiful mess of a world. All this time, I'd been trying to temper and tame my passion for mountains and tea and road trips and cheesecake and people. I'd known God my whole life, had known Christ for a decade, and had focused on Jesus's suffering and sacrifice. I'd been afraid to love anything too much for fear that I'd disappoint God and prove myself too worldly, too attached to the everyday stuff of creation that would hinder my race toward heaven and the life hereafter. I'd been afraid, and I'd held my heart back. Suddenly it occurred to me that this fear, this withholding, might be sin. Maybe I'd had everything all wrong.

A man read a cookbook, and I met God again, as if I'd never met God at all, as if all my worship had been an attempt to tame a gorgeous world that did not need taming, but adoration.

As he closed the reading, the professor apologized and pulled out a handkerchief, leaving me thinking of Moses and his need for a veil after his meeting with God on Mt. Sinai. I ran to a bookstore and bought the book.

In my own reading, I missed much of *The Supper of the Lamb* the first time through, not knowing words like *stock*, nor types of wine, nor half of the kinds of food mentioned. Back in my shared apartment, I began to smell herbs in the kitchen and compare knives. With my next meal, I attempted to make a roux from butter and flour. I consulted Ruth, who patiently endured several charred pots of rice and helped me craft a festive crock-pot roast for our last feast of the summer.

By September I was stocking my own kitchen with cookware and utensils from yard sales, hanging pots from the bright orange pegboard adorning the wall of my first kitchen. Although a beginner myself, I taught the rudiments of pancakes and soups and stir-fry to any willing student. They'd stir and flip; I'd read them Capon. I visit those former students on road trips now, and they cook for me, as we remember the orange pegboard and the tiny electric stove. It was a seedling of a kitchen, a place to start.

I've spoken to that professor, since, and he remembers reading Capon, not the tears. I've spoken to former classmates who recall the book but not the experience of that class. Other professors grumbled that summer: the course was titled "Foundations of Reformational Theology," and Capon is not remotely Reformational—in fact, he'd be more at home with Catholic sensibilities than with Calvin. That professor was not asked to teach that course again. No one else in my college ministry circles would ever experience a class like that one. And no one experienced it like me—this book, this reading, this moment seemed to be perfectly placed. The priest I needed arrived, and nothing has been the same: not in the kitchen, not in the garden, not in all creation.

The following summer I landed a job living in a beachside house with college students. The woman who hired me was a renowned chef who would cook breakfasts and dinners for thirty. And I was her assistant. One of those students was my friend Hank. How odd it felt, working in that summer house, the first time I put chicken bones in a pot with water, carrot bits and celery and onion trimmings. Something from almost nothing. It seemed just as odd as the first time my sprouts grew tiny green leaves in the jar on the windowsill. The wizardry of vegetables and bones in water, on the stove, with rosemary and thyme makes me smile every time I make stock. And the next magical addition is a roux of flour and butter added to that stock, becoming gravy. And the culmination of stock, gravy, scraps, and flour is turkey pie, for a dear friend.

It would be years before I learned to bake bread and years more before I learned to make homemade noodles that I believe even exceed my grandmother's in quality. My father tells me to hush my mouth, remembering those dinners at the Lion's Club. He doesn't believe better noodles are possible, any more than I would've believed it twenty years ago. Of course, my grandmother didn't know about fresh rosemary or hand-crank pasta machines from Italy, or food processors.

It would be years also before I heard the phrase, "sacramental theology," which I'm still not sure I grasp so much as I live and breathe it. Only recently have I learned of the Catholic view of "mediation," or seeing God through the lens of Creation, versus the traditional Protestant suspicion that if we love the earth too much we will fall into idolatry and worship the Creation instead of the Creator. The years in-between have been such good years, filled with ever-expanding circles of flavor and interests. Any real curiosity about food will spread to gardening, and any real curiosity about gardening requires learning to compost. A few years ago, I began to explore how fabric is made, how colors are blended. All of these touch on an ever-expanding affection for God's people and every corner of the world which is in need of love. Far from idolatry, the more I live, the more I look at a blade of grass and know that for this Jesus died and was risen, glorious indeed, for this and for everything.

The table is nearly set when a car pulls into the drive and my kids run out to see if it's Hank, if he's hungry, if he's figured out what we are serving. I pull out the cranberry sauce from the refrigerator and a small salad. The pie comes out of the oven and I place it on a handmade trivet at the center of the table.

Capon warns in his book that *The Supper of the Lamb* is a way of life, not merely a recipe that requires eight chapters of diversions to reach a conclusion. I read the book and reread it, as this way of life becomes mine. And I will tell you the truth: I've never grown tired of exploring the minute corners of life. I tossed a handful of lettuce seeds into the potted rosemary plant several days ago, and the sprouts stretch green leaves upward, and the anticipation grows. It might not work, but I had the seeds handy, and I was hungry for green things. I am hungry, still.

And I tell you another truth: Robert Farrar Capon has no respect for piecrust at all, feeling certain it is a cheater's way of approximating pastry dough. I may never make Capon's pastry dough, though the recipe is right here in the book. If piecrust is cheating, then it's the holiest cheating I've ever met, and I praise it. He is not perfect, my favorite priest. But this turkey potpie most certainly is.

Then Hank walks in the door, my children hanging from his arms. I ask who would like to light the candles and they rush to the table. Hank takes the seat of honor and my husband, his best friend, takes the chair beside him. We sit down and hold hands, and with our eyes wide open, we take one another in. We breathe in the scent of pie, and we say grace.

I. City Slicker's First Pot Pie

INGREDIENTS

2 rotisserie chickens

1 small bag baby carrots

1 celery stalk

Scraps of onion or onion peel

1 peel of half a lemon and squeeze of lemon

4 whole cloves

1/2 cup of red lentils

1/2 cup of rice

Scant pinch cayenne pepper (optional)

1 store-bought piecrust

1 bag of frozen peas

Gravy that you purchase with your chickens

Extra mashed potatoes or 2 nice-sized raw potatoes

1 sprig of parsley (optional)

Salad to accompany

RECIPE

Meal one: Meat and salad

Pull the chicken from the bones and place the breast meat in a ziplock bag to slice for sandwiches, another day, or eat roast chicken for dinner, with a salad.

Meal two: Soup

Put the bones and skin in a pot and cover with cold water.

Add a few carrots, and if you have them, add a few scraps of celery, onions, onion peel, and lemon peel, cloves.

Simmer for 1 to 2 hours.

Scoop out a few cups of broth and simmer the remaining carrots in the broth.

Cool the rest of the broth and sift out the solids. If you wish, you can pick the remaining meat bits from the bone for chicken salad or for your pet— but throw away the bones.

Now you have chicken scraps, carrots simmered in broth (until you can pierce with a fork), and broth for soup.

To make soup, sauté an onion and a stalk of celery, then add broth, red lentils, rice, and half the cooked carrots.

Add a small portion of the chicken scraps when the rice is tender, and adjust the spices.

If the soup is boring, add a squeeze of lemon and a scant pinch of cayenne pepper.

Meal three: Pot pie

Cube the chicken scraps and place them on the piecrust. Top with the cooked carrots and the frozen peas. Cover with gravy and top everything with the mashed potatoes, spread carefully on top. Bake at 350 until the gravy is bubbling around the edges, perhaps 40 minutes.

II. Advanced Real Pot Pie

You can see that you are not far from making this from scratch, right?

INGREDIENTS

City Slicker's First Pot Pie ingredients, excluding rotisserie chickens and gravy (see above)
1 chicken
2 lemons
1 sprig fresh rosemary, or 1 tablespoon dried rosemary
1 generous teaspoon salt

1 tablespoon butter or chicken fat drippings
1 tablespoon flour
Chicken broth
Lemon juice or white wine or cider to taste (optional)
Potatoes, cubed and/or mashed

RECIPE

Roast your own chicken with two lemons, rosemary, and salt in the cavity.

Make your own gravy: heat a skillet with butter or chicken fat drippings. Add flour and whisk—add chicken broth to form gravy.

If the gravy is boring, add lemon juice or white wine or cider and cook until it is thick.

If you make your own crust, you can make a double-crusted pie and simmer your cubed potatoes with the carrots.

Once you've made the basic pie, ask yourself if you might like to add other leftovers to your pie: sweet potatoes? Cranberry sauce? Stuffing? As long as your gravy is good and you have plenty of meat, vegetables, and gravy, why not?

You can also see how easy it is to plan four or five meals from one or two roasted birds. Add a meal of fettuccine with a white sauce, chicken, carrots, and peas, topped with grated parmesan, with a side salad.

I prefer Julia Child's method of making piecrust from *The Way to Cook*, under Pastry, *Pate Brisee Fine*, page 381.

CHEF FRED RAYNAUD has been the recipient of the Chefs Academy Award, the Chaîne de Rôtisseurs Award of Excellence, the Escoffier Award, and the American Culinary Federation Gold and Silver Medals in National culinary competition, as well as many restaurant awards. His culinary efforts have also led to his recognition by the Chaîne de Rôtisseurs and the International Corporate Chef Association as a dynamic leader in the hospitality industry, and he has appeared on numerous TV shows, including *San Diego Sun Up*, *California Date Book*, the *Good Morning Show*, *Hour Magazine*, and the *Family Channel*. He is Corporate Executive Chef for a major national food service company, where he is responsible for R&D, concept development, and the training of the company's two hundred-plus chefs.

10

In Praise of Hollandaise

You can't make an omelet without breaking eggs.
—French proverb

Why is it that every restaurant in town is packed with a twenty-minute wait at one o'clock on a Sunday afternoon? The reason is simple—hunger! It's the hardest hour of the restaurant week, and it's the same every Sunday. I should know—I have spent the last thirty years feeding those public hunger pains.

My Sunday mornings usually go like this: I get up at five o'clock and call the kitchen to make sure the morning crew arrived on time. This is about fifty-fifty, hit or miss due to the typical crew's intense desire to go out and party all night. I rush in to the restaurant to ensure everything is going well, and then I head to the main kitchen and begin to set up for Sunday brunch. If I am lucky, the cook has already pulled the ice carving out of the freezer to temper. If I am really lucky, they did not break it on its way out of the freezer. (I can't tell you how many times in the last thirty years I have had to grab my chainsaw and carve out a new sculpture only to get it up minutes before we were ready to open.) If it's a good morning, everything is in place, everyone's a hero, and we're ready to roll by ten o'clock. Brunch is open and the crowds come streaming in.

I can almost hear their growling stomachs. After being seated, they shoot up from their tables and spread out like locust upon a field of wheat. The crowd scatters, some head to the carving and omelet station, the waffle station, or the salad and fruit tables. Others head to the hot food line. They feast on hand-rolled cheese blintzes topped with fresh raspberries and almond butter sauce, or grilled swordfish laced with roasted-red-pepper-and-mango salsa.

One of the most popular items is the classic eggs Benedict, delicately graced with a delightful hollandaise sauce. That's the station my wife heads for—she loves eggs Benedict. But most cooks don't. It's not that we don't care for the dish; it's the many hurdles we have to overcome to prepare it.

The two culprits in eggs Benedict are poached eggs and hollandaise sauce. I've trained my cooks to poach the eggs and then submerge them in ice water for later use; this method alleviates the chaos and time-crunch of poaching on the spot. But the making of hollandaise sauce is not so simply done.

At the heart of making a truly magnificent hollandaise sauce, there is a principle and technique that many young cooks fail to grasp and struggle to master. It's this challenge which excites me about hollandaise. I call it Holy Emulsion. Because within the building blocks of a hollandaise sauce, there is a picture that unfolds, a picture that gives you a glimpse into the mystery of the universe.

Let me explain. Hollandaise is an emulsion sauce. An emulsion is formed when one substance is suspended in another—in this case, clarified butter (oil) is suspended in water. The need for an emulsion arises when two or more ingredients naturally repel each other, when their chemical properties will not mix. In the case of a hollandaise sauce, the two *unequally yoked* items are the acids, water (cider vinegar and lemon juice), and oil (clarified butter). We all know that oil and water do not mix; they need a stabilizer, an emulsifier.

An emulsifier brings together two liquids that are otherwise incapable of mixing, merging the two liquids to form a single homogeneous substance. Examples of emulsions include crude oil, butter and margarine, hand lotion, mayonnaise, and of course, hollandaise. Emulsions tend to have a cloudy appearance because the boundary between the oil and water, the interface, scatters the light that passes through the emulsion. They can be stable or unstable. Simple vinaigrette, for example, is an unstable emulsion that has to be shaken continuously or it will quickly separate.

An emulsifier or emulgent is a substance that stabilizes an emulsion. Egg yolks, mustard, gelatin, certain algae, and even glucose and nuts are all emulgents. Whether an emulsion turns into a water-in-oil emulsion or an oil-in-water emulsion depends on the volume of the substances being combined and on the type of emulsifier.

Emulsifiers can't work their magic without energy, however. Anyone who has made a large batch of hollandaise will attest to having a sore arm the next day—it's the price of preparing hollandaise! And it is this agitation, tension, and constant whipping that enables the emulsifiers within the egg yolk (lecithin) to bring together the acids (water) and the oil (butter) in the formation of the sauce.

Let's take a deeper look at the preparation of this sauce, starting with the age-old problem of incompatibility—oil and water simply will not mix. This dilemma parallels a problem that has plagued creation since the fall of man in the Garden of Eden. It is the curse: eternal separation between God and humanity. Because of the curse, humanity was expelled from the presence of God, and an eternal void entered into the heart of man. God and humanity had become two unequally yoked entities, two substances that repelled each other. Like the acid and oil in our hollandaise, they were separated and in need of a mediator, an emulsifier to unite God and man again.

Even the prophets of old cried out for a solution to this dilemma: "All we like sheep have gone astray; we have turned, every one, to his own way; and the Lord has laid on him the iniquity of us all" (Isaiah 53:6). Who is this great emulsifier that would unite mankind with God again? The answer is given symbolically in the humble yolk of an egg.

An egg is truly a remarkable thing. In its simplest definition, the egg consists of three parts: the white (albumen), the yolk, and the shell. The egg can be compared to the Godhead, and in this analogy, the yolk is clearly the Son of God. In the first step toward making hollandaise, which is also the first step toward redemption, the shell is cracked and broken open, and the yolk is separated from its rightful place. The yolk is tossed into a cold stainless steel bowl. Lonely and isolated, with one mission in mind: the yolk must unite two substances that chemically cannot be united, our *sinful* nature with a *Holy* God. In order to do this, the yolk must endure terrible suffering.

The creator of the sauce places the stainless steel bowl over hot simmering water. The creator then adds a vinegar mixture to the yolk, pulls out a wire whip, and begins to beat the egg yolk, breaking its skin. The heat of the water intensifies and the yolk begins to cook under turbulence and torture as the whip moves, until there is no form or life left in the yolk. Then, at just the right moment, the creator of the sauce removes the bowl from the boiling water and begins to whip in the warm butter (the oil of God). Suddenly, as if by a miracle, an emulsion begins to take place. The yolk that was once dead comes back to life. The acidic mixture, once separated from the presence of the oil, is now united by the work of our mediator, the yolk (Jesus).

Just so, it was the process of agitation and tension (beaten and crucified) that enabled the emulsification to take place. Even the addition of vinegar recalls the moment on the cross when Jesus called out in thirst and was given vinegar on a sponge just before his last words, "It is finished." When the oil of God is fully incorporated into the cooked mixture, the sauce is complete: it is finished! "For there is one God, and one mediator [emulsifier] between God and men, the man Christ Jesus; Who gave himself a ransom for all, to be testified in due time" (1 Timothy 2:5–6).

All around us, the Lord proclaims his eternal truth. Look around—milk, cream, butter, mayonnaise, hollandaise—all emulsions symbolically pointing to Christ.

Give Jesus the chance to make you a new creature, a sauce fit for a king, and he will do it. Only after your life is reunited with God will it have its fullest meaning and fullest flavor. God will bring a fragrance and beauty to your life that will refresh all those around you, like the most delicate hollandaise laced atop a moist poached egg.

Cilantro Citrus Hollandaise

INGREDIENTS

4 egg yolks
1 tablespoon lime juice
3 tablespoons orange juice
1 tablespoons grapefruit juice
1 1/2 cups clarified butter, warm but not hot
1/4 cup cilantro, chopped
Salt, kosher
Pepper, ground, white or cayenne
Chipotle chili (optional)

Yields 2 cups

RECIPE

Whisk together egg yolks with lime, orange, and grapefruit juice.

With one hand whisk over a bain-marie (a simmering pot of water in which you place your mixing bowl) until sauce is light and fluffy. With your other hand, away from heat, slowly—in a drizzle—add clarified butter.

Season with chopped cilantro and salt and pepper to taste; keep warm.

If you'd like, a chipotle chili may be added to the mixture (puree in food processor or with a stick blender first).

For a sweeter version, substitute good orange marmalade for the orange juice.

For an intense orange or even tangerine flavor reduce ¾ cups of juice over low heat until you have about 1 tablespoon of light citrus syrup. Add lime and grapefruit to this.

Be creative! Swap in other acids—tomato, pineapple, yuzu, or a simple Meyer lemon. Swap in other herbs—mint, basil, tarragon, or dill; they all add their own flair. Just picture the dish you're going to grace it with!

Alissa Herbaly Coons is a recovering vegetarian currently feasting on farm-fresh goat in Waterloo, Ontario. A recent graduate of the Seattle Pacific University MFA program, she is working on a series of essays on migration and belonging in the context of her Hungarian heritage, including a celebration of *savanyúság* ("sour things"), such as the vat of sauerkraut fermenting in her kitchen. In her free time, Alissa hunts for old editions of the *Joy of Cooking*, feeds fresh produce to her number-theorist husband, and fantasizes about crafting goat cheese and growing her own melons. Recent highlights in her food life include making a pilgrimage to Julia Child's Kitchen at the Smithsonian, discovering the existence of the marrow spoon, acquiring a chest freezer, and nourishing her newborn daughter. Originally from Montana, Alissa has also lived, studied, and worked in Hungary, Germany, Nigeria, Switzerland, and Texas. Her writing has appeared in *The Christian Science Monitor* and *The Montana Journalism Review*.

11

Tasting the Animal Kingdom

Then God said, "I give you every seed-bearing plant on the face of the whole earth and every tree that has fruit with seed in it. They will be yours for food."

—Genesis 1:29

I have carried a deep ambivalence about my place in the food chain since the summer I raised a flock of chickens at age thirteen. I was a town child, raised with backyard tomato plants in Kalispell, Montana, and limited exposure to genuine agriculture. For a family science project, my mother brought home a dozen Araucana chicks, which we placed under a heat lamp in a box in the kitchen. They were the size of marshmallow Peeps, and they were warm and downy and tottered around their cardboard nest on delicate miniature feet. That first day, my sister and I named each chick, cupped their springy bodies in our palms, and let our hearts swell to the chorus of their cheeping. At dinnertime, when our mother pulled a bag of chicken breast out of the freezer, I underwent a crisis of faith.

In the Sunday school lessons of my childhood, I learned of fruitarian Eden and of the sin that necessitated the Old Testament complications of blood sacrifice and dietary rule keeping. The church basement rooms where I learned these lessons were often filled with the scent of ham being warmed for a post-service potluck or traces of bacon grease left over from a communal breakfast—the legacy of the apparent free-for-all introduced by Peter's New Testament vision. Acts 10 notes that Peter fell into a hunger-induced swoon, and "He saw heaven opened and something like a large sheet being let down to earth by its four corners." The sheet contained all kinds of four-footed animals, as well as reptiles of the earth and birds of the air. Then a voice told him, "Get up, Peter. Kill and eat." Peter himself was perplexed by the vision, but we had it figured out: Jesus came, among other reasons, so we could eat ham for Easter.

These things occasionally sifted and shifted in my mind as I ate, but the chicks sharpened my focus. For as much character as they had, for as clean as we kept them, these chickens were filthy birds. I was unwilling to kill them, let alone eat them. Then it occurred to me that I could no longer eat anything that I was not willing to bear the responsibility of killing.

My parents were supportive. They had been vegetarian before they moved to Montana and my father shot an elk. They bought me *Diet for a New America* and a subscription to *Vegetarian Times*. I was harrowed to learn about factory farms and feedlots, and it became clear to me that opting out of the meat system was better for the earth, better for the animals, and better for my health. Being vegan seemed even more noble, but it was far more effort than I could conceive. I continued to eat eggs and dairy products: willing to exploit the animals, but not to have their blood on my hands. At the end of the summer, we moved the chickens out of our kitchen and backyard and into Seeley Lake. There they lived in an alpine chicken chalet with a meadow full of grass and herbs and insects, and laid their pale green eggs for a family of canoe makers. It was an idyllic life, for a chicken.

My own upkeep was not so idyllic. The first year was easy enough—we had a well-stocked pantry, and I was armed with sufficient idealism (and references to Eden) for the inevitable meat debates among my peers. Then my father took a job in Hungary. We arrived in our small city in winter, and fresh produce was sparse. Over our malfunctioning Soviet-era stove, my mother claimed cooking amnesia, and the rest of us attempted to fend for ourselves. In a land rich with lard, goose liver, and veal-stuffed crepes, I subsisted on Nutella and oranges and learned to live with hunger, driven on by a self-satisfied sense of vegetarian sacrifice.

Later in high school, I moved to Germany, where I ate an abundance of homemade bread and learned to make a mean onion tart. When I returned to the States for college, I started cooking in earnest, reading cookbooks for pleasure, and reveling in the possibilities of plant products. This yielded years of good vegetable soups, bread, and baklava, all shared in the company of friends.

When I married Michael, he essentially adopted my diet, eating the occasional piece of meat when dining out or when we visited his childhood home, where the freezer is stocked with packages of his father's cows, each labeled by name. As a goodwill compromise at our first several Thanksgivings, we ordered a free-range Hutterite turkey, the epitome of wholesome meat, which my sister prepared and served to the meat eaters among us. Although I have sautéed tofu samples for the uninitiated, I have never inflicted faux-meat on anyone. Tofurky, with its pretentions to meat, seems somehow idolatrous. Also, it's trying too hard.

When we met, Michael was keeping kosher and living primarily on Reese's peanut butter cups. Our biggest fight during our first year of marriage was over the Sinai Kosher sausages he ate at Costco. He thought that consuming two per trip was reasonable; I was convinced that he was eating himself into an early grave. But there was hope for his carnivorous soul: at age twenty-eight, he discovered asparagus.

However, just as he was finding vegetables, I started losing momentum, sliding into a slow decline of nachos and grilled cheese. The unraveling of my vegetarianism began in earnest four years ago in Italy, on a trip with Michael and his mother. My mother-in-law, who in her restless youth was married to an Italian-American with mafia ties and access to an excellent family restaurant, was on a mission to find authentic Italian food. "I want to eat where the locals eat," she insisted.

And so Michael drove us into the Venetian hinterland, the mists off the salt marshes sublimating in the soft April twilight. We passed first one, then another, promising local-looking restaurant. Half an hour later, we found the one she had been waiting for. We pulled into a gravelly parking lot and approached a seedy stucco building festooned with cigarette ads. Inside, there was no menu, and the woman who showed us to a table left us in a kind of muted awkwardness as she sent out someone who was more accustomed to dealing with foreigners. The chef was cheerfully doughy, and although unresponsive to our English, French, Spanish, and Hungarian, he seemed eager to feed us. He addressed us in German.

"Fisch oder Fleisch?" he boomed.

I paused to translate, and then in my high-school German mumbled something about a vegetarian option. "Ja, natürlich, Salat," the chef said and continued to wait for our choices. Something inside of me cracked then, and out of my hunger, I said, "Fisch, bitte." Michael also ordered "Fisch." His mother took the "Fleisch."

I had been thinking about adding fish to my diet for a couple of years but hadn't mustered the will to actually start eating it. I was feeling increasingly malnourished, and losing my intense appreciation of the pleasures of vegetable matter. I had tried a few bites of salmon at an IKEA cafeteria once, trying not to taste its animality. That moment in the restaurant, I prayed that whatever came would be skinned, filleted, and bland, made palatable by its anonymity.

What actually came, if I had had the courage to say it then, was exquisite: a bowl full of fresh pasta loaded with fruits of the sea: baby squid, shrimp, and mussels, followed by a plate of larger squid, prawns, and various fish. I was overwhelmed. Anything with legs or eyes moved to Michael's plate. But the rest! My keen resistance, more than half my life spent defining my diet on the animals that I wouldn't eat, was a mouthful away from coming undone. I suspended my judgment and ate the remaining fish. The fatigue I bore in my mind, the weight of sheltering myself and restraining my choices, began to lift. The glass of limoncello may have helped, too. As I paced myself through the specimens, I prayed to be well and to be honest about the requirements of my existence. Then I was hit with a pang of regret for the meals I might have shared and hadn't, especially my friend Borja's roasted chicken—the sole dish he mastered during the year we shared a kitchen—that every night I would turn down. How much else had this sense of restraint kept from me? A catalog of feasts opened in my mind, and I decided to start slowly. As the resurrected Christ did with his disciples on the shore, I would eat fish.

The restraint I practiced in my vegetarian life had been good training—two years ago, I was diagnosed with sensitivities to gluten, dairy products, and eggs, perhaps due to the excessive role they played in my former diet. As efficiently as I had quit chicken and bacon, I now quit pizza and ice cream. When I gave up my deeply entrenched bread, cheese, and yogurt habits, I lost weight that I did not have to spare, and I found that I needed to replace more than half of my calories with other foods. I could only eat so much fish, and I was yearning for something satisfying to eat. I was desperate to feel well.

One day Michael drove me to Whole Foods to see what kinds of exotic allergen-free products we could procure. I circled the store in a swoon of self-pity and increasing hunger. We picked up tapioca flour and xanthan gum—essentials for the science project of gluten-free baking. The towering displays of imported cheeses, the heady aroma of wheat flour and butter emanating from the bakery—it was all too much. Between the cheese shrine and the case of chocolate éclairs, I came upon the rotisserie chickens. They were roasted to a deep golden brown, and the air was filled with a scent that couldn't help but explain God's well-documented desire for burnt offerings. We purchased half a chicken and drove it home.

The packaging promised that the bird had led a good and healthy life, and the scent of its body, sacrificed for a single dinner, filled my head. I cried a little in the car and I made Michael promise not to tell anyone or tease me about the chicken. He had never given me a hard time about being vegetarian, but he seemed shocked and a little proud that I was preparing to eat this chicken. I took a portion of breast meat and tasted a small bite. The flesh was dry and overly bland, so I added some of the spiced skin—skin that I knew had held mite-infested feathers and came off in flakes when the chicken was alive but that now completed the flavor of each bite I took. Michael, hovering with concern, encouraged me to take a little more. When I was finished, I felt fine, even satisfied. Still, buying a pre-cooked chicken seemed cheap, a kind of cheating. I was not equipped to start raising and slaughtering my own birds, but I needed to take responsibility for the process. I decided that there would be a second chicken, and that the second chicken would be different.

The next weekend our friends Liz and Scott and their toddler, Charlie, came to visit. They had undergone a food crisis of their own in the previous year. Charlie was born with severe reflux and digestive problems, and he had been in and out of the hospital, at times fighting for his life. Understandably, Liz and Scott have reordered their lives around preparing food that will help Charlie grow and thrive; Liz understands dietary desperation better than most. She saw the panic in my eyes as we picked the chicken out together at my neighborhood health-food store, and she volunteered to prepare the meat. But this bird was marked for me. I needed to prepare it myself, to know its body, to weigh its life and flesh in my hands.

I left the chicken to thaw in the kitchen sink, and it floated there, barely submerged, remarkably buoyant for the gravity of its condition. A few hours later, I split open the packaging, and the water flushed pink with blood, a faint hint of what must have happened at slaughter. When I took the chicken out of the bag, its wings relaxed into the water; and as I held the fleshy body, I remembered bathing my nephew in this sink at Thanksgiving a few months after his birth. The similarity in the size and weight and feel of the chicken and the baby shivered through me. I did what every young mother cleaning poultry must do, as my sister must have done that weekend as she prepared the Thanksgiving bird—I banished the thought. I reached inside the carcass to remove what I took to be the liver, grazing my hand on the bird's sharp ribs as I pulled it out. Three washings later, the water was no longer tinged with blood. I rubbed the carcass with salt and pepper, and I prepared to cook.

Between the 1946 and the 2006 editions of *The Joy of Cooking*, I approximated a recipe, browning the chicken in hot olive oil, turning it awkwardly over with a pair of wooden spoons. Next I sautéed some sturdy vegetables in the bottom of the cast-iron pan, set the chicken on top of them, dropped in a bundle of herbs, and baptized the lot with two cups of water before setting it in the oven to roast.

When the chicken came out, we came to the table and collectively hesitated. None of us had carved a whole bird before. Someone older, wiser, or more experienced had always sliced the meat. We didn't need to carve it, as it turned out. The flesh was tender and fell off the bones. It was good. And it was good for Charlie, who Liz calls a canary in the coal mine of our food system. Scott, who once had a summer job on a farm, talked about learning how to slaughter and butcher a goat, how he saw the twitch of the goat's muscles after death, felt the blood and warmth drain from its body, and was filled with reverence.

After dinner, I looked at the jagged remains of the bird and knew what must be done next. I stripped the remaining meat from the bones, bit by bit, and then dismantled the skeleton, cracking the bones into pieces, dropping them into my stockpot. With chicken fat under my nails and the scent of bird-death on my hands, I thought of my parents and of all the poultry they prepared for us when I was a child—my mother's delight at finding sale chicken and buying it in bulk, my father's satisfaction in salvaging the remaining meat after a meal of whole turkey or chicken. As I picked over the carcass, seeing for the first time my hands as a continuation of his hands, I found the oysters. I had forgotten they existed, the rounded pockets of tender flesh sunken into little bone basins above each leg. I dug them out with my thumbs and wondered if my mother had any idea what she started when she put that batch of chicks in my hands.

The final stage of handling this chicken I undertook alone, late in the night, according to the comparative *Joy* method. The earlier text seems to take the reader's familiarity with stock for granted whereas the later edition explains the culinary and nutritional value of homemade stock to a generation of readers rendered indifferent by bouillon cubes. Taking my stockpot back to the stove, I added onionskins, carrot tops, and celery and covered the remains with water. For hours, I boiled the last nutrients out of the chicken, claiming the goodness of its skeleton for myself and for the soups of my future, a small act of faith in my slow reconversion. As I strained the broth and finally discarded the bones, I found the wishbone, whole in the pot, which had slipped unnoticed through my earlier bone breaking. I held it for a moment, and then I left it intact.

One-Pot Paprikás Chicken

Chicken stewed in a rich bath of caramelized onions and sweet paprika
is one of my favorites. For this recipe, I've combined the basic wisdom of
the paprika chicken recipes in the 1946 and the 2006 editions of the *Joy of
Cooking*, added a few flavorful vegetables and condiments, and adapted the
dish to be a self-contained meal. If you're looking to make a more traditional paprikás, omit the sauerkraut and potatoes, go heavy on the lard and
sour cream, and serve over egg noodles.

INGREDIENTS

Several tablespoons fat/oil/butter/lard, as you like it

Salt

Black pepper

2 1/2 pounds chicken parts (I like using 4 large bone-in, skin-on thighs or
quarters of a whole chicken for this), rinsed and then blotted dry

2 onions, finely sliced

4 cloves garlic, minced

3+ heaping tablespoons paprika, the freshest possible, preferably Hungarian

2 cups sauerkraut, roughly chopped

4 cups small, new potatoes, cut into bite-sized pieces, with peels

1/4 to 1 cup water or broth (1/4 cup if your pot is self-basting, more if it's
not)

Several generous dashes cayenne pepper, or 1 to 2 teaspoons of hot chili
paste (Erős Pista or chili-garlic rooster sauce)

1 cup sour cream (the results will still be good if this is omitted)

RECIPE

Begin by melting enough fat to generously coat the bottom of a large and heavy pan over medium-high heat.

Sprinkle salt and pepper on the chicken and add it in the pan without crowding it. Cook each piece for approximately 5 minutes per side or until golden. Set the chicken pieces aside on a plate to catch the juices.

Add the onions to the fat, stirring frequently, until they begin to caramelize.

Stir in the garlic and paprika, and return the chicken and juices to the pot.

Add the sauerkraut, potatoes, and water. Reduce the heat to medium, cover, continue to stir frequently, and cook for approximately 1 hour, until the potatoes attain the desired consistency and the chicken reaches an internal temperature of at least 180° F.

At this point, add paprika, cayenne, salt, and black pepper, to taste.

Just prior to serving, stir in the sour cream.

NANCY J. NORDENSON holds an MFA in creative writing from Seattle Pacific University and is the author of *Just Think: Nourish Your Mind to Feed Your Soul*. Her work has appeared or is forthcoming in *Harpur Palate*, *Comment*, *Under the Sun*, *Desert Call*, and *Relief* and has received a Pushcart nomination. As a freelance medical writer, she writes for a variety of venues including continuing medical education programs, advisory groups, and national and international medical symposia. Nancy and her husband live in Minneapolis, Minnesota, and have two sons, to whom she feeds Swedish pancakes whenever they come to visit. She can be contacted through her Web site at www.nancynordenson.com.

12

Things that Fall and Things that Stand

1

A bridge has fallen in the city where I live.

I was a thousand miles from home at the time, and my mother phoned to tell me about it. "There's been a tragic accident," her recorded voice said. "On 35W, the bridge collapsed into the Mississippi."

My husband, two sons, and I had crossed that bridge hundreds of times. We back out of our driveway, drive east five blocks, and turn left onto the northbound interstate that brings us to the concrete and steel eight-lane span across the Mississippi River. We crossed it to go to work and visit friends, to get to soccer games, Dinkytown, the Loring Pasta Bar, and the East Bank of the University of Minnesota. And we crossed it to return home.

I played the message again.

2

My mother taught me to make Swedish pancakes in her kitchen long before I had a kitchen of my own. Each pancake is about six inches in diameter, lacy like a doily, in variegated shades of beige and brown like the meat and skin of an almond, and thin as a French crepe. My father, siblings, and I gladly kept the cold cereal in the cupboard on the special days my mother heated up her pan.

Swedish pancakes, topped with either lingonberries or maple syrup, are a special tradition now for my family also. The breakfast is anchored not to a particular holiday but simply to a chosen morning. One of us knows the time is right, says so, and the plan is set.

1

My twenty-year-old son was OK, my mother's message assured me. My father located and talked to him before they called me. They didn't want me to worry.

I dialed my parents' number. "What happened?" I asked, hoping to hear that I had gotten it wrong. But no: at rush hour, less than sixty minutes earlier, the bridge simply fell.

Interstate 35 runs north-south across the United States, from Duluth on the west end of Lake Superior down through Minneapolis and St. Paul, where it splits temporarily into 35 West (35W) and East (35E), respectively, and on through Des Moines, Kansas City, Wichita, and Oklahoma City, finally ending in Laredo on the bank of the Rio Grande. It crosses, among others, the Minnesota, Missouri, and Red rivers, the Kettle, Winnebago, South Skunk, and Washita, the Frio, and Nueces.

Driving north across the 35W Mississippi River Bridge, from the river's west to east banks, seemed no different than driving on any other expanse of freeway. The bridge ran flat from one river bluff to the next, like a Popsicle stick laid between two bricks, with no graceful arches or taut suspension cords to alert travelers to the deep moving water below. The bridge is set on the far edge of downtown, where the river curves south and the bluffs start their rise from its banks, fooling the eye traveling at fifty-five miles an hour into believing that the continuous scenery is all one frame without an ancient cleft in bedrock running through its middle.

But driving south on the bridge could take your breath away. Here the river curved toward the traffic, its bridges fanning out to the right: the Stone Arch, Third Avenue, and Hennepin. St. Anthony Falls crashed below. The city birthed on the Mississippi sprang up blue and glittering, reflecting sky and water in glass and steel.

2

The recipe for Swedish pancakes—"Arthur's Favorite Pancakes"—passed from my grandmother to my mother to me.

Arthur's Favorite Pancakes

2 eggs

1 cup milk

2/3 cup flour

Arthur was my grandfather. Born in 1900 in Nyland, Sweden, he moved to America at the age of twenty-three and settled in Minneapolis, where he married Jenny, my grandmother, who was also from Sweden. Arthur worked for the phone company and occasionally preached in his native language at a Swedish church with an immigrant congregation. When my mother was nine, three churches in Sweden asked Arthur to be their pastor, so the family boarded a ship and set sail. They planned to stay indefinitely, but then Nazi Germany attacked Norway, and they heard the gunfire near the border to their west. Yielding to the pull of U.S. safety, they recrossed the Atlantic and returned to Minneapolis.

I have an old family movie of Arthur, circa 1969, walking from my childhood home toward his car, a turquoise and white Chevrolet. He's dressed in a navy suit, white shirt, and dark tie. A white handkerchief is folded into his breast pocket. His thinning salt-and-pepper hair is neatly combed. The coloring of his long face testifies to sunshine and good circulation. Jenny died a couple years earlier and he walks alone. As the camera follows him, he waves and smiles. He chuckles. I remember sometimes he laughed so hard he could hardly speak. His smile pulled his dimples in tight. His face taught me joy, as if it were my birthright.

1

"Mom, there's sirens and smoke everywhere," my son said when I called him after talking to my parents. He was downtown, walking toward the river.

Less than fifty minutes earlier, he had backed our car out of the driveway, driven east, and taken that north ramp onto 35W. He and his friend were on their way to see another buddy who lived in Dinkytown, just across the bridge. They had planned to leave about twenty minutes earlier, but the friend's father needed a quick favor. Their original plan placed them on the bridge at about 6:05 p.m., the time it fell. Due to the delay, they approached the bridge about 6:25, but by then, the bridge lay in the river and the road was closed.

Stories like this were everywhere. A friend's nephew drove south on 35W to cross the river, but at 6:02 he decided to turn off and take a different route. My sister's coworker crossed the bridge at 6:04, felt the car shake, and thought something was wrong with her tires or the engine. When she reached the other side, she looked in her rear view mirror and saw the bridge drop behind her. Another coworker suddenly chose to forego the 35W Bridge and instead took the Tenth Avenue Bridge, just downriver, a route he never took. As he drove across that smaller, older bridge, he looked over and saw the interstate bridge fall.

2

To start, crack open the eggs and beat them, using a metal whisk, into a pale yellow slurry. Next, pour milk into the measuring cup and add this to the eggs. Whisk again. Finally, spoon the flour into the measuring cup, level it with a knife, and dump it into the egg-milk mixture. More whisking and then the thin batter of no more substance or color than melted vanilla ice cream is ready to cook.

There is more to making the pancakes than following the recipe. The recipe matters, of course, but its list of ordinary ingredients and simple instructions won't show you how to move your wrist while swirling the batter in the pan or how to wait for the dancing water.

1

When the bridge fell, I was staying in a college dormitory in Santa Fe for a graduate school residency. An undergrad student in a dorm lounge sacrificed his televised baseball game to let me watch news coverage of the breaking story. Paula Zahn—on her second-to-last day at CNN, her first day being 9/11—showed viewers live pictures of smoke rising up from the river and an aerial view of the bridge missing from the line-up of its diminutive fellow bridges, like an octave without a middle C. I looked at these pictures as if a stranger, unable to orient myself to the shift in reality. I was accustomed to seeing my city at eye level, unblurred by smoke and settling dust.

Zahn reported people stranded on the span remnants, rescue boats in the water, and survivors being carried up the riverbank. The bridge's middle span had dropped right into the water, its weighty fall causing a wind. The north and south ends, sheared off, hung at precarious angles. A school bus, full of children, stopped right at the edge of a downward-pointing span. A semitrailer burned next to the bus, and a railroad car lay crushed underneath the bridge's north end. Police cars, ambulances, and fire trucks lined both sides of the river. Divers searched the moving water, but not for long, she said. Stormy weather was moving in.

Fifty to one hundred cars and trucks had been on the bridge at the time, a small number for rush hour. A witness suggested that resurfacing work on the bridge had limited its traffic capacity to one lane in either direction, and therefore, the number of vehicles was far less than on an ordinary Wednesday.

2

"Tell us about the miracles," my sons often said to my mother when they were little, even though they'd heard the stories again and again. My parents used to travel from St. Petersburg, Florida, to Minneapolis to visit us, and they stayed in a makeshift guest room in our basement. Early in the morning, the two boys would run down the stairs and into their room. They jumped on the bed and slipped under the covers. Arthur starred in at least two stories.

In one of the stories, a teenaged Arthur was alone in the forest of Ångermanland, Sweden and had become trapped under a large rock. Unable to free his leg, he prayed and fell asleep. When he awoke, he found himself free and sitting on top of the rock. The mystery of how he got there sent giggles and goose bumps into my little boys.

The other story was less an adventure tale than a domestic tale. When the grown-up Arthur moved his family to Sweden, their family had little money. One day, Arthur had to take a bus and leave for a few days on church business.

"You can't go," said my grandmother. "We don't have much food and the potatoes are gone."

"But I have to go," said Arthur.

He knelt on the floor right then and prayed for potatoes. "God will provide," he said as he stood and went out the door. No sooner had he reached the gate at the end of their yard than the bus pulled up. The bus driver opened the door and lifted up a sack of potatoes. "A lady in town thought you might be needing these," he said, handing the sack to Arthur.

1

Two days later and still in Santa Fe, I sent my son in Minneapolis a morning text message—"just checking in." By late evening he still hadn't responded. He usually texts back quickly, but he's busy and worked long hours as a waiter, and there are all kinds of reasons why he didn't respond, yet I put two and two together and came up with eight million and started to tremble inside.

What could have happened now? If a bridge can fall in the city where I live, a bridge he was nearly on when it fell, then anything can happen. Worry got the best of me and I called him.

He picked up within a few rings and said he was walking to his car on his way home from work. His shift had been long, the tips decent. He carried take-out food from the restaurant. I made light of calling him rather than waiting for him to call or text me, trying to cover my worry. No problem, he said.

2

My husband starts the coffee. Usually there is a Swedish brand or a dark French roast stashed away for just such an occasion. He inserts a white coffee filter into the coffeemaker's brew basket and measures out the coffee, one heaping scoop for every two cups, although our sons encourage him, "Make it stronger." He pours water into the top of the maker and presses the start button.

He turns on the television, flips through the stations looking for news, and then turns it off. Headlines won't penetrate the next hour or two. Laundry lies silently in piles a floor below. A floor begs to be swept.

1

After talking to my son, I walked back to my dorm room, full of awakened nerves. I sat down at the worn wooden desk, opened my laptop, and played music from a CD of hymns recorded by a band of brothers I know.

"Come thou font of every blessing / tune my heart to sing thy grace / streams of mercy never ceasing / call for songs of loudest praise."

Tremble: be still.

"Be thou my vision / O Lord of my heart / naught be all else to me / save that thou art."

Throat, tight and dry: gulp life like a baby's first breath.

A Quaker hymn played last. *"The peace of God restores my soul / A fountain ever springing."* I hummed, then sang, so very quietly. *"How can I keep from singing? / How can I keep from singing?"*

Was it the words affirmed over centuries of collective history and decades of my personal history? Or the familiar melodies? The guitars and harmonica and voices in harmony? Artistic beauty, wrote philosopher Jacques Maritain, slips light into the mind without effort.

Heavy heart: run away in joy.

2

On each side of the rectangular birch table, I place a heavy Fiestaware plate: purple like concord grapes, navy like lapis stone, cornflower blue like the morning sky, and orange like poppies. I often skip a tablecloth or placemats because I like the look of the colors on the light wood palette. I set out coffee mugs in a mix-match style: orange with navy, cornflower with purple, purple with orange, and navy with cornflower. The table explodes color like newly opened watercolor paints.

Silverware comes next. My left hand wraps around cool stainless steel while my right removes a knife, spoon, and fork from the cluster to place at their respective sides of each plate. I fold four green napkins and slide one under each fork. I set out a white china pitcher filled with cream. A small rectangle of pale yellow butter goes on a china dish. A white bowl holds sugar cubes. Two blue candles stand lit in crystal holders.

My mother served the pancakes on china plates, all white like a canvas on which to stroke and drip the red-violet paint of lingonberries. My Swedish step-grandmother, who crossed the Atlantic on an airplane to marry Arthur four years after my grandmother died, served the pancakes on white china bordered in blue flowers. She swirled lingonberries into whipped cream and heaped it all into a glass bowl like an ice cream sundae.

1

"I am not afraid." A few weeks later and back in Minneapolis, I read these words written by a man I admire in response to the bridge falling. He's a pastor and a father and I know he was doing what parents do. They say to their trembling children, "Here take my hand. I'm not afraid." Then the children lose their fear; their parent's courage displaces it.

But I can't write that same compact declaration, and I read in his words a challenge to do so. I can list the reasons why I'm not afraid that bridges—or towers—fall, citing risk statistics and articles of faith. Even so, the human tremble rises up at the prospect of bad news. I'm old enough to know that a parent's love, faith, and fear are often in a crazy internal knot even as he or she firmly grips that younger hand.

2

The way my mother's wrist swirled through the invisible parabola as she gripped the frying pan and spiraled the batter into a circle across the pan's surface made all the difference in what ended up on our plates. Her standards for symmetry, laciness, and delicacy elevated the perfect swirl to the level of artistry.

The swirl yields its prize, however, only in combination with the perfect frying pan. The pan must be heavy enough to withstand and conduct the heat evenly, but not so heavy the wrist can't easily hold and move it. Before I got married, my mother made sure I had the right pan, just as her mother had done for her. We stood in the department store's cookware section while she picked up each candidate, testing its feel in her hand and its maneuverability as she did the swirl.

I take out this pan now and turn on the gas flame under my stove's lower right burner. I've learned over the years that pointing the burner's control knob to the one o'clock position ensures a flame not too high, not too low.

1

A *Newsweek* web exclusive suggests that the bridge fell due to pigeon dung, an acidic excrement known to corrode nearly any metal. Other headline stories blame a flawed design, cracks and corrosion, substandard concrete, years of strain from trucks bearing weight beyond the legal limit, and ignored inspection warnings.

Engineers are trying to recreate the bridge from its wreckage along the river's edge, south of its original site. The first bolt to break or supporting beam to buckle may never be determined, but it's easy to speculate that a general carelessness among the stewards of public safety was an early domino to fall.

2

The pan heats over the flame. I pass my fingers under running water and then hold them over the pan and watch the action of the water droplets when they drip onto the pan's surface. These sizzle and evaporate; the pan needs more heat. A minute later I try the water trick again, and this time the drops do their dance, skipping and leaping on the pan's surface.

For the first pancake, I place a small sliver of Crisco in the pan, about the size of the fingernail on my little finger. It melts nearly instantly, and I use a metal spatula to spread it over the pan's surface. For subsequent pancakes, the sliver will be about half that size. Butter would smoke and burn in a pan this hot.

I transfer a spoonful of batter to the pan's center with my right hand, and with my left, I lift the pan off the burner. I swirl my wrist as my mother did, and the thin batter rushes to its rightful size and shape. After about eight seconds, I slide the spatula underneath, and flip. The first one always lacks the lace pattern and browns unevenly, but it primes the pan for those that follow.

As each pancake comes out of the pan, I stack them on a plate covered with a pan lid to keep in the heat. A stack of about fifteen signals that its time to call my husband and sons. They inhale deeply and smile at the dual aroma of coffee and pancakes.

1

Thirteen people died in the bridge collapse and about one hundred were injured. One of the men who died drowned while helping others get out of their cars. Another man died when his semi hit the side of the bridge. The truck's movement to this position perhaps stopped the school bus full of children from going off the sheared edge. The current theory is he careened his truck into the bridge side, at the cost of his life, for that very purpose. All the children lived.

One woman who survived said that when her car stopped falling, people were everywhere helping those in cars and in the water get out and to safety. She called them her angels. A friend of my older son—tall, broad shouldered, always smiling and laughing, infused with a joy kindred to Arthur—was near the bridge when it fell and bolted down the riverbank to help pull people out.

2

"Come and sit down," I say. "Start eating." The pancakes are never eaten in solitude as a bowl of corn flakes or toast and jam often are. Neither are they carried on a plate from room to room, pushed into the hungry mouth by the forkful while getting dressed or gathering papers for the day ahead. My husband and sons each take a seat. I stand behind mine.

Now God be thanked. Reality shifts and Beauty, already present, welcomes Peace and Life and Joy to the feast; we bow our heads to their transcendent First Cause. We lean into the stream of mercy that sings over rocks, rolls and rushes across continents and bodies of water and generations.

The stack of pancakes circles the table. I run back the ten steps to flip another pancake. I keep cooking while they eat, walking back and forth between flips to join the conversation. I sit down intermittently and toward the end.

We talk about school, work, friends, music, and books. The spoken word swirls around the table's center of gravity. The tender pancakes carry the gentle sweetness of maple syrup, the sharp sweetness of lingonberries. We wipe our mouths and laugh.

My husband gets up to make another pot of coffee. I check that there is still cream in the pitcher.

"Are you full yet?" I ask. "Who wants more?" The extravagance of this meal stuns me. There is always at least one more egg to crack, one more galup-galup of milk to pour from the carton, a couple more spoonfuls of flour, another sliver of shortening. The common ingredients transformed by heat and swirls and served amid bursts of color lavishly feed our hunger.

1

I went to look at the bridge site one month after it fell. The Tenth Avenue Bridge had reopened for traffic after being closed for several weeks. Chain-link fencing rose up from its west side and one lane had been closed off for pedestrians. The walkway was as crowded as any at the state fair.

Six stories below, the twisted metal looked as insubstantial as an erector set, as flimsy as a bobby pin. The rust caked like refried bean residue on silverware. The concrete surface lay peeled off like a sheet of vinyl flooring. The exit sign I had followed countless times stood propped on its side in debris at the river's edge.

People clamored for a spot at the fence. Cameras clicked. We grow up singing the nursery rhyme and playing its game—"*London Bridge is falling down, falling down, falling down*"—but what do we really know of such things?

2

The pancake stack disappears. The last of the coffee sits in the mugs. A few drips of syrup and lingonberries glisten on the wood's surface. We are happy about each other and we are full. My mother told me Arthur's last words before he died were, "Gud är så god." (God is so good.)

I know not to waste suffering or fear. I know to use them as hard lessons, to extract the nugget of what I have yet to learn or what I need to learn yet again or what I can only hope to someday learn. But how not to waste *these* moments?

We'll soon get up from the table and do who knows what and drive who knows where for all the rest of our lives. But here, now, the whole-ness of this moment, dense and round as a concrete piling driven deep into bedrock, anchors our paths. This is what it feels like when all is well. A mnemonic of experience as real as any. Might not a person just tip right over from the weight of fear or angst without this ballast at the other end?

Swedish Pancakes ("Arthur's Favorite") with Lingonberries

INGREDIENTS

Pancakes

2 eggs
1 cup milk
2/3 cup flour
Shortening

Lingonberries

1 pint fresh or frozen lingonberries
1 ½ cup cold water
1 ½ cup sugar

RECIPE

Pancakes

In a mixing bowl, whisk the eggs, milk, and flour together.

Heat a heavy skillet over medium-high heat until drops of water sprinkled on the pan "dance" on its surface.

Coat the pan with vegetable shortening.

Pour about 2 to 3 tablespoons of batter into the center of the pan. Quickly, pick up the pan and tilt it as needed so that the batter forms a thin circle.

Place the pan back on the heat and cook the pancake until it is lightly browned on the bottom.

Flip and cook again until that side is also lightly browned.

Between pancakes, as needed, add a small amount of shortening to prevent pancakes from sticking to the pan. Serve with maple syrup or lingonberries.

Lingonberries

Place lingonberries and water in an uncovered saucepan. Bring to a rolling boil.

Add sugar, stirring well to dissolve.

Bring the mixture back to a boil, then reduce heat slightly and maintain a steady, but gentler, boil for about 8 minutes.

Pour into a heat-resistant bowl and let cool. Refrigerate.

LAUREN F. WINNER is the author of *Girl Meets God*, *Mudhouse Sabbath*, and *Real Sex: The Naked Truth about Chastity*. She has appeared on PBS's Religion & Ethics Newsweekly and has written for *The New York Times Book Review*, *The Washington Post Book World*, *Publishers Weekly*, *Books & Culture*, and *Christianity Today*. Lauren has a PhD in history, teaches at Duke Divinity School, and travels extensively to lecture and teach. When she's at home, you can usually find her curled up, on her couch or screen porch, with a good novel. This essay is an excerpt from *Mudhouse Sabbath*.

13

Fitting Food

Eating attentively is hard for me. I'm single, I'm busy, and I just don't give very much thought to what I eat. My most beloved cooking implement is the microwave. I hate going to the grocery store. I like picking up Thai food. Once in a while, I do a real doozy in the kitchen—risotto with portobello mushrooms, some sophisticated salad, chocolate mousse. But these bursts of culinary bravado are occasional and almost always designed to impress a guest.

As a practicing Jew, I kept kosher—which is to say I observed *kashrut*, the Jewish dietary laws. Keeping kosher cultivates a profound attentiveness to food. Because I kept kosher (the word comes from the Hebrew for "fit" or "appropriate"), I thought about the food I ate. I thought about what I was going to eat, and where I was going to procure it, and how I was going to prepare it. Eating was never obvious. Food required intention.

Only after I stopped keeping kosher did I fully appreciate that kashrut had shaped more than my grocery lists. It also shaped my spiritual life. Keeping kosher transforms eating from a mere nutritional necessity into an act of faithfulness. If you keep kosher, the protagonist of your meal is not you; it is God.

The laws of kashrut are found in Leviticus and Deuteronomy. As with the Sabbath laws, the rabbis embroider and elaborate the dietary code in the Talmud.

There are two basic rules:

Some foods are simply forbidden: fish without both fins and scales, creepy-crawly insects, mammals that don't chew their cud and mammals that don't have cloven hooves. This means no shellfish, no pork chops, no prosciutto, no chocolate-covered ants, no lobster bisque. No bacon with your morning omelet. No Virginia ham. (All fruits and vegetables, by the way, are kosher. Eat as many chickpeas, pomegranates, bing cherries, and green beans as you want.)

Dairy products and meat products may not be eaten at the same time. The strict separation of meat and dairy is based upon Deuteronomy 14:21: "Thou shalt not seethe a kid in his mother's milk." The rabbis interpreted that verse broadly. Not only should a baby goat not be steeped, stewed, or sautéed in its mother's milk, no meat should be cooked with any dairy product. Indeed, meat and milk may not be eaten at the same meal. Nor can a pot used to cook dairy ever be used for anything *fleishig* (that's the Yiddish word for "meat," a cognate of our word "fleshy"). So forget about cheeseburgers. Forget, also, about your plan to make cream of mushroom soup in your blue stockpot tonight: three years ago you simmered Bolognese sauce in that pot, and now it is a meat pot forever.

In addition to those two basic principles are a host of narrower rules. Never eat blood. Eat only animals that have been slaughtered according to Jewish law (the law requires the most painless slaughter possible, a quick and neat slash to the jugular vein). Don't eat an animal that has died of old age.

Curious rules indeed. But they are far from arbitrary. A cosmology and an ethics underpin each injunction; to keep kosher is to infuse the simple act of feeding oneself with meaning and consequence. The codes of *shechitah* for example—the rules that govern the ritual slaughter of animals for food—insist on compassion. Yes, we human beings have to kill other living creatures in order to eat, but let's make that killing as painless and humane as possible. Even the injunction about the kid and its mother's milk is symbolic. Rabbi Abraham Joshua Heschel observed that boiling a baby in the milk of its mother mocks the reproductive order and life itself. Rabbi Arthur Waskow has suggested that to separate meat products from milk products is to constantly recall a distinction between death (meat) and life (milk).

But one shouldn't romanticize kashrut. It must be admitted that kashrut can, at times, be a royal pain in the neck. Keeping kosher requires at least two sets of dishes, one for meat and one for dairy. You have to buy your own brisket and steaks and ground round at a kosher butcher. At the grocery, you'll scrutinize packaged good, trying to determine which are certifiably kosher (Pepperidge Farm, Ben and Jerry's, and Coca-Cola all have rabbinic sanction, and most of their products are kosher; Kraft cheddar cheese and Quaker's S'mores granola bars are not). And then there's the problem of dining with your non-Jewish friends. In their homes, or at non-kosher restaurants, you're stuck drinking water and possibly munching on raw veggies. Keeping kosher is also expensive—meat slaughtered by kosher butchers is pricey, and then there are all those extra plates. Most of all, kashrut requires almost constant vigilance and thought. This chicken casserole calls for cream—how can I avoid the forbidden mingling of meat and milk? (For each cup of cream, substitute a cup of chicken stock mixed with one egg yolk and a dash of cornstarch.) *The Eating Southern and Kosher* cookbook suggests that you make gumbo with tofu instead of shrimp.

For Christians, this may seem quaint and intriguing but ultimately irrelevant. Throughout Christian history, interpreters have agreed that the moral precepts of the Old Testament—in particular, the Ten Commandments—are binding upon Christians, but the civil and ceremonial codes, from the dietary laws to the holiday injunctions, are not. And the New Testament rather dramatically makes clear that Christians are free to eat as many clams and oysters as they like: in the Book of Acts, a hungry Peter has a vision of a sheet of food descending from heaven. The sheet is filled with food that is kosher and unkosher, clean and unclean—potatoes and chicken and spinach, but also pork chops and lobsters and prawns. A voice instructs Peter to "kill and eat," but Peter protests, insisting that he will never eat unclean unkosher food. The voice from heaven then says, "What God has made clean, you must not call profane." This story is symbolic, to be sure. The voice is talking not just about food, but also about people; the instructions are not simply to eat, but also to invite both Jews and Gentiles into the Kingdom of God. Still, the story has epicurean consequences, too. Peter, a Jew who has come to follow Christ, is free to eat any and all of those once forbidden foods.

While Christians are not bound by the particularities of Deuteronomic dietary law, we may still want to pay attention to the basic principle that underlies kashrut: God cares about our dietary choices. This should come as no surprise; you only have to read the first two chapters of Genesis to see God's concern for food. Humanity's first sin was disobedience manifested in a choice about eating. Adam and Eve were allowed to eat anything they wanted, except the one fruit they chose. And the New Testament makes clear that God cares about the most basic, quotidian aspects of our lives. (Our God, after all, is the God who provides for the sparrows and numbers the hairs on our heads.) This God who is interested in how we speak, how we handle our money, how we carry our bodies—he is also interested in how we live with food.

At its most basic level, keeping kosher requires you to be present to your food. Of course, so does the Atkins diet. The difference between Atkins and kashrut is God. We try out the Atkins diet because our physician cares about what we eat. We limit ourselves to kosher food—to return to the etymology, appropriate or fitting food prepared appropriately—because God cares about what we eat.

So, down to brass tacks. I am not about to stop eating shellfish again. But I am trying to bring some thought and intention to the food I eat. The impulse comes from Judaism, but for the specifics I have turned to a number of different teachers who, though not Jewish, have an intuitive appreciation for the logic of kashrut.

One of my food teachers is an Episcopal priest-cum-chef, Robert Farrar Capon. In 1968, Capon wrote a slender book called *The Supper of the Lamb*. It's part cookbook, part theological meditation—something like M. E. K. Fisher meets the desert fathers. (The book is, in fact, organized around a lamb recipe, and the title's biblical allusion is not accidental.)

The second chapter of *The Supper of the Lamb* begins with the slightly absurd instruction to spend "sixty minutes or so" chopping an onion. One onion, sixty minutes. The hour is to begin with the chopper looking at the onion, encountering the onion, having a "material . . . meeting" with it. After noticing its shape, its top and bottom, its blemishes, you proceed to removing its skin, moving so carefully that you do not puncture, let alone slice, the flesh of the onion itself. And on and on

Capon leads us, through a veritable onion meditation. By the end of the chapter one wonders if a single hour is enough time.

What is Capon's point? Presumably not that we should all set aside sixty minutes every time we sauté a Vidalia. Rather, he is making "a case for paying attention." After an hour with your onion, you might begin to see "that the uniqueness of creation are the result of continuous creative support, of effective regard by no mean lover." The lover of course is God. "He *likes* onions, therefore they are. The fit, the colors, the smell, the tensions, the tastes, the textures, the lines, the shapes are a response, not to some forgotten decree that there may as well be onions as turnips, but to his present delight." And so the reminders stack up on top of one another (rather, one might note, like the layers of a cake). Food is part of God's creation. A right relationship with food points us toward him.

Another of my food teachers is Barbara Kingsolver. In an essay called "Lily's Chickens," Kingsolver explains that she eats seasonally. When tomatoes and plums are in season she eats them. She avoids the unseasonable temptations of modern American supermarkets, which ship in greenhouse tomatoes and lemons and plums and asparagus all year round. Kingsolver only eats tomatoes in January if she canned some back in June.

Why is Kingsolver so committed to this culinary calendar? Because shipping food from greenhouses around the world is America's second-largest expenditure of oil. (The first, not surprisingly, is our daily reliance on cars.) As Kingsolver explains, "even if you walk or bike to the store, if you come home with bananas from Ecuador, tomatoes from Holland, cheese from France, and artichokes from California, you have guzzled some serious gas." To eat seasonally (and locally) is to enact a politics of reduced consumption.

But seasonal eating has an almost sacramental effect as well. Though Kingsolver may not have had spiritual aims when she began eating seasonally, she nonetheless introduced a liturgical calendar to her life. Her year, just like the Jewish year or the church year, now has a rhythm. Tomatoes mean summer. Potatoes and beans suggest winter. Kingsolver's seasonal diet sacralizes not just food, but time.

I do not practice seasonal eating with the rigor I once brought to kashrut. Last night, for example, I found myself eating a slice of pizza topped with chunks of avocado. (It's November.)

But I have begun the move toward seasonal eating. I'm embarrassed to admit that the first step in seasonalizing my diet was study. When I read Kingsolver's essay, I realized that because I am so accustomed to Whole Foods and The Fresh Market with their year-round displays of bright, perfect produce, I had no idea which fruits were in season when. I had to head to the library and read up on vegetable birthdays. (No strawberries in November, of course, but apparently persimmons are abundant here in Virginia in the fall.)

Now, like some of my Jewish friends who keep kosher at home but eat more liberally at restaurants, I try to keep a seasonal kitchen but allow myself to indulge when I'm out on the town. For the first time since I became a Christian, I have found myself thinking about what food I put in my body, and where that food has been—in whose hands, in what countries—before it got to my plate. Like Capon's musings on the onion, this reflecting on and participation with my food leads ultimately back to him who sustains, provides, and feeds. Seasonal eating is not for everyone, and it is certainly not the only discipline that can infuse Christian eating with attention and devotion. Some of my friends find that fasting one day a week imbues their six days of meals with a spirit of gratitude and joy. Others try to make all their food from scratch. Every loaf of bread is baked at home; every salad comprises vegetables from the garden in the backyard.

On Sunday morning as I watch my priest lay the Communion table for the gathered believers, I remember why eating attentively is worth all the effort: the table is not only a place where we can become present to God. The table is also a place where he becomes present to us.

Lauren's Fresh Cherry Cobbler

Recently, I went cherry picking with two friends. The cherries definitely needed baking—it was a little too early in the season, and the fruit was a little too tart. I paged through cookbook after cookbook—a dozen or so must have been on the floor before I was through. While I found many recipes for wonderful sounding treats made with cherry pie filling, I found nothing calling for fresh cherries. So much for seasonal eating. Here's what I threw together:

Preheat oven to 375°F. Pit and slice about 4 cups of cherries. Mix that up with 1 ¼ cup sugar, 2 to 3 tablespoons of flour (just enough to give the mixture some viscosity; cornstarch would probably work just as well, but I didn't have any on hand). Put the cherry mixture into a 9x13-inch baking pan. Then combine 1 ½ cups oatmeal, 1 cup brown sugar, 1/2 cup flour, and a pinch or two of cinnamon; cut in 1 cup butter. Sprinkle this crumbly mixture on top of the cherries and bake about 45 minutes. Serve with vanilla ice cream.

Next time I might use a little less sugar . . .

KIRSTIN VANDER GIESSEN-REITSMA is the editor of *catapult magazine* (www.catapultmagazine.com), a bi-weekly online publication of *culture is not optional (*cino). She and her husband Rob formed *cino when they realized that others shared their post-college sense of isolation and desire to keep learning in community about living faithfully in the everyday stuff of life. *cino's work has extended to the biennial Practicing Resurrection conference, the quarterly print *road journal*, and a growing series of topical books that includes *Eat Well: A Food Road Map* and *Do Justice: A Justice Road Map*. Rob and Kirstin also helped found World Fare, a volunteer-staffed fair trade store in Three Rivers, Michigan, that networks their small-town community to work for local and global justice. By way of tentmaking, Rob and Kirstin share a position at Calvin College in Grand Rapids, Michigan, doing research, education, and programming around discernment and popular culture, which includes organizing the Festival of Faith & Music. Kirstin refreshes her body and mind by gardening, biking, singing, camping, reading fiction, cooking prolifically, and gathering combinations of wonderful people around tables and bonfires.

14

Choice Cuisine

First, I decided that I didn't like tomato soup—just grilled cheese. Then, I decided I didn't like a bun with my sloppy joe—just slop. I can trace the path of developing my own unique identity as a person directly through the food choices I started making when it came to our standard family menu. No pizza burgers for me, please. No PB, just J. Yet I don't ever remember my parents being exasperated with me, just graciously patient.

In the life of a child, food is often the first fork in the road, from which many tines of rebellion and secession diverge. Thankfully, declining the tomato soup doesn't inevitably lead to a crack habit. For the high-school version of myself and my now-husband Rob, our search for identity in relationship to and apart from our families led us to the abundant table of some of our high school teachers—two families who chose to share a home in the suburbs of Chicago. Around that table, we regularly became intoxicated not on cheap beer, but on theology and literature and music and kindness.

My husband Rob and I still know exactly what to expect when we're having a meal with these friends. The dining table is laden with eclectic, heavenly smelling dishes. Someone blesses the food—they all take turns, even the three-year-olds. And then, passing a steaming bowl, Bill inevitably says, "I can't believe we eat this well." When he says this, Bill isn't referring to the fanciness or expense of the food, but to the wholesomeness of the preparation, contents, and community.

My own concept of "eating well" has evolved a great deal since I started honing my sloppy joe preferences. My parents were frugal, and I inherited their cost-conscious ways. I took pride my sophomore year of college in coordinating a grocery list for eight housemates on a budget less than a quarter of what the cafeteria meal plan cost. The staples of our youth—tuna noodle casserole, shepherd's pie, mostaccioli—efficiently fed our bodies and souls through a tumultuous year. The ritual of sitting down together each weeknight around our mismatched kitchen to eat familiar comfort food produced a much-needed sense of stability in the midst of break-ups, health issues, disagreements, and existential crises. And it was all practically sustained by shopping the sales and buying generic, just as my parents had done.

As proud as I was of managing a thrifty food budget, in the intervening years, I've developed a greater awareness of the social cost of food. The price that pops up with a bar code scan at the register is not the only thing that differentiates one choice from another. Long before I check out, the food I purchase accumulates a tab sheet of environmental costs. Likewise, the process that takes place after each bite leaves my fork and enters my body involves a balance sheet of physical debits and credits.

I think about the dietary laws given to the Israelites and realize that these were not arbitrary rules, but rules to teach God's people stewardship of the land and of the body. God was teaching the people how to live out Kingdom values even in the mundane, how to tell the true story of their identity in times of plenty and of want. If we start looking for patterns that correlate with today's food issues, we can infer that Kingdom values include food systems that are sustainable for humans, animals, land, plants, water, and air. That is, the resources we consume to produce our food should be proportionate; no part of creation should be abused so some human beings can have more than they really need.

While we know the law has not been abolished by Christ, we also know we are the benefactors of grace. Jesus came to explain to us in person the not-so-secret secret of life in God's kingdom: it's all about love. Love God and love your neighbor: these two commands are the summary of the law. Life in Christ is not about following the rule for the rule's sake, but about having the desire to do so out of love for God and about trusting that God knows the deepest longings of our hearts. As Rob and I have journeyed together through high school, college, and into the cultivation of our own household, we've attempted to continue the biblical narrative of love and grace and abundance in our everyday choices, including our food choices, through both fat and lean times.

During one of the lean times, Rob and I had the privilege of eating a meal with Dr. Vincent Harding, a friend of Dr. Martin Luther King Jr. and an amazing historian and theologian. Dr. Harding was scheduled to speak at a Martin Luther King Day event at the college Rob was attending at the time. The school offered to pick up the tab for dinner if we would serve as Dr. Harding's chauffeurs and companions for the evening.

At the recommendation of a professor, we ended up at The Brick House, a converted Victorian-era house blooming between the cracks of a concrete industrial district. Through three hours of appetizers, main courses, drinks, and desserts, the conversation and the food were fantastically slow. We asked each other questions about where we had been and Dr. Harding asked us about where we were going. As he spoke, the truths he shared struck me as perfectly aged delicacies, precisely paired with each course of the meal. At the end of the night, Rob and I had a sense of being completely satiated, both physically by the most expensive meal we'd ever eaten and spiritually by one of the most wise people we'd ever met. I couldn't believe we had eaten so well.

Back at home, the day after our fabulous Brick House feast, I turned to the more modest ingredients of our home kitchen. My job as a part-time church office manager provided our only income while Rob was a full-time student, and both of us were also more-than-full-time volunteers. In that season of our lives, even our "home" kitchen was borrowed:

a well-used room at the center of my grandparents' lake cottage, usually empty in the winter, but at that point in time it was a refuge for two young explorers trying to forge a new and decidedly unlucrative path in the world. My parents, proud of and yet understandably concerned about our simple lifestyle, frequently found ways to supplement our meager pantry with edible staples and treats. Each visit to my childhood home ended with a plastic bag, filled with an assortment of food items they just happened to have purchased in excess of what they needed.

Ramen was common, as was rice and beans, even for the weekly culinary peak of Sunday dinner. But that particular Sunday, I thawed the six-pound pork loin my dad had bought for us, at a too-good-to-be-true sale at his local grocery chain. I hauled out the heavy cutting board, nearly two inches thick, and a knife from the motley cottage collection—a knife that somehow always seemed sharp, perhaps from the plentiful leisure time that characterized life on the lake. I chopped carrots, potatoes, and onions for the Crock-Pot, looking forward to the delicious product of my labor but also reflecting with some amount of guilt on how the pork loin from the grocery store didn't reflect the food values I would live out if we could afford to do so. I had been learning more about factory farming. I was quite certain that the pigs who gave their parts to be packaged in plastic for the grocery store weren't being stewarded according to the values of the God of the Bible, but according to the values of the gods of commodity. Should I have refused the gift from my dad, excited as he was and hungry as we were?

In the wooden rhythm of the knife against the cutting board, my mind wandered back to our conversation with Dr. Harding. Over a glass of port, he had told us how his years of community organizing had convinced him that when love and theology conflict, love should always be our priority. I assembled liquid and seasonings and trimmed the fat from the gifted meat—the centerpiece of our dish, but with a history of violence that could not be cooked away—and I knew I'd stash Dr. Harding's wisdom away like a favorite recipe.

In the years since that evening at The Brick House, I've surrounded myself with a community of people who are also passionate about the relationship between faith and food. I've attempted to articulate and practice good theology more fully when it comes to what I purchase, prepare, and put into my body as nourishment. Guided by the ecological spirit of the Hebrew Bible's dietary laws, Rob and I have focused on local produce, dairy products, and meat. Attempting to embody biblical advice against consuming meat that's been offered to idols or gained through violent means, we seek to undermine industrial agriculture's anti-relational commodification of animal life by building relationships with small family-owned farms.

Even as we make intentional choices to eat less meat and invest in more sustainable farms, I still struggle with the question of eating meat in general. I read in Isaiah about the renewed earth in which even the "natural" violence of animals is healed, and I can't help but believe we'll all be vegetarians in the Kingdom to come. Then shouldn't I be pursuing that value now in preparation? Perhaps I should be praying for the will to desire that goal. But in light of Dr. Harding's revelation, I know that even if I arrive there some day because being a vegetarian is consistent with my theology, I probably won't ever give up eating meat with my family. As much as I try to invite my family to participate in the joyful realization of our shared Christian faith values at the table, I'm committed never to reject—or even fail to appreciate and sincerely bless—a meal we eat together.

This commitment, reinforced by the words of Dr. Harding, takes on particular importance in my relationship with my dad. As I've continued to form my own identity apart from my parents, I've graduated from food preferences to politics. My dad and I often find ourselves debating the finer points of gun control policy, arguing about the validity of war as a national defense strategy, expressing our opinions about political candidates—and almost always coming down on opposite sides. However, faced with the task of collaborating on a menu, our taste buds fall into lockstep over portabella fries and crème brûlée, grilled zucchini and phyllo pastries. To share and prepare recipes, to stand around the grill in the summer, to witness his delight when I try his newest creation—I know my love for my father finds its best home in these things, in spite of our differences in other areas of life, like politics and pork loins. And as imperfect as my practice may be, love is the thing, the only thing.

My journey through childhood, high school, and marriage has been characterized by endlessly discovery about how to live in this world as a beloved child of God. On that journey, I've had the gift of being a child of very human parents who have done their best to equip me with tools for faithful servanthood. As children do, I've taken those tools and made them my own. I've discovered in so doing that it's not tomato soup

I dislike—just soup from a can. As I create and revise my own fresh version of the recipe from my own backyard tomatoes, home grown herbs, and farm-fresh milk, I'm not rejecting my childhood, but deepening the lessons my parents have taught me: grow something good to eat, even if it's just one tomato plant. Appreciate wholesome food, enjoyed around a table with other people. Develop long-term relationships with the best recipes.

Which brings me back to the notion of eating *well*. We eat best when we perceive the wholeness of the act, brokenness and all, struggling to cultivate a feast worthy of the Kingdom while humbly acknowledging that all perfect goodness begins and ends in God alone. And how can I not be humbled when I realize that the food I choose has the power to sustain my land, my neighbors, and my relationships? To be the embodiment of my love? It is toward these ends that I seek to steward our modest financial resources, to tell the best possibly story about who I am in Christ. I can only hope the merciful Judge will one day say, "I can't believe you ate so well. Won't you join me at the table?"

Grilled Zucchini

A great way to use up a lot of zucchini at the peak of the season and keep the heat of cooking out of the kitchen!

INGREDIENTS

6 medium zucchini
1/4 cup olive oil
1/4 cup balsamic vinegar

Serves 6

RECIPE

Cut each zucchini lengthwise into about 6 spears each.

Place zucchini, oil, and vinegar in a flat dish, toss to coat, and let sit for at least 30 minutes.

In the meantime, heat a grill to medium-high. Place zucchini spears on the grill and turn until they're slightly blackened on the edges.

Enjoy hot off the grill or chill to eat plain or in salads.

Deborah Leiter Nyabuti has friends who call her the Queen of Soup-Making. She has also been named a DeKruyter Graduate Scholar in Communication for her interests in faith and communication. She pursues her varied research interests as a doctoral student in communication at Purdue University in West Lafayette, Indiana, where she holds an Andrews Fellowship. Her essays, poems, and other writings have appeared in a variety of venues, including *catapult magazine*, the *Road Journal*, and the book *A Fine Frenzy: Poets Respond to Shakespeare*. Whenever she can, she squeezes in time to travel, to read and write creatively, and to study Swahili from sources other than *The Lion King*. She believes with T. S. Eliot, Julian of Norwich, and her loving husband that "all shall be well and all manner of thing shall be well."

15

Cooking Chicken Wat

I pull out the cookbook and study the recipe. It calls for three pounds of chicken pieces. I'm in grad school now—that's too much meat and it's too much money. I decide to add more vegetables instead, potatoes and peas this time. I also remember the last time I followed this recipe. The next day, in the lunchroom, eating the leftovers, I nearly cried over the spices, including the three tablespoons of cayenne pepper. This time I decide to take a friend's advice and use sweet Hungarian paprika to moderate the spiciness. I don't want sweat rolling down my face in front of my new boyfriend when eating a dish from his side of Africa. At dinner that night, I get rave reviews. "No one in Africa would believe you made this dish!" he tells me, clearly meaning it as a compliment.

That was four years ago, when I began to cook for the Kenyan native who has since become my husband. When I mention my adventures in Ethiopian cooking to those living around me, I get a variety of responses. "I didn't know they had food in Ethiopia," some would jokingly say. Others, more thoughtful, say, "You don't always connect countries like Ethiopia with cuisine." I often respond by inviting them over to share the dish with me, hoping that they'll be able to learn a bit more about East Africa's culture by experiencing its spicy flavors.

I'm Dutch-American and was raised on largely spiceless American food, but a semester abroad and many subsequent successful culinary experiments, especially from cultures in nations we in the West call "developing," broadened my palate before I even met my husband. Smelling the zesty vegetables of an Iraqi baked dinner, tasting the creamy zing of a Thai curry with coconut milk, and hand-chopping the many vegetables for a Guatemalan Juliana soup have gradually taught me humility toward other kinds of food and the cultures from which they spring. I've learned, for starters, that delicious food is a part of the culturally and economically diverse realities of continents far from my own. Beyond this, I've also discovered I can learn a lot from these cooks about how to prepare excellent food economically. When I cook curry, the cayenne pepper and other spices provide the flavor, so only a couple of tablespoons of oil are needed. In rice pudding, the natural sweetness of ground fenugreek, cardamom, and cinnamon decrease my need for so much sugar in the dessert. I've learned how to stretch costly meat by scattering small pieces among many more vegetables and complex starches in stews and soups. In the Juliana soup, I hardly notice there's only a single chicken breast's worth of meat when it's surrounded by so many chopped turnips, zucchini, carrots, potatoes, kale, and corn.

The steadiest companion in this culinary journey for me has been *Extending the Table*, a Mennonite cookbook full of authentic recipes from all over the world. Still in graduate school, I'm more thankful than ever for these lessons, and I am starting to come full circle, applying the lessons I learned from making delightful foods like chicken wat to the cultural cuisine of my own home and country. Armed with these lessons in flavor from cultures around the world, I'm able to make healthier choices while cooking with local ingredients and creating more authentically American food.

As I experiment with my food fusions, finding myself adding Mexican spices like adobo into African recipes thick with coriander, I wonder what truly makes a cuisine authentic. I wonder whether my experimentation would be considered kosher to the people whose native foods I'm messing with. These complexities remind me of Anne Tyler's thoughtful portrait in her novel *Digging to America*. In one part of the story, one of the protagonists, the matriarch of an Iranian-American family, visits a relative who has married a white American, and she is offended at how blithely (and, she feels, awkwardly) the American husband has "taken over" Iranian food and terminology. The matriarch feels it is rude, whereas her relative's perspective is that her husband is approaching her cultural background with love and respect.

These questions of cultural identity and how we approach other cultures are complicated. I can't come to another person's culture without wearing the glasses of my own cultural position and perspective. This means there's a danger in my cooking chicken wat: in my desire to learn another culture's food, I could become a food imperialist. After all, the various cuisines of developing countries emerge out of necessity as well as delight. The very fact that some of the spices for my Ethiopian stew aren't grown locally in North America, yet are available to me, is a factor that, at best, takes me out of the food's original context and, at worst, potentially implicates me in the same kind of imperialism that centuries ago led Europeans to dominate other cultures in the process of exploring for new and different spices. And my take on Eastern African cuisine will always be a non-native one.

Yet, as long as I'm bringing a perspective (and its baggage) with me, I might as well admit that position's strengths as well as its weaknesses. While I seek to find balance between local and global ingredients, it's pointless to deny that I have a wealth of choices before me when it comes to food, and that I have been shaped by that position as well as by my own heritage's approach to food. And I'm actually deeply thankful to live in a place in which I have been given the materials to explore other cultures through their food.

I don't know the answer to these complex tensions, but I'm gradually starting to understand how important it is to bring an awareness of them to my international cooking experiments. I do know that as a blond-haired, light-skinned American of Dutch/English/German/Swiss/Scottish heritage, nothing can make me a native East African, not even taking on an African last name. And even if it were possible, cooking chicken wat isn't enough on its own to make me truly appreciate and understand a culture that's so different from my own. Being truly Christ-like in an approach to foods and the cultures out of which they arise takes more effort than cooking a few dishes now and then from my copy of *Extending the Table*. But I know, for me, this has been an essential first step. "Taste and see," we Christians are told at Communion; that directive is true in our relationships with our global neighbors as well as in our relationship with God. Sometimes literally tasting is a necessary part of the process, a step toward seeing. I'm looking forward to tasting and seeing where God will take me next.

Chicken Wat (Ethiopian)

It may look like this stew has a lot of ingredients, but most of the ingredients are spices. The original recipe is from *Extending the Table* (see below), but I've added my own substitutions and twists. The stew is very spicy, so if you're not used to lots of spicy heat, lessen the spices (particularly the cayenne pepper) and make sure you use the sweet Hungarian variety of paprika. The vegetables I add seem to absorb the spice more than the chicken does, so be prepared for that as well. The stew is good over rice, alongside a white cornmeal concoction from Kenya called ugali, or with African or Indian flat breads (injera and chapatis, respectively). The recipes for all of these sides can be found in *Extending the Table*.

INGREDIENTS

2 ½ to 3 pound chicken pieces (you can use less than this if you use boneless chicken and/or add vegetables)

2 tablespoons lemon juice

1 teaspoon salt

2 tablespoons oil, margarine, butter

2 cups onions, finely chopped

1 tablespoon garlic, minced

1 teaspoon ginger root, grated, or 1/2 teaspoon ground ginger

1/4 teaspoon fenugreek, crushed

1/4 teaspoon ground cardamom

1/8 teaspoon ground nutmeg

2 tablespoons Hungarian sweet paprika

Berbere (a simple formulation):
    1 teaspoon ground ginger
    3 tablespoons ground red pepper (*Hot!*—you can lessen this or
       substitute quite a bit of sweet paprika if you don't like as much heat)
    1/4 teaspoon ground cloves
    1/2 teaspoon ground cinnamon
1/2 cup water
Vegetables (optional)
1 egg per person (optional)

RECIPE

Remove the skin from the chicken and then sprinkle the chicken with lemon juice and salt.

Let this stand while preparing other ingredients.

In large saucepan, melt the oil.

Add onions, garlic, and ginger root, cover, and cook on low heat until onions are soft, but not browned.

Add fenugreek, cardamom, ground nutmeg, and paprika. Stir well and add 1/4 cup of the Berbere spice mixture.

Stir over low heat for 2 to 3 minutes.

Pour in water. Bring to a boil over high heat, stirring continuously.

Add the chicken to the sauce, turning the pieces until they are entirely coated. At this point, you can also add any vegetables you would like. I often use chopped potatoes, peas, green beans, and corn.

Reduce heat to medium-low, cover, and simmer until chicken is tender, about 45 minutes, turning once or twice to coat chicken evenly.

When it becomes too dry, add a little water.

Sauce should be the consistency of heavy cream.

If you like, you can prepare 1 hard-boiled egg for each person. Peel the hard-boiled eggs and then cut shallow slits in the eggs to allow the color and flavor of the sauce to permeate the eggs.

Add the eggs to the sauce and simmer for 10 minutes.

Stew can be made a day ahead of time and then refrigerated, and the eggs can be boiled and added when reheating, but be aware that the stew gets spicier the longer it sits.

Adapted from Charmayne Denlinger Brubaker and Phyllis Horst Nofziger, in Joetta Handrich Schlabach, *Extending the Table: A World Community Cookbook*.

Jacqueline Rhodes is a native of Memphis, Tennessee. She is the proud mother of five children and currently resides in Grand Rapids, Michigan.

16

The Soul of Soul Food

It is an annual late-August ritual for the very few and privileged: mini-vans, family wagons, and U-Hauls are stuffed to the brim with furniture and books and clothes and all that is required to transform a cinder block dorm room into a comfortable living space for the next six months. The night before our pilgrimage to East Lansing, my firstborn loaded the family van with a mix of green and white MSU Spartan paraphernalia and high school keepsakes. Brittane wanted to get an early start, but not too early.

"Mother, sophomores cannot be the first students on campus—that is so freshmen. But we should get there early enough to take care of a few business matters," she explained.

I had no idea how early "early enough" was, but I was willing to oblige my homegrown drama queen. She was the kindergartner who eagerly started the first day of school by encouraging her teary-eyed parents to "leave already—don't you two need to go to work?"

She studied her back-to-school checklist to make sure every item had been scratched off. Then she walked into the kitchen, list in hand, and said, "Mother, you didn't make my dinner." She lingered on the word *dinner* like a sleepy four-year-old, dividing the word into two notes, the second syllable almost an octave lower than the first.

"What dinner Britt? Were you hoping to have a big family dinner? You were only home a few days."

131

"No, Mother, my own dinner with all my favorites—I really *need* a good soul food dinner before I go back to school. I won't be able to survive till Thanksgiving!"

I felt as if I had violated the Black-Mother-Sending-Her-Child-Off-to-College code of ethics. "OK, Brittane, but *you* are going to help!"

"I'd love to," she replied. "I need to learn how to cook some of this stuff anyway!"

Preparing collard greens, candied yams, dressing, fried corn, baked macaroni and cheese, fried catfish, baked BBQ chicken, and cornbread is a labor of love. And, although helping hands would speed up the process, my children are of the microwave-and-fast-food generation. They know very little about the art of cooking soul food.

Recipes in my family were passed from mother to daughter for generations, like precious family secrets. Yet these recipes were taught without words. When I was old enough to stand at Ma'Dear's apron, she would say, "Pay attention, child, so one day you can make this cornbread." The rule was to been seen but not heard, and so I watched and learned in an almost sacred silence.

Ma'Dear's kitchen was quiet—my kitchen is full of noise. Music, laughter, dancing, distractions, and words. And Brittane, with every intention to help, was swept away by the latest video on MTV.

Several thoughts arrested me as I rummaged through the cupboards to assemble the ingredients and tools of the trade. In my mind I flipped through the novel of my life, the pages already filled in with childhood memories of me and Ma'Dear in the kitchen and the pages yet blank but footnoted with the anticipation of experiencing the kitchen with my own grandchildren. While Brittane peeled the sweet potatoes, I wondered what my great-great grandmother, Mama Arkie, would think of my life with its hectic, noisy, word-filled pace. In her day, silence was safety. Slave mothers trained their children to be quiet and out of Master's way. Now kids are encouraged to become wordsmiths before preschool. The art of observation has been discouraged and the sacredness of silence is disappearing like my memory of Ma'Dear's recipes.

I have got to write some of this stuff down, I thought to myself. Shamelessly, I often opt to buy the boxed, inferior version of everything for the sake of time. Why is it that I utilize the most modern, time-saving technology known to humankind and yet I never have enough time? I can't even find the time to make homemade cornbread. It's tragic.

As I mixed the cornbread batter, careful to add a pinch of salt on the egg, careful to fold in the melted lard, careful to use a seasoned cast iron skillet, carefully *and* effortlessly recreating history, I felt as stirred as the batter in the wide-mouthed bowl. My mom taught me how to make this bread, because her mother taught her and because her mother taught her and so on and so on. But I hadn't taught Brittane. She's watching MTV.

The realization hit me hard. Had I been negligent? Had I dishonored my foremothers: Mammy, Aunt Jemimah, Big Mama, Ma'Dear?

The image of a full-figured black woman adorned in a red bandana and a flour-stained apron has long been a source of controversy and embarrassment in the African American community. But for me, an African American woman born and raised in the south, Mammy has always been the epitome of tenacity and creativity. When Jim Crow segregated the South right down to the last morsel of food, Mammy raised generations of teachers, lawyers, nurses, and social activists on the scraps from the butcher's floor. With the fat, feet, tails, ears, organs, skins, and snouts of animals, Mammy ensured the survival of a people who without her ingenuity would have perished. She testified to the glory of God by retelling the creation story and by reenacting creation herself: bringing order out of chaos, making something out of nothing, and saying, this is good, very good.

Soul food is the "survival-of-a-people" food. Culture, history, heroes, and heroines are connected to this food.

But soul food is not without controversy. It is a painful reminder that blacks were considered "less-than," unworthy, undeserving, and subhuman. Like the front seats of the bus, the best foods, the choice meats, were reserved for whites. Nutrition is also a concern. Favorite soul foods, such as chitterlings (pig intestines), hog mog (the lining of a pig's stomach), and sous (pig scraps boiled into a jelly-like substance) are criticized for their nutritional value. How do we reconcile the relationship between our beloved foods and their glaring health risks? And if we stop preparing these edible heirlooms, do we disconnect from our heritage?

While we may argue over dietary choices, for others it is a moot point. Racism continues to limit access to healthy food options in many communities of color. It is hard to replace fat with fresh and processed with produce when you are limited to the convenience store on the corner. Although we know that breakfast is the most important meal of the day we sit idly by while children start school on empty stomaches. Then we wonder why—why the achievement gaps, why so many children placed in special education, why so many discipline issues? Could they be starving? Not only suffering because of poor nutrition but also choking on the systemic, institutionalized racism that has denied access to their culture, history, heroes, and heroines. Systems, structures, and policies serve as blockades for some while protecting others.

Racism is insidious and far more complicated than individual acts of personal prejudice. Racism affects opportunities to attend college, prospects for employment, and quality of life. It affects where we live, who we love, what we buy, and yes, what we eat. It even taints our image of who we are and what we deserve.

We can side with conventional wisdom by blaming parents or government or the church. But loving thy neighbor does not command us to assign blame, it calls us to love. Love. I've finally realized that *love* is the soul of soul food. When black mothers had little to no material thing to offer, they poured all the love they could muster into the food they prepared.

Mama Arkie's love continues to nourish her offspring even now through the golden brown cornbread soon fetched from *my* oven. In twenty minutes, the aroma of the bread signals that it is ready. As I flip the bread out of the skillet and onto the plate, I'm reminded of Brittane's earlier comment about "needing" this meal. It is as if she intuitively knew what I am only now able to articulate. Soul food gives us roots to stand tall and wings to soar high. African American women transferred their hopes and dreams for change, their anguish, their will to survive, and their tremendous faith into the dishes they prepared for blacks and whites. They mixed a tablespoon of strength and a cup of determination, drawn from the depth of their soul, into their cooking. I hope that I am doing the same for my daughter.

Today Aunt Jemimah, Mammy, and my great-great-grandmother Arkie's spirit nourishes the sons and daughters they could have only imagined. May their spirit live on through Brittane. May physical and spiritual starvation end with us. And may the tradition of preparing and serving food connect us to our past, present, and future.

Cornbread

INGREDIENTS

5 tablespoons melted-butter-flavored Crisco

2 cups all-purpose flour

2 cups yellow cornmeal

2 tablespoons sugar

2 teaspoons baking powder

2 ½ cups milk (some people prefer buttermilk)

2 large eggs

2 teaspoons salt

RECIPE

Preheat oven to 400° F. Place a 10-inch cast iron skillet in the oven with 5 tablespoons of Crisco.

Meanwhile, mix the batter: whisk the flour, cornmeal, sugar, and baking powder together; add milk and eggs; sprinkle the salt over the eggs; and mix the batter with a fork.

Take the skillet out of the oven and be sure to coat its bottom and sides with melted Crisco.

Pour the hot Crisco into the batter and stir with a fork.

Pour batter into the skillet and spread it evenly with a spatula. Bake for 25 minutes or until golden brown and firm.

Wendell Berry has been called the prophet of rural America. His thirty-plus books of essays, poetry, and fiction champion a vision of community that considers the connections between our natural environment and the whole range of human activity. He proclaims that humankind must learn to live in harmony with nature or perish. In addition to his writing, he continues to farm the land along the Kentucky River that his family has worked for two centuries. This essay is an excerpt from *What Are People For?*

17

The Pleasures of Eating

Many times, after I have finished a lecture on the decline of American farming and rural life, someone in the audience has asked, "What can city people do?"

"Eat responsibly," I have usually answered. Of course, I have tried to explain what I mean by that, but afterward I have invariably felt there was more to be said than I had been able to say. Now I would like to attempt a better explanation.

I begin with the proposition that eating is an agricultural act. Eating ends the annual drama of the food economy that begins with planting and birth. Most eaters, however, are no longer aware that this is true. They think of food as an agricultural product, perhaps, but they do not think of themselves as participants in agriculture. They think of themselves as "consumers." If they think beyond that, they recognize that they are passive consumers. They buy what they want—or what they have been persuaded to want—within the limits of what they can get. They pay, mostly without protest, what they are charged. And they mostly ignore certain critical questions about the quality and the cost of what they are sold: how fresh is it? How pure or clean is it, how free of dangerous chemicals? How far was it transported, and what did transportation add to the cost? How much did manufacturing or packaging or advertising add to the cost? When the food product has been manufactured or "processed" or "precooked," how has that affected its quality or price or nutritional value?

Most urban shoppers would tell you that food is produced on farms. But most of them do not know what farms, or what kinds of farms, or where the farms are, or what knowledge of skills is involved in farming. They apparently have little doubt that farms will continue to produce, but they do not know how or over what obstacles. For them, then, food is pretty much an abstract idea—something they do not know or imagine—until it appears on the grocery shelf or on the table.

The specialization of production induces specialization of consumption. Patrons of the entertainment industry, for example, entertain themselves less and less and have become more and more passively dependent on commercial suppliers. This is certainly true also of patrons of the food industry, who have tended more and more to be mere consumers—passive, uncritical, and dependent. Indeed, this sort of consumption may be said to be one of the chief goals of industrial production. The food industrialists have by now persuaded millions of consumers to prefer food that is already prepared. They will grow, deliver, and cook your food for you and (just like your mother) beg you to eat it. That they do not yet offer to insert it, prechewed, into our mouth is only because they have found no profitable way to do so. We may rest assured that they would be glad to find such a way. The ideal industrial food consumer would be strapped to a table with a tube running from the food factory directly into his or her stomach.

Perhaps I exaggerate, but not by much. The industrial eater is, in fact, one who does not know that eating is an agricultural act, who no longer knows or imagines the connections between eating and the land, and who is therefore necessarily passive and uncritical—in short, a victim. When food, in the minds of eaters, is no longer associated with farming and with the land, then the eaters are suffering a kind of cultural amnesia that is misleading and dangerous. The current version of the "dream home" of the future involves "effortless" shopping from a list of available goods on a television monitor and heating precooked food by remote control. Of course, this implies and depends on a perfect ignorance of the history of the food that is consumed. It requires that the citizenry should give up their hereditary and sensible aversion to buying a pig in a poke. It wishes to make the selling of pigs in pokes an honorable and glamorous activity. The dreamer in this dream home will perforce know nothing about the kind or quality of this food, or where it came from, or how it was produced and prepared, or what ingredients, additives, and residues it contains—unless, that is, the dreamer undertakes a close and constant study of the food industry, in which case he or she might as well wake up and play an active and responsible part in the economy of food.

There is, then, a politics of food that, like any politics, involves our freedom. We still (sometimes) remember that we cannot be free if our minds and voices are controlled by someone else. But we have neglected to understand that we cannot be free if our food and its sources are controlled by someone else. The condition of the passive consumer of food is not a democratic condition. One reason to eat responsibly is to live free.

But if there is a food politics, there are also a food esthetics and a food ethics, neither of which is dissociated from politics. Like industrial sex, industrial eating has become a degraded, poor, and paltry thing. Our kitchens and other eating places more and more resemble filling stations, as our homes more and more resemble motels. "Life is not very interesting," we seem to have decided. "Let its satisfactions be minimal, perfunctory, and fast." We hurry through our meals to go to work and hurry through our work in order to "recreate" ourselves in the evenings and on weekends and vacations. And then we hurry, with the greatest possible speed and noise and violence, through our recreation—for what? To eat the billionth hamburger at some fast-food joint hell-bent on increasing the "quality" of our life? And all this is carried out in a remarkable obliviousness to the causes and effects, the possibilities and the purposes, of the life of the body in this world.

One will find this obliviousness represented in virgin purity in the advertisements of the food industry, in which food wears as much makeup as the actors. If one gained one's whole knowledge of food from these advertisements (as some presumably do), one would not know that the various edibles were ever living creatures, or that they all come from the soil, or that they were produced by work. The passive American consumer, sitting down to a meal of preprepared or fast food, confronts a platter covered with inert, anonymous substances that have been processed, dyed, breaded, sauced, gravied, ground, pulped, strained, blended, prettified, and sanitized beyond resemblance to any part of any creature that ever lived. The products of nature and agriculture have been made, to all appearances, the products of industry. Both eater and eaten are thus in exile from biological reality. And the result is a kind of solitude, unprecedented in human experience, in which the eater may think of eating as, first, a purely commercial transaction between him and a supplier and then as a purely appetitive transaction between him and his food.

And this peculiar specialization of the act of eating is, again, of obvious benefit to the food industry, which has good reasons to obscure the connection between food and farming. It would not do for the consumer to know that the hamburger she is eating came from a steer who spent much of his life standing deep in his own excrement in a feedlot, helping to pollute the local streams, or that the calf that yielded the veal cutlet on her plate spent its life in a box in which it did not have room to turn around. And, though her sympathy for the slaw might be less tender, she should not be encouraged to meditate on the hygienic and biological implications of mile-square fields of cabbage, for vegetables grown in huge monocultures are dependent on toxic chemicals—just as animals in close confinements are dependent on antibiotics and other drugs.

The consumer, that is to say, must be kept from discovering that, in the food industry—as in any other industry—the overriding concerns are not quality and health, but volume and price. For decades now the entire industrial food economy, from the large farms and feedlots to the chains of supermarkets and fast-food restaurants, has been obsessed with volume. It has relentlessly increased scale in order to increase volume in order (probably) to reduce costs. But as scale increases, diversity declines; as diversity declines, so does health; as health declines, the dependence on drugs and chemicals necessarily increases. As capital replaces labor, it does so by substituting machines, drugs, and chemicals for human workers and for the natural health and fertility of the soil. The food is produced by any means or any shortcuts that will increase profits. And the business of the cosmeticians of advertising is to persuade the consumer that food so produced is good, tasty, healthful, and a guarantee of marital fidelity and long life.

It is possible, then, to be liberated from the husbandry and wifery of the old household food economy. But one can be thus liberated only by entering a trap (unless one sees ignorance and helplessness as the signs of privilege, as many people apparently do). The trap is the ideal of industrialism: a walled city surrounded by valves that let merchandise in but no consciousness out. How does one escape this trap? Only voluntarily, the same way that one went in: by restoring one's consciousness of what is involved in eating; by reclaiming responsibility for one's own part in the food economy. One might begin with the illuminating principle of Sir Albert Howard's *The Soil and Health*, that we should understand "the whole problem of health in soil, plant, animal, and man as one great subject." Eaters, that is, must understand that eating takes place inescapably in the world, that it is inescapably an agricultural act, and how we eat determines, to a considerable extent, how the world is used. This is a simple way of describing a relationship that is inexpressibly complex. To eat responsibly is to understand and enact, so far as we can, this complex relationship. What can one do? Here is a list, probably not definitive:

1. Participate in food production to the extent that you can. If you have a yard or even just a porch box or a pot in a sunny window, grow something to eat in it. Make a little compost of your kitchen scraps and use it for fertilizer. Only by growing some food for yourself can you become acquainted with the beautiful energy cycle that revolves from soil to seed to flower to fruit to food to offal to decay, and around again. You will be fully responsible for any food that you grow for yourself, and you will know all about it. You will appreciate it fully, having known it all its life.

2. Prepare your own food. This means reviving in your own mind and life the arts of kitchen and household. This should enable you to eat more cheaply, and it will give you a measure of "quality control": you will have some reliable knowledge of what has been added to the food you eat.

3. Learn the origins of the food you buy, and buy the food that is produced closest to your home. The idea that every locality should be, as much as possible, the source of its own food makes several kinds of sense. The locally produced food supply is the most secure, freshest, and the easiest for local consumers to know about and to influence.

4.   Whenever possible, deal directly with a local farmer, gardener, or orchardist. All the reasons listed for the previous suggestion apply here. In addition, by such dealing you eliminate the whole pack of merchants, transporters, processors, packagers, and advertisers who thrive at the expense of both producers and consumers.

5.   Learn, in self-defense, as much as you can of the economy and technology of industrial food production. What is added to the food that is not food, and what do you pay for those additions?

6.   Learn what is involved in the best farming and gardening.

7.   Learn as much as you can, by direct observation and experience if possible, of the life histories of the food species.

The last suggestion seems particularly important to me. Many people are now as much estranged from the lives of domestic plants and animals (except for flowers and dogs and cats) as they are from the lives of the wild ones. This is regrettable, for these domestic creatures are in diverse ways attractive; there is such pleasure in knowing them. And farming, animal husbandry, horticulture, and gardening, at their best, are complex and comely arts; there is much pleasure in knowing them, too.

It follows that there is great displeasure in knowing about a food economy that degrades and abuses those arts and those plants and animals and the soil from which they come. For anyone who does know something of the modern history of food, eating away from home can be a chore. My own inclination is to eat seafood instead of red meat or poultry when I am traveling. Though I am by no means a vegetarian, I dislike the thought that some animal has been made miserable in order to feed me. If I am going to eat meat, I want it to be from an animal that has lived a pleasant, uncrowded life outdoors, on bountiful pasture, with good water nearby and trees for shade. And I am getting almost as fussy about food plants. I like to eat vegetables and fruits that I know have lived happily and healthily in good soil, not the products of the huge, bechemicaled factory-fields that I have seen, for example, in the Central Valley of California. The industrial farm is said to have been patterned on the factory production line. In practice, it looks more like a concentration camp.

The pleasure of eating should be an extensive pleasure, not that of the mere gourmet. People who know the garden in which their vegetables have grown and know that the garden is healthy and remember the beauty of the growing plants, perhaps in the dewy first light of morning when gardens are at their best. Such a memory involves itself with the food and is one of the pleasures of eating. The knowledge of the good health of the garden relieves and frees and comforts the eater. The same goes for eating meat. The thought of the good pasture and of the calf contentedly grazing flavors the steak. Some, I know, will think of it as bloodthirsty or worse to eat a fellow creature you have known all its life. On the contrary, I think it means that you eat with understanding and with gratitude. A significant part of the pleasure of eating is in one's accurate consciousness of the lives and the world from which food comes. The pleasure of eating, then, may be the best available standard of our health. And this pleasure, I think, is pretty fully available to the urban consumer who will make the necessary effort.

I mentioned earlier the politics, esthetics, and ethics of food. But to speak of the pleasure of eating is to go beyond those categories. Eating with the fullest pleasure—pleasure, that is, that does not depend on ignorance—is perhaps the profoundest enactment of our connection with the world. In this pleasure we experience and celebrate our dependence and our gratitude, for we are living from mystery, from creatures we did not make and powers we cannot comprehend. When I think of the meaning of food, I always remember these lines by the poet William Carlos Williams, which seem to me merely honest:

> There is nothing to eat,
>   seek it where you will,
>   but the body of the Lord.
> The blessed plants
>   and the sea, yield it
>   to the imagination
> intact.

Tanya Berry's Green Beans

INGREDIENTS

Olive oil

Several cloves diced garlic

2 (15-ounce) cans Roma (flat Italian) beans with liquid, or 1 quart fresh beans with enough water to cover the beans, cut into 1-inch pieces

Salt

Pepper

Hot sauce

Serves 6 to 8

RECIPE

Coat a heavy-bottomed pan with olive oil and turn the heat to medium-high.

Add diced garlic and sauté until just soft.

Cut the beans into 1-inch pieces and add to the pan.

Add salt and pepper.

Bring the pan to boil, and then turn the heat to low and simmer until the liquid is nearly gone and the beans are tender. This may take up to an hour.

Add a few drops of hot sauce.

Check for seasoning and serve.

KELTON COBB joined the faculty of Hartford Seminary in Connecticut in 1995, and teaches courses in theology and ethics. He has a keen interest in the overlap between these two disciplines, understanding that a theology gives rise to moral actions, and that moral actions assume a theology. His current interest is in examining how it is that Western Christianity has learned to be moral. He is the author of *The Blackwell Guide to Theology and Popular Culture*. He and his wife, Heidi, have two sons, Henry and William—named after their grandfathers, not the princes of England.

18

Table Blessings

Everything God has created is good, and no food is to be rejected, provided grace is said for it: the word of God and the prayer make it holy.

—1 Timothy 4:4–5

In the past three years I have made a number of road trips between Denver and New Jersey, traversing terrain that has a reassuring persistence. From Kansas City to Reading, Pennsylvania, the land is planted in corn—1,500 miles and hundred of thousands of acres of corn, interrupted only occasionally by a city like St. Louis or Indianapolis with their suburbs and industrial belts.

I asked a friend from Illinois what was done with all that corn. "It takes a lot of it to keep the world in cornflakes," he said. He had made a good point. We in North America are big cornflake eaters—not to mention our appetite for other forms of processed corn, such as Fritos, Doritos, Captain Crunch, and numerous other variations on nature's bounty. All of those acres of corn are annually converted into a thousand different products intended to stimulate our jaded taste buds. All that corn is picked, husked, and processed in ingenious ways and made ready to eat from the box.

It has to be that way. We do not have time for slow food; our schedules cannot accommodate it. One of the advantages of the twentieth century is our liberation from the slow drudgery of plowing, sowing, harvesting, milling, and cooking from scratch. Factory food frees us from all that bother. It is easy to buy, easy to unpackage, easy to warm up, easy to look at, and easy to eat. It fuels our pursuits without wasting our time.

All of which raises an interesting question. Since North Americans place such a high premium on gastronomic convenience, why do some people still insist on praying over the food they are about to consume? Even people who seldom if ever go to church often pause for a blessing before supper. Perhaps the custom reflects the remnants of a religious upbringing—the vestiges of some vague consciousness of God that food can provoke in us. Maybe a bowl of cornflakes represents to us a certain providence in the universe, and in its presence, a reverent pause is almost a reflex action; food, ready to be eaten, triggers in us something like an unavoidable, ontological religiousness. Then again, perhaps there are more functional explanations; such as that saying a prayer is an indirect way of complimenting the cook or calming the kids.

For whatever reason a table blessing is remembered, however, it provides a thoughtful gap in our tight schedules where God can conceivably intrude. We refer to it as table "grace," after all. And saying grace strikes me as one of those irrational instances in which ritual triumphs over convenience, in which our consumption of fast food throttles down long enough for God to be acknowledged.

Martin Buber tells the story of an old Hasidic master who asked a rabbi what puzzled him most about his neighbor. "I heard him say," said the Hasid, "that he was surprised that merely saying grace is not enough to make men God-fearing and good."

"I think differently," the Hasid reflected. "I am surprised that merely *eating* is not enough to make men God-fearing and good. For it is written: 'The ox knows its owner, and the donkey, its master's trough.'"

The kitchen table, heaped with food, is our trough. Most of us, if we pray at all, become God-fearing enough at that trough just long enough to manage a cursory, "Thank you, God, for this day and for this food.

Amen." Then we pile the foodstuff onto our plates, gobble it down, excuse ourselves, and resume our schedules refueled. Fast prayers for fast food. We don't linger long enough truly to acknowledge God's generosity in our bounty.

During the summer months my grandmother always saw to it that some produce from my grandfather's garden graced the table. His carefully cultivated tomatoes, bell peppers, chayote squash, string beans, or peaches were his contribution to the ceremony of mealtime. When we sat down to eat, I was prepared to be refreshed, not merely refueled. All of my senses were assaulted—with color, aroma, flavor, texture, and sound. I recall my grandfather's prayer, a formula that always began: "Our most gracious and loving Father, we praise and thank thee for the gift of thy son Jesus and for life eternal through him. We thank thee for guidance and for strength and for blessing us with this food . . ." Table grace for my grandfather was a confession of faith, of ultimate loyalties. Food reminded him of his dependence on God. Food reinvigorated his faith and prompted him to confess it. Before he ate, he acknowledged his life as a gift from God.

In his letter to Timothy, Paul suggested that prayer makes food holy. The saying of grace sacralizes the food. That is what "blessing" is, after all. To bless food is to make it sacred.

The *Treatise* records the regular practice of the Jews and early Christians as they prepared to share a meal. First, the family and guests gathered around the table. A clay pitcher full of water was carried in from the back room. The father, or host, waited for silence, then declared, "Blessed art thou who has given us command concerning the washing of the hands"—whereupon each person in the group stretched out his or her hands to receive water poured from the pitcher. After drying their hands, they sat down. The prayer was resumed with a confession of their loyalty to God and to God's kingdom. Included in the prayer was a reminder that the seasonal rains necessary for the growth of corn, grapes, and olives were contingent on human service and love for God—no devotion, no rain. The earth yields fruit at God's command, the prayer affirmed, and fertile land is a gift. That is essentially the content of the prayer that preceded the actual blessing of the food.

Next, the food was brought in and set down on the table. The host studied each dish because there was a special blessing to be applied to each category of food. He commenced the blessing: "Blessed art thou, O

Lord our God, King of the universe. . ."; then, with his mind's eye first on the loaf of bread baked from barley flour, he said, ". . . who brought forth bread from the earth . . ."; then for the pot of lentils he prayed, "who created different kinds of seeds . . . ," and for the plate of onions and radishes, "who created different kinds of herbs. . . ." For the locusts fried in a batter of honey and flour, he continued, "by whose word all things exist . . ."; for the bowl of figs, "who created the fruit of the tree . . ."; for the wine, "who created the fruit of the vine . . . ." And for the baked fish, he exclaimed, "Blessed be the One who created this baked fish; how beautiful it is!" Each item of food and drink appropriately blessed, according to the formula recalling the unique means through which God provided that item, the host concluded, "For all came into existence by God's word. Amen." The host then raised his head, broke a loaf of bread, and distributed portions of food to each person at the table. Finally, everyone ate.

After the meal, spices were sprinkled on hot coals to produce a fragrant incense. The host proceeded with a benediction which was either spoken or sung as a hymn. The content of the benediction was essentially a thanksgiving for the food, for the gift of good land, and for the temple. It was often concluded with the host testifying, "I have never seen the righteous forsaken. Amen."

What is striking about these Jewish table blessings is the reverent care given to such a common activity. Hands were washed not only for sanitary reasons, but in order to make them ritually pure for handling food, which was understood to be a gift from God. As a gift, food was holy, and to avoid desecrating it, the people washed. Eating was a sacred ritual. So that the vastness of God's gift of good land and the food harvested from it could be more fully appreciated, the one saying the blessing paused over each dish. The individual blessings recognized the magnitude of the gift by elaborating its variety: the fruit of the vine, the fruit of the tree, the different kinds of seeds, the herbs—each focused on the origin of the table's bounty in a way that praised God for the earth's glorious fertility. And its words of appreciation outstripped any cursory "Thank you, God, for this food."

Buber has recorded one Hasid's story of Abraham's reply to a guest who had eaten at Sarah and Abraham's table. When the guest had finished and wiped his chin, he rose to thank Abraham. Abraham asked the man, "Was the food that you have eaten mine? You have partaken of the bounty of the God of the universe. Now praise, glorify, and bless the One who spoke and the world was."

The Hasid went on to comment, "Whoever enjoys any worldly pleasure without benediction commits a theft against God."

It is not easy to picture food as holy. And the way we treat all those cornfields is anything but holy; the unnatural forms we force the corn to take are an insult to the good land on which it is grown. The fast factory food liberates us to live in the jet age, but it does not teach us that food is holy. Fast food teaches us that food is fuel; consequently, we are much better at cursing food than at blessing it.

Buber recounts the tale of an old rabbi, Abraham Yehoshua Heshel, who was considering the prospect of his death. Pushing back from the table after the noon meal, he recited the benediction, then stood up and began to pace slowly. Alone in the room, he pondered with knitted brow what God's verdict would be on his accomplishments. Suddenly his face glowed. Abraham stopped by the table covered with crumbs, reached out, and gently stroked it with his hand. "Table, good table," he said, "You will testify on my behalf that I have properly eaten and properly prayed at your board."

That evening, Abraham Yehoshua Heshel instructed his son that when the time came he desired to be buried in a coffin built from the boards of his dismantled table.

The food we eat, and the way we handle it, may tell God a good deal. The table blessing is not simply a nice custom. It is a sacramental litany. Food and nourishment are made holy when received with a blessing.

GINA OCHSNER is the writer-in-residence at Corban University and also teaches with the Seattle Pacific Low-Residency MFA program. Gina has been awarded a John L. Simon Guggenheim grant and a grant from the National Endowment of Arts. Her stories have appeared in *Image*, *The New Yorker*, *Tin House*, *Glimmertrain*, and the *Kenyon Review*. She is the author of the short story collections *The Necessary Grace to Fall*, which received the Flannery O'Connor Award for Short Fiction, and *People I Wanted to Be*. Her latest work, *The Russian Dreambook of Colour and Flight*, was longlisted for the Orange Prize.

19

Filled to Brokenness: Notes on Hunger

The other day I stood in the kitchen chopping onions. To keep the onion juice from burning an open cut in my hand, I wore signal orange gloves, and to keep from crying, I wore my daughter's bright purple swim goggles that forced tight angles on everything in my periphery. As the kids drifted inside from a long round of airsofting wars, they each looked at me and giggled. The sight of the goggles and gloves, standard issue superpower accessories, then spurred a debate: if each of us could choose a super power, which would we choose? The oldest, a boy, wanted to shoot arrows with his eyes. Our daughter wanted to have the power of pretty, which would enable her to stop foes dead in their tracks with a flirtatious wink of her eye and cant of her hip. The youngest son wanted to fly—where to, he didn't much care.

"What about you, Mom?"

From behind the goggles, I blinked in surprise. "I want to be invisible," I said. Their collective disappointment was palpable.

"Invisible?" The oldest asked. "That's so middle-aged."

I shrugged and kept chopping. How do I explain the unextraordinary desire to disappear to kids whose entire beings shout, "Look at me!" And I do—I look at them with wonder and nostalgia, remembering when I could scale steep tree trunks and hang from the limbs, when like them I played hide-and-seek until darkness swelled up as a mist from the ground and neighborhood mothers one by one leaned out front doors and called us, name by name, to our homes.

It would be hard to articulate what changed between the girl I was and the girl I am. Because even then I wanted to vanish into thin air. And I believed, then, that such a thing could be possible. But it would be hard to explain to these kids now, pawing through the cupboards for Handi-Snacks and applesauce packs, how this desire to disappear was inextricably linked to what they are doing right now: eating food.

For so many of the women in my family, the kitchen was a place of thankless repetition, a place where capable women made functional, serviceable food. For my mother, as a young girl living in Prospect, Oregon, the meal needed to have plenty of starches to soak up the whisky her father, Papa, would likely have consumed on his way home from the power plant. Most importantly, the meal needed to be on the table when he rattled the back door, otherwise he'd go to the woodpile and drink. And so, as a young girl, my mother learned that meal preparation was a preventative act, part of a vast system of damage control, not a nutritive act. Too often she'd witnessed Papa come home to an empty table and the fights that then flared up between her parents. My mother recalls falling into a troubled sleep at night, unsure if the silence between her parents' words signified reconciliation or a regrouping for more verbal warfare.

When my mother tells these stories, I resist the urge to condemn, to label—*alcoholic, co-dependent*—to set the dynamics of her family as a rigid template for the one I grew up in. And yet it's hard to dismiss the patterns between what she recalls of her childhood meal times and what I recall of my childhood meal times. It's hard not to wonder if I'm doomed to repeat these same patterns. Because the fact of the matter is this: when I stand in our kitchen, I am at war. There are two of me standing here: the young girl who wants only to evaporate into a mist and the much older girl whose gravity-bound sense of duty won't let her. There are two girls standing here chopping onions: the one who has always felt that food was meant for fun and outdoor picnics, church potlucks, and Thanksgivings where relatives arrived laden with casserole dishes in their arms and outrageous stories at their lips. And then there's the girl who has learned to fear food. She does not trust herself to make good and wise decisions in its presence. The older girl recognizes that she's old enough now to know better and that it is time to rewrite the little girl's family story. The older girl senses that it starts in the smallest of ways, oddly enough, with words and with food.

When I turned thirteen, I joined an all-girls church club called the Missionettes, a group whose chief function seemed to be memorizing Bible verses. I gravitated toward those verses that involved food, and I discovered that God seemed to favor his servants who ate little, who fasted. Going hungry seemed to galvanize their prayers. The idea that the voluntary denial of a basic necessity might be a testament to one's devotion or an indicator of one's holiness haunted me. Conversely, I discovered that eating and drinking to excess was a special kind of sin called gluttony, which I pictured as a large-assed woman stuffing herself with See's chocolates. Nearby the companion sin, sloth, a pudgy, three-toed, incontinent house pet, lolled about. Together they watched mindless game shows. Together, gluttony and sloth held soft hands and violated the Puritan work ethic which held that one mustn't ever quit working, achieving, aspiring.

Sometime after I turned fourteen, a girlfriend who lived down the street told me about nuns who lived for seven years on nothing but the Eucharist, that tiniest morselette of Christ's blood and body. This tidbit of information bolstered my burgeoning notion that holiness and devotion were best achieved by acts of denial, acts that could be measured by the flattened stomach which came from going hungry. It did not escape my notice that these nuns were greatly admired by all who knew them. They were eating God and it was enough for them, and they did all this in complete seclusion. It all sounded too perfect and utterly impossible.

"It's like a modern miracle," my friend explained. And because I believed in miracles, because I wanted seclusion that carried God's tacit approval, I decided to severely limit the food I ate. I would deny myself the pleasure of eating anything I truly loved: Fig Newtons, black licorice, Ho Hos and Twinkies. Inch by inch, I would disappear as I embarked on holy, good work. It was an idea that seemed to parallel the all-cabbage, all-carrot, no-eating-anything-fun diets of my mother's friends.

And no diet, I learned by watching an instructional video, can be effective without incorporating a regimen of exercise. I had seen my next-door neighbor run around the gravel track at our schoolyard, the peevish looks of irritation on his face when he paused for a short rest. "Why do you run so much?" I asked him one hot afternoon in September. I was crossing the field to go home and he had just stopped to check his pulse. His scowl lifted to a look of astonishment.

"To stay in shape," he said. "I wouldn't want to get fat, would I?"

The next week I took up running. After a few blocks, my lungs burned, my legs felt heavy, I had a stitch in my side. Still I kept on, the shoe manufacturer's company logo thrumming through the waffle-soled shoes and into my shins: *no pain, no gain*. I remembered that this is what we do if we don't want to get fat. I reminded myself that I was doing good, divinely approved work. Not only that, but two miles past the dark soil of the onion flats, nobody could see me. Under the tight canopies of filbert orchards I was disappearing from a world of rules and expectations, of longings that could in never be fulfilled, a world I did not know how to or wish to navigate.

Past a low shoal of grain elevators and long fields of grazing cows, I followed a string of telephone poles. An electric buzz hummed through the sagging cables and I imagined that this is what happened to the household anger and frustration announced in the clattering of pots and pans, the shrill cries and hoarse barks of unhappy parents and despairing children; it all collapses into this unintelligible music. And if I ran long enough, I found that these sounds were steady and rhythmic, like my feet on the pavement, each slap and buzz and whoosh pushing away the sounds of my family's unhappiness and my own peculiar despair which had quietly taken up residence inside of me.

Over the next few months my body visibly changed. Certain slants of light cast my shadow several paces behind me, and I thought I was, at last, leaving my clumsy body behind. I was subduing my vexing, stubborn flesh that continually held me back. I was becoming pure and raw and hollow as hunger itself. I could run without effort over country roads and through orchards. And so that autumn, I signed up for cross-country. As I continued to lose weight, my clothes sagged on my body. The lightness I had felt in my feet evaporated. I'd swallow air, gulp it down, thinking I could fill my stomach with clouds and fly away. But when my body quit moving, I could hear it talking to me, begging me to let it rest. Begging me to feed it. My joints ached and my hair broke when I combed it with my fingers.

"This not-eating stuff—knock it off," Dad would growl after the grace, the muscles in his jaw pumping.

"Just eat. It's good for you," said Mom gently.

And it was good for me—nutritious, well balanced, a careful representation of the four food groups, the meals she prepared contained what her own mother's had lacked. How my finicky ways and general ill-ease at the table must have baffled and offended her post-Depression sense of thrift that said eat whatever is ripe, whatever wanders into the crosshairs or onto the line. Catch it, gut it, give thanks for it, because it gave its life so that we could further ours.

And so I ate. Chewing furiously and drinking glass after glass of water. But all that water wouldn't put out the fire in my stomach; nothing could douse the fear and rage and righteous indignation. I felt betrayed somehow. Fat on our bodies, I thought we had all agreed, was bad. It was the physical manifestation of laziness; it announced a soul beset by the troubling spiritual conditions of sloth and gluttony. So why did they chastise me for not eating? And why, I silently fumed, were my parents now micromanaging when I ate and how much?

For every action there is an equal and opposite reaction, I learned in science class. This law I revised to suit my own thinking: certain actions necessitate certain other actions. If I were forced to eat, then I would rid myself of the food, by fair means or foul. It didn't take too many reverse Heimlich drops on the backs of upright chairs, acrobatic maneuvers that produced stars and little else, to induce something like an epiphany. I remembered seeing an after-school special that had featured a troubled but fabulously successful anorexic withering to a bony tragedy. How I envied her self-control, that so-elusive fruit of the spirit, her discipline, but most especially her creative food-removal techniques. I studied the movie as if it were a how-to seminar. The human throat really does have a release lodged at the back, the ultimate tool for damage control, as it were. All it took to trigger this gag reflex were a few aggressive pokes with the index finger.

Oh, bliss compounded! I understood at once how I could maintain the illusion of two separate girls, two separate lives: the dutiful daughter who ate when told and the paper-thin anorexic whose moral superiority wouldn't allow her to eat. I saw how I could not only eat what I was forced to, but I could even eat what had previously been forbidden.

And so I lived a double life. I'd starve by day, and at night, I'd wake and move zombie-like to the kitchen. In the dark I'd claw and tear open boxes of saltines and graham crackers. I'd bolt down cartons of ice cream. I'd eat without tasting, swallow without chewing. Then, giddy with sugar and dizzy with self-loathing, I'd grope my way toward the bathroom. Curled around the commode, I'd throw everything back up. Quietly, quietly. Then back to bed I went, where uneasy dreams ferried on an ocean of acid awaited me.

In the morning I'd wake, my stomach bloated and roiling with a sensation I knew only to call guilt and shame. Even in the smallest of acts: eating and not eating, I was a failure. I could taste this failure, bile, burning at the back of my throat. As I hurried through the morning routine—gathering books, hunting for shoes, skipping breakfast—the resolve to work off the previous night's failure firmed like concrete.

For several months I lived like this: going to bed at night, hungry, knowing dimly that the chances were good that like a fool to her folly, a dog to its vomit, I would repeat my mistake. Unsurprisingly, by spring I hit a plateau in my Personal Plan for Transformation. The weight stopped dropping. Nothing I did could move the scale's needle. Terror gripped me. If I couldn't keep losing weight, then the unthinkable would happen: I would start gaining it. With visions of our neighbor plowing doggedly around the little track, I understood that weight gain had to be avoided at all costs. Everybody frowns at a fat girl, and everybody, I was sure, included God.

Those were the months I could not concentrate, could not read a paragraph in a textbook without thoughts of calorie counts galloping across my internal radar. I had completely lost my capacity for joy, for astonishment, for awe. If the birds sang, I didn't hear them. A comet could drop on the neighbor's roof, a cow could jump the moon, and I wouldn't have noticed. All I cared about was keeping detailed lists of food eaten and calories consumed, and running laps. I wasn't satisfied with the hollow girl I saw in the mirror. And I sensed that I never would be.

One day, after a weary week of semester finals, a track meet in which I almost didn't finish a race, and many long nights of purging, I found myself in the therapist's office. I hated my body, I hated who I was, what I was doing. At seventeen, I was tired of living.

"OK," I said to Randy that afternoon as I handed over my weekly food lists. "Maybe you're right—I'm sick. My way of doing things isn't working out."

"What are you going to do?" Randy asked, his legal pad balanced on his knee.

"I'm giving up," I said.

Randy beamed. His eyes welled up a little.

"What?" I asked.

"You have no idea how long I've been waiting for you to say that."

That was just the start. Over many more years of counseling, I slowly forged a truce with food. I realized I had to stop thinking that I could simply quit food the way some people quit smoking. My body really did need to eat. Food is fuel, Randy had coached me to say. I couldn't eat less during the day, but I could learn to eat smarter. And I tried. Each morning I stood in front of the mirror and I forced myself to maintain a level gaze at my reflection and mumble: "Food is my friend. It is like medicine. I will treat it wisely; I will not abuse it." I forced myself to sit in cafeterias and break rooms and eat among other people—something I had rarely done. I covertly observed eating patterns, what "normal" serving sizes looked like and what a balanced meal might contain. After eating these meals in public, I kept my hands in my pockets, resisting the urge to run to the bathroom.

But old habits die hard. I still binged late at night. Worse and most distressing: what I ate didn't satisfy me. I could empty an entire cupboard and still want more, convinced that hunger knocked at my ribs. How was it that when I devoured the most, I felt so hungry? I wanted to be filled with a lasting substance so that I would never hunger again. Emptiness and fullness were two sensations I could never accurately gauge; they seemed beyond my control, even beyond my ability to understand. Night after night I'd wake in darkness, convinced that I was hungry, and without asking why, I'd head for the refrigerator, that humming lighted carnival of illicit calories.

My hands dutifully fumbled their way toward the only action they knew to perform as a trained response to the ritual call. My mind and body had become a closed and silent loop of hands, mouth, feet; hunger, failure, shame. But life, my life, any life, had to be more than the sum of basic functions, more than this meaningless cycle. If life wasn't meant for something more, then what was this hunger for more really about?

At a neighborhood Bible study I attend, we are reading Romans, one of Paul's letters that I have avoided for a long time. I'd always figured Paul's writings—Paul—would be far too righteous to be relevant. What I've found instead is a man wracked by the contradictions of living in an imperfect corporeal body while longing for the more perfect spiritual body. He was a walking fulfillment of several paradoxes. A Jew who at one time took pleasure in persecuting Christians, Paul became a Christ follower. Though a lawyer by calling and training, he often supported himself by making tents. A skilled and impassioned orator, his words more than once provoked audiences to the point that he found himself imprisoned. In fact, we know that while he was chained at the ankle to a guard, Paul wrote of having much and having little and knowing how to be content in both states, a paradoxical condition requiring a faith beyond sight, a faith beyond sensory evidence: here's what I can see in my hand, what I feel in my belly, what I can count in my savings fund. And yet Paul does not discount the needs, desires, or failings of the body. In one of his last letters (2 Timothy), which he writes from prison, Paul is near death, and he most likely knows it. It is a touching letter—loving, wise, and heartfelt. Paul concludes by asking for his cloak, a request that marks him as a man who understands and lives within the ordinary un-sublimated body.

But Paul recognizes, too, that we are made of spirit stuff and our spirits have yearnings and needs, just as our bodies do. One such yearn-ing is for perfection. It is a pull architected into us. Because we are made of body and spirit, a painful negotiation between the two ensues, each element—body and soul—making its own demands. Our bodies may desire perfection, completion, and satisfaction, but built as they are of imperfect, impermanent material, our bodies' longing will never be fully fulfilled. Fortunately, we are more than our bodies, Paul reminds us. And our spirit's desire for better, for perfection, can and will find completion—someday. The spirit's desire for that fulfillment is in and of itself, a godly hunger. But Paul laments the fact that too often God's children try to sate the spirit's pangs by attending to the body, a medium simply not robust enough for the task.

When I read Paul's pain-filled letters I sympathize, I synthesize.

I think of all the time spent running on a treadmill, convinced that I was redeeming myself in a physical, tangible way, as I worked off the previous day's failure. I consider my implacable fear that if I continue to fail, if I keep gaining weight, if I cannot subdue my unruly body, I will be utterly unloveable, especially to God, who is perfect. With Paul I anguish, knowing whatever I do, I am pegged to this body, enslaved. But I also know that the day is coming when the tent will become a kite and I will be free of my clumsy cargo.

I'm learning that in Uzbek culture Issyk-non, a sweet flat bread, is considered so sacred that to step on or trample the bread underfoot is a punishable crime. Likewise, in certain parts of Latvia, if a piece of bread falls to floor, it is customary to brush it off and kiss it, so as not to offend the bread. My host explained, "Bread is our life." Given the amount of effort and time required to make bread from the moment rye is gathered, threshed, and processed into flour, this affection for bread seems quite justified. And it's easy to imagine how bread, in the mind, in the imagination, in song and myth, swells to symbolic proportion.

I have felt it happen for myself. In my stomach, bread absorbs whatever is there, expanding to fill whatever space it is afforded. It's why bread is offered at the beginning of a meal, I've been told. It is why, I suspect, when Jesus wanted to feed thousands, he multiplied loaves of bread. It is why Jesus called himself the bread of life. He wanted to be consumed; he wanted to fill the hungry. More importantly, he wanted to show us that in order for him to fill a life, he first had to be broken. Before I can be filled, I too, must be broken. *OK, God,* I pray in the morning. *Go ahead and do it. Break me. Grind me into a paste.* Big words for a bold spirit, but then my body asserts itself, maintains its old and stubborn arguments. It still wants to thresh out old territory on its own bodily terms, hoping to arrive at different destinations and outcomes.

Creature of habit that I am! How I wish I could write that I'm cured, utterly healed of my bodily imperfections, these habits. How I wish I could say boldly that body and spirit have found perfect balance and that I hunger in proper measure and proportion for the right things at the right times. But it wouldn't be true. This road to recovery more closely resembles a switchback mountain pass than a steady trajectory labeled "progress." I am still parsing out the difference between being invisible and being transparent, allowing others to see me as I really am. I am better and I am worse. A clumsy story, I am continually in revision. But I take comfort in a verse like Isaiah 55:2, which seems tailor-made for someone like me: "Hearken diligently unto me and eat ye that which is good, and let your soul delight in fatness."

I will feed you, my heavenly father says. Come, sit, and eat. And so I will, bringing my hungers with me.

Piragi (Latvian Ham Rolls) for Celebrations and Holidays

INGREDIENTS

3 packages dry yeast
1/2 cup warm water
2 cups milk
20 tablespoons unsalted butter (2 ½ sticks)
1 teaspoon salt ("one tip of a knife")
10 tablespoons plus 1/2 teaspoon of sugar
1/4 teaspoon cardamom
8 cups flour (sifted wheat flour recommended)
6 eggs, beaten
2 white onions, finely diced
1 pound ham, finely diced
1 pound bacon, finely diced
Black pepper to taste ("one tip of a knife")

Makes about 80 servings, but sizes vary. My Latvian friends tell me that 3 or 4 suffice per person, but on holidays, who's counting!

RECIPE

Dough

Dissolve the yeast in water.

Heat the milk in a saucepan until it is almost boiling.

Add butter to the milk.

Combine salt, sugar, and cardamom in a large bowl; add the heated milk and butter to the bowl.

Add 1/2 cup of flour, and then mix well.

Stir in the yeast, and then stir in 5 eggs.

Next, gradually mix in the remainder of the flour. Beat well, until smooth, cover, and put in warm a place to rise until it doubles. This may take an hour or more.

If it is a cold day outside, I put the dough in the oven and turn it on very low.

Filling

While waiting for the dough to double, finely chop the onions, and dice the ham and bacon.

Sauté the bacon until most of the fat is rendered.

Add the finely chopped onions and sauté limp.

Stir in ham and pepper. Allow to cool.

Egg wash

Beat 1 egg with 1/2 teaspoon of sugar.

To fill the piragi

Divide the dough into heaping tablespoon-size pieces and flatten the pieces into four-inch rounds. Fill the rounds with a heaping teaspoon of the filling mixture.

Fold over into half-moon shapes. Place seam-side down on baking sheets covered with parchment paper.

Brush each filled dough piece with egg wash. Bake in an oven at 400° F (literally in a "powerfully" hot oven) for 10 minutes (375° F if using a convection oven), until lightly brown on top.

AMY FRYKHOLM is a writer with a passion for soup kitchens, local food, exotic recipes, and almost anything served in a bowl with a spoon. She is also the author of *Julian of Norwich: A Contemplative Biography* and *Rapture Culture: Left Behind in Evangelical America*. She writes for the *Christian Century* and lives at 10,200 feet in the mountains of Colorado.

20

Fasting Toward Home

On a December night in Krasnodar, a small city in southern Russia, I stood in the warmth of Olga Nikolaevna's narrow kitchen. Potatoes, carrots, and beets boiled in a large pot, steaming the windows. As she pulled them from the pot to cool, she handed me a knife and cutting board and began to tell me about her days as a Hare Krishna and her long spiritual restlessness. While she talked, she showed me how to peel the vegetables and cut them into perfect tiny squares. After my first attempt, she shook her head and took the knife. "Like this, Amochka, smaller." She demonstrated deftly, then turned the knife back over to me. But the sticky starch of the potatoes clung to my fingers, and my squares were more like tetrahedrons.

"Why don't you peel and I'll chop?" she offered. When all of the vegetables were in the bowl, Olga added pickles, fresh dill, sunflower oil, salt and pepper. The she mixed the salad until the vegetables were stained pink from the beets and glistened with oil.

Olga was a professor of history at Kuban State University where I was an exchange student. She had been assigned to give lectures in Russian culture to the Americans. As part of our instruction, she had invited us to the central cathedral and introduced us to her mentor, Father

Alexander. Olga, who had been raised in a secular household in a secular Soviet Union, was a recent convert to Orthodoxy. Trying to answer a spiritual hunger, she had spent time not only as a Hare Krishna, but also as a Buddhist and a Hindu. As the Soviet Union collapsed and her marriage teetered on the brink, she found herself drawn to Orthodoxy, a religion that seemed to grow—like her beets—directly from her own soil. Father Alexander, himself a recent convert and a university professor, understood as well as anyone what it meant to come home to a new faith.

The meal that Olga was preparing that evening was a "fasting meal." She had just begun observing the period that the Orthodox call "Little Lent," what I had always called "Advent." In Little Lent, the Orthodox abstain from meat and dairy products for four weeks before the feast of Christmas. She prepared all of her usual foods in their simplest forms: borscht with vegetable broth instead of pork, salads with oil instead of mayonnaise and sausage. She practiced this as a quiet reminder that she was preparing body and soul for Christmas.

The body and soul formulation was not something that I had ever taken seriously. As a lifelong, devout Protestant, I had thought a great deal about my soul. As an American, I had obsessed a great deal about my body. But I had rarely considered body and soul in mutual relation. Everywhere I went in Russia as an exchange student—and I was drawn instinctively to churches—I witnessed a fuller understanding of the body and soul in communion. "Sometimes if I cannot pray," Olga had said at the entrance to the cathedral, "I come to the church and light a candle."

At that time, I would have called Olga's gesture an empty ritual. I might have considered an inability to pray a personal failing, and I wouldn't have thought it could be remedied or substituted by lighting a candle. But Olga allowed this bodily action to stand in the place where her mind and heart might lag, and I found the possibility moving.

In the Orthodox churches I visited, I observed a sensuality of worship: smells, sights, sounds, beautiful colors and sensations, as if the whole self were being invited into delight. I had always thought that the truest worship happened deep inside the self, a place best reached, perhaps, by shutting down the senses. This other, fully participatory worship was strange to me, and my body did not know how to respond.

In the same way, I had never thought of Advent as a fast. To me Advent was a time to make Christmas cookies, sing carols, and go to holiday parties. In truth, by the time Christmas arrived, I'd had enough of it. As for fasting, I admired the willingness of others to experience self-deprivation and thought of it as something athletic, a tremendous act of the will. In *Celebration of Discipline,* Richard Foster talks about how to manage thirty-six hours without food and how to tell if the body is going into starvation mode. I saw fasting as a way of going inside the self, shutting it down—its wants and needs set aside in the name of a greater good.

One summer, more than a decade later, I received an assignment to interview Orthodox Christians who had converted from Protestantism. On an August morning, I went to visit an Orthodox monk named Father Christodolous at a makeshift monastery in Denver. I arrived for early morning Mass and slipped into the back of the small chapel located off the kitchen. By the time I arrived, Mass had been in progress for a while. There were only a few people present, a middle-aged couple, a few young men, and myself. Father Christodolous led the prayers, a woman chanted the lessons, and then the *antidoron* was distributed. (The antidoron is bread that is offered to non-communicants, like me.)

After the Mass, though a stranger to the monastery, I helped put on coffee and prepare snacks. At the instruction of the woman who had chanted the lessons, I sliced apples and put jam in a small china bowl. Together she and I carried the breakfast into the bright sunshine of the garden. We set out whole almonds, apples, sesame crackers, jam and honey, a meal that observed the fourteen-day fast preceding the Dormition of Mary (the Orthodox version of the Feast of the Assumption). As we sat unsteadily on our chairs in the thick grass, Father Christodolous said, "The liturgy is like a taste of the eternal. Let's linger in it for a moment."

We sat in silence, nibbling and sipping.

I was again intrigued by the simplicity and generosity that accompanied the fasting. Here was no heroic feat of will over desire. Instead, a community simply acknowledged together its common preparation and its common focus. I had been welcomed as a guest, but not treated with any special accommodation. I was merely invited to join the fast, as it was.

And this kind of fast wasn't about hunger. The meal Olga served me that long-ago night in Krasnodar—complete with fresh bread, homemade pickles, and strong tea—had not been an exercise in self-deprivation. On the contrary, I had left nourished, so nourished that the moment lived vividly in my memory. This meal in Father Christodolous's garden, surrounded by gentians and rhododendrons, again offered hospitality and warmth; I was welcomed and fed.

Was fasting, I wondered, a form of nourishment? Was it related in some way that I couldn't quite grasp to hospitality?

When I returned home, I decided to incorporate a small fasting practice into my own life. I decided to abstain from dairy and meat on Wednesdays and Fridays, as I knew the Orthodox do. I looked forward to those days as time set aside for more attention to food, not in an obsessive way, but for simply noticing.

A few months into my practice, I found myself at the cutting board trying to cut potatoes and carrots into squares. I felt connected to Olga thousands of miles away and thought of the millions of people whose food was this simple—not necessarily because they were fasting, but because they were poor. On fasting days I didn't ask myself what I "wanted" to eat, a question that could often be more of an irritant than a delight. I just ate. That was a freedom I had rarely tasted.

All of these lessons seemed to lead me in the right direction, but I then decided that if some was good, more must be better. This had been my lifetime pattern toward all things related to food. My friends and family will tell you that I'm something of an overachiever in this area. I've been known to follow to a tee Julia Child's eight steps for hard-boiling an egg, despite the fact that my grandmother's simple "stick 'em in with the potatoes" method has never failed me. I've followed diet trends since I was a teenager, and my head is a thicket of contradictory rules about food. Over my lifetime, I've counted calories, grams of protein, carbohydrates, fats, and sugars. I don't just shop at the grocery store like some people do—I have an elaborate system of food pickups at three distinct locations to get the freshest food possible.

So this was the obvious next step: "Big Lent," the six-week fast before Holy Week and Easter, was quickly approaching. I extended my new practice to my daily table.

I struggled through the first few weeks. I ate a lot of oatmeal, salads, and sautéed vegetables. I thought about food incessantly and tried to plan my way through the difficulties of fasting when no one else around me was fasting. Then one night, about three weeks into the fast, I woke up in a panic. I was hot, sweaty, and my mouth and throat were inexplicably dry. No amount of water could slake my thirst. The next morning, light-headed and miserable, I gave up the fast. My house of cards collapsed.

In hindsight, there were several problems with my plan. One problem was that I was determined to undertake this challenge, but I had no mentor to help me. In Orthodox Christianity, such a safeguard is nearly always available. Olga had Father Alexander. Father Alexander had other priests at the cathedral; the community that gathered at the monastery in Denver had each other. I had no one. I had tried to reason through my many questions by myself. When I was in company, should I ask for accommodation? Should I share what I was doing with others, or was it better to keep it private? Do Sundays count? In some communities, fish and eggs are allowed on the fast. Should I allow them or was that cheating?

And then there was my own family. My young son and my husband had about as much interest in an Orthodox fast as in a root canal. They didn't complain about their vegan meals when it was only two days a week, but now I found myself sometimes cooking two separate meals or providing both fasting and nonfasting options. The fast complicated ordinary life, to say the least.

Instead of curiously seeking, the primary mode of my Wednesday and Friday practice, I was stubborn and determined, setting one flimsy card grimly upon another, with little to support it.

This fasting attempt was also like another kind of house, one I have seen on the border between Colorado and New Mexico. From the highway, I can see turrets and balconies glistening, but they're made of scrap metal and the lids of aluminum cans. Broken glass and bottle cap mobiles sparkle from every tree branch in the garbage-strewn yard. Every time I drive by, the structure and its environs have grown more elaborate. If I look at it in one light, it looks beautiful. If I look at it in another light, it looks like trash. Reflecting on my attempts that particular Lent, I realize that I created it in my own image: an ornate, but flimsy structure, part junk and part art. A whirligig in the sunshine.

What would it take to learn Olga Nikolaevna's fast? Apparently fasting was not just a matter of forgoing meat and dairy products. There was both more, and less, to it. Olga's fast had been extended to me in a delicate and gentle gesture of hospitality, and yet the meal she served me was simple—roots, oil, salt.

Perhaps, if I try again, I will return first to Father Alexander's garden. There I will ask for help. Even in the asking, I will need, I can tell, to turn over some fresh earth in myself. What if, after all, fasting is not an act of will, but instead an act of kindness and hospitality—to myself, to others, to the world? Perhaps fasting is learning to listen to the quiet whisper of the eternal—*slow down, abide with me. All you need is here.* Perhaps I too can learn that fasting is a way of coming home.

Olga's Fasting Salad

INGREDIENTS

4 medium beets, washed and ends trimmed

2 large potatoes, washed but not peeled

2 carrots, washed but not peeled

2 small pickles, diced

3 tablespoons oil (olive, sunflower, or salad oil)

1 tablespoon spicy mustard

2 tablespoons fresh dill, chopped

Salt and pepper to taste

Capers (optional)

Parsley (optional)

Peas (optional)

Steamed, chopped green beans (optional)

Green onions (optional)

Sunflower seeds (optional)

RECIPE

Cover whole beets in cold water; bring to a boil and boil 30 to 40 minutes until tender.

In a separate pot, boil potatoes and carrots (cut potatoes in half if they are very large) until tender, 15 to 20 minutes.

Cool the vegetables; peel and then chop them at a very small dice.

Combine the boiled, diced vegetables with the pickles.

Mix the oil, mustard, and dill together and then add to the vegetables.

Stir and season with salt and pepper to taste.

LaVonne Neff has had careers in education and publishing. She has earned three master's degrees, written numerous books and magazine articles, and raised two daughters. In her reading life, she enjoys mysteries, detective stories, and terrifying sociological books about how bad the world has become. She also likes to cook, eat, hang out with friends, and walk her two small imperious dogs. She and her husband, David, live in the Chicago area, which is altogether too far from their daughters and their three remarkable grandchildren. She blogs at http://livelydust.blogspot.com. Her posts from the Food-Stamp Experiment are available at http://thelentenexperiment.blogspot.com.

21

My (Self-Righteous) Food-Stamp Fast

Fasting isn't my thing. First, I really like to eat. Second, hunger gives me migraines, not mystical experiences. Third, my religious history makes fasting difficult.

I was raised Seventh-Day Adventist, a church with lots of rules for healthful living. We never fasted, but then we never needed to—we already avoided meat, poultry, fish, alcohol, coffee, and tea. All the time.

In my thirties I became Episcopalian, the church Walker Percy called "invertebrate Catholics." We observed Lent, for example, but each in our own way. One year my teenaged daughter gave up homework.

Then in my forties I joined the Catholic Church, which since Vatican II is a lot less like boot camp than it was in Percy's day. The church still has rules about fasting, but they are minimal: two fast days a year (Ash Wednesday and Good Friday) for Catholics between the ages of eighteen and fifty-nine. Eight days when meat is forbidden (the two fast days, plus the six Fridays in Lent). That's all. Now that I'm in my sixties, and since I rarely eat meat anyway, I hardly notice.

Still—whether from the lingering influence of having read *Celebration of Discipline* thirty years ago or from a more recent dose of Catholic guilt—last year I began wondering if maybe I shouldn't enjoy food quite so much. This was a troubling thought for one whose life text is Ecclesiastes 5:18: "It is fitting to eat and drink and find enjoyment in all the toil with which one toils under the sun."

But the recession had hit, and I was noticing that even in my comfy suburb, people were overwhelming the food pantries—people who would love to enjoy their food and drink but were unable to find any toil, under the sun or otherwise, to make it possible. My husband and I, though still comfortable enough, had just taken a big hit to our income too. What would it be like, I wondered, to have to live with "food insecurity"—the current jargon for everything from insufficient food to almost no food at all?

My first thought, immediately rejected, was to try to eat on $1 a day. Some 22 percent of the world's population live on $1.25 a day or less—not just for food, but for everything. Several bloggers have done it (to find them, google "blog $1 day food"). I did not want to join them.

Well then, how about $2 a day? About half the world's population gets by on a daily income of less than $2.50. That still didn't sound realistic.

And then I remembered food stamps. We needed them for a few months back in the 1970s when we were grad students with two small children and very little income. If I wasn't willing to eat like a Haitian peasant or a Sudanese refugee, could I at least try living for a few weeks on a food-stamp budget?

A quick Google search informed me that the program formerly called food stamps is now known as the Supplemental Nutritional Assistance Program (SNAP). Monthly allowances are based on U.S. Department of Agriculture estimates of how much a healthy diet costs. The USDA suggests four plans: thrifty, low-cost, moderate-cost, and liberal. Food-stamp recipients, if their income is extremely low, are entitled to an amount similar to the thrifty plan. Most get less.

According to the USDA chart, my husband and I would need at least $79.80 a week to eat thriftily. Illinois's maximum SNAP benefit at the time (early 2009) was $74 a week. We decided we'd try to eat for $77 a week, $11 a day, $5.50 apiece.

I would record all our food purchases, along with recipes and experiences and attitudes, in a daily blog for six weeks. We would do this during Lent: if we were going to be miserable, we might as well feel righteous about it. Also, Lent comes in late winter when Illinois has no fresh local produce anyway.

A month in advance, I began planning and blogging. Hoping to enlist friends to suffer with us, I listed the good effects our experiment might have. "Join us and diminish your body-mass index, blood pressure, and cholesterol," I wrote. Five days after I posted that, Dr. Mehmet Oz destroyed my illusions. "The best way to gain weight in America," he told Oprah's audience, "is to go on food stamps." Uh oh.

But hey, good health wasn't my motivation. I was doing this because I wanted to know how it feels to be too poor to eat in restaurants, shop at Whole Foods, or pick up a nice bottle of wine for Sunday dinner. I would watch every penny, eat lentils instead of wild-caught Alaskan salmon, celebrate with a bottle of Two-Buck Chuck.

In short, I wanted to be a pampered tourist on a short-term excursion to the land of poverty.

"If you really want to know how it feels to be poor," said a friend as we ate at an Indian restaurant the Sunday before the experiment was due to begin, "first come clean my house for two dollars an hour, then clean three or four other houses, and then go home and try to cook a meal for your family for less than twelve dollars."

Her comment struck home. "I'm all for showing solidarity with the poor," I wrote on my blog on Tuesday, "but this experiment is not going to do it." I then listed some ways my life would be different if I were a real-life food-stamp recipient, or if I truly didn't know whether my paycheck would last until the next one arrived.

> If I were poor, I wouldn't have time to cook meals from scratch, compare prices in different stores, clip coupons, or collect recipes.
>
> If I were poor, there probably wouldn't be an inexpensive grocery store in my neighborhood. There might not be any grocery store at all. I'd have to rely on convenience stores and small neighborhood shops, which often cost more than the chains and have much less variety.
>
> If I were poor and uneducated, I might not realize what foods I need or what foods I should avoid. I might not be skilled

at budgeting, and I probably wouldn't have a PC with Excel to help track expenses.

If I were poor, I wouldn't have an assortment of appliances to make food preparation and storage easy. Nor would I have attractive plates, glasses, flatware, and tablecloths to make even the simplest fare seem like a feast.

Most of all, if I were poor, this would be no experiment. Cheap eats would be my life.

The next day, Wednesday, I began the experiment anyway. Even though I was beginning to realize that my poverty would all be pretense, I still wondered what I would learn. And six and a half weeks later, right on schedule, I abandoned my food-stamp budget and prepared an Easter feast.

In between, I cheated. I ate in restaurants a couple of times. We bought some wine and, since food stamps don't cover alcohol, didn't include it in our tally (it was cheap wine, though). We took an entire week off at the end of March to go to the Northwest and celebrate our fortieth anniversary.

Also, I complained. This experiment "would be a lot more fun if it weren't so long," I grumbled. "And penitential. And guilt-inducing." Besides, it was raining too much.

In addition, I fantasized. Back in the early 80s, when our budget was so tight that if I found an extra dollar I rushed out and bought potatoes, I found myself dreaming of dressing like Princess Diana. Partway through our food-stamp experiment, I began having a similar dream. I wanted to go out to dinner—not to the moderate-priced restaurants I could no longer afford, but to Charlie Trotter's. I imagined us ordering one Grand Menu ($165) and one Vegetable Menu ($135), plus the Wine Accompaniment (about $125 times two). The meal would cost considerably more than our entire thirty-nine-day budget. "Maybe I can save money by borrowing one of Princess Diana's old dresses," I wrote.

Even so, I resisted. I persevered. For thirty-nine days we stuck to our "fast," each of us spending an average of $4.70 a day for home-cooked food. About two-thirds of our meals were vegetarian. The other third included small amounts of fish, turkey sausage, or—once—chicken. We ate a lot of Italian-inspired meals: risotto, gnocchi, pizza, spaghetti, lasagna. We had cheese tamales, tostadas, omelets, ratatouille, lentil soup, and black bean stew. We ate piles of vegetables and fruit bought for pennies at Aldi. I baked endless loaves of bread. We did not suffer. We did not gain weight.

What did I learn?

Well, I quickly found out that living on such a strict grocery budget made me grumpy. I disliked having to comparison shop, adjust my menu by price instead of taste, buy foods that were obviously not produced in environmentally sound ways, and eat the same boring foods day after day. I really hated having to keep track of every penny.

I confirmed that this experiment would give me no brownie points. Despite all my scrimping, I daily recognized how far I was from true poverty. I had—and still have—no idea what food insecurity feels like.

I learned that I am spoiled. A woman I do not know left this comment on one of my blog posts. I wish I could credit her by name, because I appreciate her honesty. As one of the working poor, she saw right through me:

> I can get a big old can of ravioli for $2.89 and fill my family's tummies in a matter of minutes. And for many, many families, this is the most the parent can manage at the end of the day. I know it's not the healthful choice, but at the end of a day of shuttling kids and working for minimum wage and trying to figure out how to pay for the needed car repairs, this is about all we have left.
>
> Please, do not assume that the same quality and prices and time and energy required for food preparation are available to all people. Quite frankly, this group of articles has come off as self-righteous and lacking a genuine understanding of what life is like for those of us who search for affordable food 365 days per year because we *have to*, not just for forty days because we're doing an experiment. Perhaps a little more compassion and spending some time with "the least of these" would be a good idea?

Yes. God, be merciful to me, a sinner! I had just lived for five and a half weeks on a food-stamp budget, but my emphasis was all wrong. "Look what I can do," I was saying, when I should have been asking, "What can I do for people in need?"

The prophet Isaiah speaks God's condemnation of people who fast for the wrong reasons. "Such fasting as you do today will not make your voice heard on high," he says. What counts is not giving up things, but giving of oneself:

Is not this the fast that I choose:

to loose the bonds of injustice,

to undo the thongs of the yoke,

to let the oppressed go free,

and to break every yoke?

Is it not to share your bread with the hungry . . . ?

Then you shall call, and the Lord will answer;

you shall cry for help, and he will say, Here I am." (Isaiah 58:4, 6–7, 9)

I didn't fast this year. I may not fast ever again. I'm still thinking about how to share my bread with the hungry. There are now well over a billion of them, and every day the number gets larger.

Mac and Cheese for Grown-Ups

INGREDIENTS

4 ounces dried short pasta

Salted water

1/4 cup oil or butter

1/4 cup flour

1/2 teaspoon salt

1 bottle (12 ounces) cheap light-colored beer, or milk if you prefer the old
   familiar taste

4 ounces grated cheddar cheese, preferably sharp or extra sharp

1 teaspoon mustard, hot sauce, Worcestershire sauce, or something else
with zing

Parsley (optional)

Tomato, chopped (optional)

Coarsely ground black pepper (optional)

Makes 2 big servings or 4 little side-dish servings

RECIPE

Boil up some salted water, drop in some of your favorite pasta, whether
macaroni or some other kind, and cook until it doesn't crunch—usually 8
to 10 minutes depending on the shape of the pasta.

Meanwhile, make the sauce: melt oil in a saucepan and then add flour and
salt, stirring until the mixture is smooth.

Slowly pour in the beer, stirring the mixture over medium heat until it
starts to thicken.

Add cheese and keep stirring until the sauce is smooth.

Finally, stir in something to add zing, whatever sounds good to you.

Drain the pasta, stir it into the sauce, and serve. Garnish with parsley or
tomato, or sprinkle on pepper.

CAROLINE LANGSTON, a native of Yazoo City, Mississippi, is a widely published writer and essayist. She has an MFA from the University of Houston, and her fiction has been anthologized in the Pushcart Prizes and *New Stories from the South* series. She has been a commentator for NPR's *All Things Considered* and is a regular blogger for *Image: A Journal of the Arts and Religion*'s Good Letters blog. She lives with her family in Cheverly, Maryland.

22

The Joy of the Fast

I ate my first fasting meal two years before I was received into the Eastern Orthodox Church. Twenty-five years old, I was halfway into a six-week group trip to India for which I had won a scholarship, and both my health and spirits had started to flag—from the ever-present dust and crowds, from the bottled water that was sealed to look hygienic but likely was not, from the overwhelming beauty and ceremony (and threat, if I am honest) of a Hindu culture that my own evangelical Christian faith and experience gave me few tools to understand.

After spending the first half of the trip in northern India, we were in the southern city of Bangalore, which sits on a high, sunny, windy plain. That day, instead of another long trek through temples and hours of being jostled back and forth in our tour bus on ragged roads, we drove outside the city to visit the Nrityagram Dance Village, a commune that was more or less dedicated to the study of classical Indian dance. After observing a performance, our hungry, thirsty group was served lunch— on tin plates, I recall—under a portico whose sides were open to land and sky, a breeze to scattering a dusting of grit at our feet.

The meal consisted of beans, a heaping of brown rice speckled with fresh herbs, and a slab of unadorned, grainy bread. That was all. No dairy, no meat. I recall it as one of the most delicious meals I have ever tasted.

But the food was not the point. The food was just one part of the afternoon, a complement to the good conversation that we all were suddenly having. Our travel-weary, tetchy group seemed tangibly to relax, to listen to one another, and to talk with our hosts. Rested and satisfied, we boarded the bus for the long ride back into the city.

That trip to India put me on a spiritual search that led not out of Christianity—because still, always, I believed in Jesus—but to St. George Antiochian Orthodox Christian Cathedral in Wichita, Kansas. And it was while I was a catechumen at this church founded by Lebanese immigrants that I encountered the Eastern Orthodox discipline of fasting.

Before that time, I had no concept of fasting. My family was religiously lax, Southern Baptists only culturally, brothers and sisters under the skin to "C+E" Catholics (Christmas and Easter services only). The chief statement from my mother about church was, "Well, I don't see the need to be there every time the doors open," but I had accepted Jesus Christ, become an evangelical, and turned my back on that laxity.

But fasting wasn't exactly emphasized in the Christian faith I had found, either. While both the intellectually rich sermons of the hyper-Reformed Presbyterian congregation I had joined and my InterVarsity Christian Fellowship group in college acknowledged that Jesus taught about fasting in the Sermon on the Mount, I saw few examples of fasting or abstinence in practice. In those isolated cases when a friend did mention that she was fasting or a pastor urged a "day of prayer and fasting," it was nearly always done in order to get something. Whether for the purpose of bringing rain for the crops (I grew up in the cotton-growing Mississippi Delta) or America to repentance, fasting appeared to be another form of supplication designed to make something happen, a kind of magic.

There are, of course, a great number of biblical and other precedents for treating fasting in exactly this way, and I do not want to dismiss them. It's a centuries-honored means of resisting evil and changing hearts, employed by Christians in the abolition, civil rights, and pro-life movements, to say nothing of Gandhi and other practitioners of nonviolence.

Nonetheless, I distrusted this practice, distrusted anything that might remotely resemble an attempt to cow God into granting our petition.

The one time that I witnessed fasting as a means of knowing and honoring God, of simply recognizing our dependence on him, came when I was in graduate school. On a hot October day in Houston, my Jewish roommate Leslie was heading off to synagogue for all-day Yom Kippur services, and she mentioned that, in keeping with tradition, she would be fasting until sundown.

As it happened, halfway through the morning services, with sunlight glaring through the glass windows of Temple Emanu El, Leslie began feeling faint and had to leave shul for a cup of water and a bite to eat. She was forced to abandon the fast she had undertaken. That, too, was a lesson for me, of the body's inescapable demands and how perhaps even in our failure, fasting can bring humility and grace.

There was something about this fast that seemed as though it had the capacity to be truly *transformative*. It was an act both individual and corporate, but rather than a simple outward direction ("Please, God, punish America for the sin of X"), this fast was also relentlessly *inward*. I realized then that the discipline of fasting is a tangible, visceral reminder that we, ourselves, are probably the greatest obstacles to change that we are going to encounter. But when done in community, it can strengthen both our individual resolve and the bonds between the faithful. And it can bring the presence of God and the experience of his nearness closer than any other expression of faith I can imagine.

Which brings me to the discipline of fasting as it is practiced among Eastern Orthodox Christians—which is to say, *seriously*. If you want to make an Orthodox Christian commit the sin of pride (and thus, in theory at least, to have to go to Confession), then complain about how hard it is to remember your decision to "give up" chocolate or eat fish on Fridays during Lent.

By contrast, Orthodox Christians observe four extended fasting seasons per liturgical year: Advent (or the Nativity Fast), Great Lent, the fast before the Feast of Saints Peter and Paul (usually in June), and the Dormition Fast, which commemorates the falling asleep of Mary, the Theotokos. That adds up to more than a third of a year. During this time, Orthodox Christians are asked to abstain from meat *and* dairy products, as well as alcohol and even olive oil, depending on what day of the week or month it is. Even during "regular" seasons, the faithful are asked to abstain from meat and dairy on ordinary Wednesdays and Fridays—Wednesdays as a reminder of Christ's betrayal and Friday in memory of his death.

The sheer amount of time on the calendar is the ironic reason why, when Orthodox Christians talk about fasting, they almost always end up talking about eating instead: if you're "doing the fast," as we tend to say in casual parlance, you often are thinking about what you can eat rather than what you cannot.

Another irony is that observance of the fast need not condemn the faithful believer to tasteless or unhealthy food, especially if one takes advantage of the Mediterranean cooking traditions of Greek and Arab parishes. I cannot say enough about the simple gratitude to God I have felt on those Lenten days when I have heaped my plate with tofu and chickpeas and spinach, when I have felt that vitamin-rich food—exactly what the secular *New York Times* food journalist Mark Bittman prescribes as the most healthy diet—hit my stomach after a long day. Not enough food to be stuffed, but just enough to be sustained, to have the strength to do good work and love others better and to increase prayer. And this is why that meal of beans and rice on the Bangalore portico has stayed in my mind for so long—it was a perfect Lenten meal.

But spiritual dangers lurk for those who heartily enter into the fasting discipline. In an effort to "get the fast right," many Protestant converts to the faith get hung up on the letter rather than the spirit of the observance. I know this because I was one of them. They scan food labels for the word *casein*, which would denote the presence of whey, and therefore milk, as an ingredient. Or, because spineless seafood is included in the rubrics of allowable fasting foods, they make a show of ordering lobster because it is permitted, never mind its exorbitant expense. I've seen at-home mothers cry trying to put together endless meals with pasta, tomato sauce, and peanut butter.

These True Believers are often impatient and scornful when they discover that a fair number of cradle Orthodox Christians do not observe the fasts very much at all—as though the children of the very immigrants who brought the faith to these shores are not "real Christians." Less rigorous ethnic Orthodox, on the other hand, often wonder about these tiresome zealots in their midst.

Among my Orthodox friends are several who are not especially diligent about fasting, but I've found that they still share a heightened awareness of the discipline's value and importance. The fast exerts its influence, even when it's not being observed—not unlike those Jews who do not keep *kashrut* but hold its principles in their minds every time they remember to wash a roasting pan in extra hot water.

In the nearly thirteen years now that I've been Orthodox, I've been on both sides of this dichotomy. After one stint in a particularly scrupulous community—where debates about such topics as whether beer constituted alcohol or "bread" actually took place—I deliberately attended a large congregation where fasting was greatly de-emphasized, and there was no danger of an inquiring acquaintance at coffee hour peering in to my coffee cup to see whether I had added milk. While I was grateful for the acceptance and mercy in all that freedom, ultimately I found that something also was lost. For without the fast, the feast is not the same.

We are all commanded to fast, yes, and some of us do so quite strictly. Many of the saints of the church lived on little more than bread and water for decades. But it is also true that giving up meat can be burden enough, and there are seasons when I've gone into the restaurant right before Holy Week and ordered the burger and fries. I'm not proud of it, but like my friend Leslie on Yom Kippur, it served to humble my heart. As I write on the threshold of Great Lent 2009, I am forty years old and pregnant, and I will not be fasting this year. Running after my preschooler and nurturing the life within are a fast unto themselves. And this leads me to one of the great spiritual principles of Orthodoxy: the importance of balance, of taking the peculiarities of each person's circumstances, and then submitting them to the counsels of our priests and the tradition. That's why close pastoral counsel—and the sacrament of Confession—are critical.

And when done *together*, in charity and community, without judgment, urging our fellow faithful on in this journey from the "far country" into the knowledge of the resurrection of Christ, we manifest the ongoing feast that we celebrate early on Pascha morning—with roasted lamb, flickering candles, and crimson eggs that remind us of the renewal of all.

Greek Chickpeas and Spinach

Our family fasts from meat during Advent and Lent, and this is one of our favorites. We serve this over rice pilaf or couscous.

INGREDIENTS

1 large onion, peeled and finely chopped

2 cloves garlic, pressed or minced

2 teaspoons olive oil

2 cups precooked chickpeas, or one 15-ounce can garbanzo beans, drained and rinsed

2 tablespoons fresh dill weed, finely chopped

1/2 pound fresh spinach, cleaned and chopped or torn into bite-size pieces

2 tablespoons lemon juice

Serves 4

RECIPE

Using a large frying pan, sauté the onion and garlic in oil over medium heat for 2 minutes.

Add the chickpeas and dill and stir-fry for 5 minutes.

Add the spinach, a little at a time. Drizzle lemon juice over all the ingredients and cover with a lid.

Cook 5 minutes or until the spinach shrinks. Stir to combine. Serve hot.

SUZANNE M. WOLFE is the executive editor of *Image* journal and an instructor in English at Seattle Pacific University. She and her husband, Greg Wolfe, have coauthored several books on literature and prayer for children including *Bless This House: Prayers for Families and Children* (Jossey-Bass, 2004) and *Books That Build Character: A Guide to Teaching Your Child Moral Values through Stories* (Touchstone, 1994). Her first novel, *Unveiling*, was published by Paraclete Press in 2004. She is currently working on her second novel.

23

This Is My Body

I have a black-and-white photograph taken in 1967 that I found among my grandmother's things after she died. In the foreground, my grandmother sits on a blanket, smiling self-consciously for the camera. To her left my brother stands in a seven-year-old boy's macho pose with hands on hips, his smooth, hairless chest thrust out, a half-grin, half-grimace on his face because he is looking directly into the sun. I cannot specifically remember this day but I recall Sunday afternoons like it—those rare, warm days in August when we piled into my mother's second-hand Morris Minor and drove up from the crowded suburbs of Manchester into the hills of Derbyshire.

Behind my brother and grandmother, set back a little way and sitting on the brow of a hill overlooking a body of water, are my grandfather and me. We are both facing away from the camera. He is leaning on one arm, semi-reclining; I sit close up against his chest, the top of my head appearing just above his shoulder. We are looking at the lake beneath us as it stretches away into the distance, a sheet of shimmering metal overtopped by the cloudless, endless sky of childhood. I hear skylarks swooping and twittering among the grasses and the indolent *basso continuo* of bees nuzzling clover. The heather flowers purple and white at my feet as the daisies modestly offer their pink-tipped centers to the sun. My fingers are yellowed with buttercup pollen, fingernails greened with their juicy stems as I fashion a Lord Mayor's chain of gold to hang around my grandfather's neck. In the pockets of my shorts are the stones I have collected, mica-veined granite, blue-green slate, and snail shells— humble, exquisite, and infinitely fragile, a hoard of happiness to be set out on my windowsill before I go to bed that night.

I am resting now in my grandfather's embrace, lulled by the tremor of his heart, unaware that a more lasting record is being taken, a thumb-nail of celluloid that will survive for forty years, a perfect snapshot of my childhood after my treasures have long been broken, lost, or discarded.

My Canadian father abandoned the family when I was eight months old, forcing my mother to return to England and move back into her parents' home with my brother and me. We lived with them in Manchester until I was eight and then moved to our own house in the same town.

In the 60s, single parenthood was a rarity. My mother had to work doubly hard to compete with men in her profession, carve out a career, and support her children without help from the government or from a sympathetic society. She worked long hours during the day and then built up a physiotherapy practice of her own by visiting people's houses at night to give them treatment. This meant that I seldom saw my moth-er, it falling chiefly to my grandparents to raise my brother and me in our pre-school years.

Until he retired when I was five, my grandfather was a typesetter at one of the major Manchester newspapers and was gone during the day. Each evening I would wait at the gate for him to return, running down the street to greet him when he crossed the road, a tall man with a long stride that he accommodated to my three-year-old legs as we walked back to the house, hand in hand.

Parting from my grandfather five years later was my first experi-ence of the hunger I have since come to recognize as loss.

Until then, I remember a time spent among growing things, things wet and loamy, green-tasting, new, my infant senses moving like feel-ers over the surface of a pristine world, hesitantly and full of wonder.

My earliest memories are of my grandfather digging in the allotment he rented from the township, the crunch of the spade biting into the ground, his foot on the blade, bearing down; the dry sift of bone meal scooped from burlap sacks, dust lazy in sunlight. And then, at the end of the day, the trundle and bump of the wheelbarrow over pavement when I was too tired to walk home, my grandfather's face the sky that bounded the horizon of my childhood.

In his greenhouse he grew tomatoes, fragile shoots he planted in humus, then puddled and pressed down, his fingers—nicotine-stained and rimed with dirt—moving delicately and deliberately. Those same hands smoothed the covers up to my chin each night, planting me in a bed of warmth and darkness, his love for me the water that fed my roots, the heat that drew me upward, all five-foot, seven-inches of me, a suddenly gangly seventh grader.

The taste and scent of baby tomatoes picked from the vine is, for me, the taste of paradise long foregone. Store-bought tomatoes are the ultimate postlapsarian tease—perfectly round, polished to a jeweled sheen, but scentless, tasteless, and inclined to soften. My grandfather used to pray before each meal: "For what we are about to receive, Lord, make us truly thankful." But like Adam and Eve before the fall, I could not be thankful for what I did not know would end. I did not dream of famine or drought, bad husbandry, disease, blight, waste, or mediocrity. I did not think the crops could fail.

Food was the outward and visible sign of my grandfather's love, and I received it as matter-of-factly as a lifelong communicant receives the host. The high priest of my childhood, his robes smelled of earth and cigarettes, the tweed of his jackets scratchy against my cheek. He taught me World War II songs, checkers, the card game "Patience," and how to pray. At meals I sat at his right hand and ate blithely, without conscious gratitude but with careless and innocent joy. My first joke was: "Gramp, how come your string beans are all string and no bean?"

Once a year, on Father's Day, I would walk down the street to the sweet shop on the corner and buy a pound of my grandfather's favorite candies. Sugar-encrusted, fruit-flavored jellies called jujubes, they tumbled from the scoop in a pulse of color, bulging the white paper bag that I carried home under my coat as carefully and furtively as if they were the Crown Jewels.

On Fridays—fish days in our pre-Vatican II Catholic household—he and I would walk to the local fish-and-chip shop. On the way there, I would hold his hand, but on the way back I would cradle the hot newspaper bundle under my sweater to keep the food warm for the table. My grandmother would complain that the stink of salt and vinegar was impossible to remove from my clothes, but to me it was the smell of happiness—sharp, pervasive, and, I thought, indelible.

I was seven when my grandfather had his first stroke and was bedridden for a time. I stopped coming to table and, instead, hid in the laundry basket in his bedroom, fasting and keeping vigil until I was discovered and hauled out.

At about the same time, I began to have episodes of vomiting, and foods that I had previously eaten without complaint suddenly nauseated me. For the first time, I became aware of the sounds my stomach made after eating and learned that this was called digestion, that the gurgling was the dirty water going down the drain after a bath, that my mouth was the hole in the tub and my body a series of pipes.

Without my grandfather's presence, food was no longer a miracle winging down in the beak of a raven or an angel appearing to Ezekiel saying, "Eat. Drink." Food had become a thing, a dead weight in the pit of my stomach, the heft of nothingness.

When we moved from my grandparents' house to our own home, the gulf between sign and signifier grew, the object becoming more lifeless, more inert. As if to prove it, I began to consume the inedible. In the course of a single term, I ate the leather strap of the purse that I kept my lunch money in at school, the texture of the strap paradoxical in its inner toughness and the outer slipperiness of the leather softened by saliva. I ate the wood of pencils down to the nub and consumed paper tissues pellet by pellet, then started on the inside of my cheek, self-cannibalizing until I bled, oddly comforted that my food of choice was always available, something of my own and not dependent on the largesse of others.

Cut adrift, I was already cutting myself off. Later, I would call such solipsism independence.

My mother worked days as well as nights, and my brother and I took turns preparing the evening meal by peeling and boiling vegetables while my mother grilled the meat. Meals became perfunctory, rushed affairs, eaten perched on kitchen stools at a Formica counter where the clash of cutlery and the sound of chewing replaced the conversation of my grandfather's table. I remember my mother's fatigue and hopelessness leaching into the silence like carbon monoxide—odorless and colorless.

We learned to tread lightly, my brother and I, over the brittle skim of my mother's fear, testing for fissures, cracks, the yaw of unstable ground, our stomachs tensed for the heart-stopping plunge. I turned to books and practiced a deadly, and deadening, asceticism; my brother became a connoisseur of cruelty, pulling the wings and legs off insects, watching their helpless, vibrating torsos describe circles worthy of Dante.

In my teens, my grandfather suffered a series of increasingly debilitating strokes, and every day after school I would cycle to my grandparents' house to visit him. I would read his favorite Psalm aloud to him—"Yea, though I walk through the valley of the shadow of death . . . ." But when I looked at his garden, now infested with weeds, his greenhouse empty and opaque like a closed eye, his allotment sold off, all things passing away, I did not believe in a Good Shepherd.

At Mass I would help him to Communion, his arm brittle and sticklike beneath my hand, his shoulders rounded, stooped, the nicks and cuts on his neck telling me that his hands shook too much for shaving. He insisted on fasting for twelve hours before taking the host, even though his illness made him exempt from such mortification and the fast had been reduced to one hour after Vatican II. Only when he was dying would he consent to allow the priest to bring him the host at home. "McEntee stubbornness," my grandmother said, the Irish cognomen carrying the full weight of her Anglo-Saxon disapproval, as if it were a synonym for mule.

At the very end of his life, he became unable to feed himself, and my grandmother became enraged by his inability to swallow and the way the food dribbled down his chin. I would feed him, spoon by careful spoon, and talk of my day and my studies and the books we loved as if words could stanch his humiliation and shame.

I was out of the country when he died. When I returned, my grandmother had removed every trace of him from the house. When I opened the closet, only the memory of his scent remained, like the barely heard whisper of my name in the dark.

I too began to fast, not with the holy asceticism of my grandfather preparing to receive the bread of life, but with the vaunting *non serviam* of the apostate. Instead of food, I digested rage; instead of flesh, I glutted on words; instead of God, Nietzsche. His *Triumph of the Will* was my manifesto, the *credo* of a believer in nothing, the faithful communicant of the sacrament of antimatter.

Or that is what I told myself. In reality, I was abandoning God as he had abandoned me—starvation as preemptive-strike theology—in order to avoid saying the unthinkable: *Eli, Eli, lama sabachthani?*

From the depths of her body's malnutrition and her soul's plenitude, Simone Weil warned, "The danger is not lest the soul should doubt whether there is bread, but lest, by a lie, it should persuade itself it is not hungry."

When I lost my appetite for bread, I stopped going to Mass. But my hunger did not diminish; it grew. I began to mistake the physical effects of starvation for spiritual purity: eating became a sin; starvation, a virtue. My body appeared gross and bestial and its incessant clamor tormented me, but unlike the desert fathers or the great saints who denied themselves in order to affirm the goodness of what they denied, my fasting nullified the world. As Simone Weil said, "All sins are attempts to fill voids."

I was a suicide posing as a hunger striker.

My teens were spent in an orgy of self-destruction and the annihilation of my mother's happiness. I refused food but submitted my body to the more insidious fruits of drugs and the dark sexual tutelage of a much older man until, one night, traveling on a bus between Paris and Calais, I saw in my hollowed and ravaged reflection the darkness I had become, with pinpoints of light showing randomly and seldom. It was an epiphany of sorts.

At Oxford University that autumn I met Greg, my future husband, and began to learn, arduously and with many setbacks, how to receive as well as to give. Gradually my soul filled out and grew stronger, and I returned to the church of my childhood, where I encountered my grandfather in the curve of an old woman's back as she knelt at prayer and in the knock of knuckle on breastbone, the murmur "*Mea culpa* . . . ." In the breaking of bread, that audible crack when the host yields to the force of human flesh, I heard the breaking of my heart and saw it lifted up in the service of something other than unredeemable loss.

When I became a mother and felt my children stirring within me I knew I was no longer alone, that my body was no longer my own. The imperative to eat became an imperative of love, each pound gained no longer a millstone but a sign of my baby's development.

For the first time since childhood I was able to revel in abundance, cradling my unborn children the way I had clasped the fish and chips beneath my sweater—my belly warm and bulky, the heat of it alive and life-giving, the mystery of me and of another. Then I would remember what I had forgotten, that the flesh is the outward sign of inner grace—symbiosis, or what Charles Williams called "co-inherence."

Holding my newborns in my arms and guiding my nipple into their questing mouths, I felt life drawing from my breasts and watched in wonder as the surfeit of my love ran over their chins when they turned away, sated and oblivious.

"This is my body."

Watching my toddlers in their highchairs taught me that food is miraculous, its myriad colors and shapes, its glorious textures, an invitation to play. Squishing peas or squeezing fistfuls of mashed potatoes, my children were Adams and Eves discovering the wonder of creation for the first time, reaffirming the gift of this world and offering it back. Called to tend the vigorous growth of their bodies, I adored every crease, concavity, and roundness, observing the dewy sheen of lips parted in sleep, caressing the cool pearlescent flesh faintly tinged with blood. With their eyes, they drank the world entire and did not disdain to bring it to their mouths and taste. Hands that clutched, held, kneaded, and stroked, also blessed, and as I obeyed their infant commands to name the things of this world, the world was made holy.

A low table and two chairs sit beneath a plum tree. On the table are a pot with purple flowers, a verdigris statue of a sparrow. There is a bench under an apple tree and a dripping stone birdbath. In my house, leaves and bits of grass litter the floor as if the garden had moved indoors. On the windowsill sit gifts my children have given me over the years: shells, rocks, pinecones, treasures to replace the ones I lost from that summer's afternoon long ago. Now all but one of my children are grown and the three oldest have moved out of the house. I tend my flowers, herbs, and tomatoes and find myself returned to the place I first knew, where the boundary between those who sow and those who reap forever blurs.

At dusk the house rides like a light-bedizened ship on a darkening sea waiting, like my heart, for my children to return.

I would like to say that my hunger has been satisfied, but this is not the case. When I am lonely, exhausted, and discouraged, the temptation to deny returns. I still find it difficult to go to restaurants, to eat in front of strangers. Often when I attend Mass and file slowly up the aisle to Communion, I feel like a gate-crasher at the heavenly banquet and take the host like a beggar pocketing a dinner roll. I tell myself that if I were good enough, I would live on the Eucharist alone and it would not burn my conscience or dissolve like air. If I were good enough, I would whisper, "Father, I am hungry; for the Love of God give this soul her food . . . ." But I am not a holy anorexic like Saint Catherine of Siena. I am just a child greedy for love.

When I read George Herbert's poem, "Love (III)," I hear the voice of my grandfather telling me that I must sit at his right hand once more, that I have been too long absent from his table. When I teach Herbert's poem, I tell my students that Herbert's faith in God is so great that even his sins are virtues marred only by prefixes that are as easily removed as dust—"*un*gratefull," "*un*kinde." In my daily spiritual practice, I am very far from Herbert's magnificent trust, yet I return to his poem again and again because, like a lost sheep, I recognize the Shepherd's voice:

> Love bade me welcome: yet my soul drew back,
> > Guiltie of dust and sinne.
> But quick-ey'd Love, observing me grow slack
> > From my first entrance in,
> Drew nearer to me, sweetly questioning,
> > If I lack'd any thing.
> A guest, I answer'd, worthy to be here:
> > Love said, You shall be he.
> I the unkinde, ungratefull? Ah my deare,
> > I cannot look on thee.
> Love took my hand, and smiling did reply,
> > Who made the eyes but I?
> Truth Lord, but I have marr'd them: let my shame
> > Go where it doth deserve.
> And know you not, sayes Love, who bore the blame?
> > My deare, then I will serve.
> You must sit downe, sayes Love, and taste my meat:
> > So I did sit and eat.

Since my self-expulsion from Eden when I was fifteen, my life has followed Herbert's poem line by line as I have sought the voice of my grandfather calling me back to communion. I know now what I knew in the paradise of my childhood when he and I walked together in the cool of the evening, when we sat looking at the still-life of an idyllic summer afternoon long ago—that all my life I have been seeking what I had already found.

In memory of John McEntee, 1901–1977

Irish Soda Bread (Brown Bread)

INGREDIENTS

3 cups wheat flour

1 cup white flour (do not use self-rising as it already contains baking powder and salt)

1 teaspoon salt

1 ½ teaspoons bicarbonate of soda

2 ounces butter if you want to deviate a bit

14 ounces buttermilk (pour in a bit at a time until the dough is moist)

RECIPE

Preheat the oven to 425° F.

Lightly grease and flour a cake pan.

In a large bowl, sieve and combine all the dry ingredients.

Rub in the butter until the flour is crumbly.

Add the buttermilk to form a sticky dough.

Place on a floured surface and lightly knead (too much allows the gas to escape)

Shape into a round flat shape in a round cake pan and cut a cross in the top of the dough.

Cover the pan with another pan and bake for 30 minutes (this simulates the *bastible pot*). Remove cover and bake for an additional 15 minutes.

The bottom of the bread will have a hollow sound when tapped, which will show that it is done.

Cover the bread in a tea towel and lightly sprinkle water on the cloth to keep the bread moist.

THOMAS MALTMAN is an award-winning novelist who teaches literature and creative writing at Silver Lake College in Manitowoc, Wisconsin. His first novel, *Night Birds*, has been awarded a BookSense pick of the Literate. His second novel, *Little Wolves*, is forthcoming. Thomas is married to a pastor in the Evangelical Lutheran Church of America, and has two daughters, Tess and Emma.

24

Famine

Down in the basement of St. John's Lutheran, Jesse stands shivering. He rinsed his shirt and jeans in a bathroom sink to disguise what happened, but the acrid odor of urine still clings to his clothing. Jesse has wet his makeshift bed of aged quilts, and the other boys wake knowing it, their senses heightened by hunger. Black-haired, with small, feral eyes obscured by thick glasses, Jesse cringes and hugs himself when I approach him.

We are twelve hours into the fast-for-famine and the basement floor is chilled and glazed with morning light. Soon the girls will return from sleeping next door at the parsonage and Jesse's humiliation will be complete. As the pastor's husband, I am here to keep order and watch over the boys during the lock-in. This is not something I foresaw.

Another boy comforts Jesse. "It's OK," he tells him. "These things happen."

"Is there someone you can call to bring fresh clothing?" I ask Jesse. Time is of the essence.

He shudders. "My dad will be mad," he says. "He's not supposed to drive since his last D.U.I."

Jesse holds a string with a cardboard picture of a Mongolian child named Boldkhuyag attached to the end. Jesse is supposed to wear the picture around his neck and every time he gets hungry say a prayer for this boy on the other side of the world. Through fasting we hope to better understand a world where 29,000 children die each day from malnutrition. In the black-and-white photograph, Boldkhuyag, clad in a simple jumpsuit, leans on something for support and gapes open-mouthed at the photographer. The similarity between these two boys, one wet and frightened, one starving, troubles me.

I can't look at Jesse without thinking of his brother, though I try not to. Joey committed suicide last semester. I only know the hearsay that spread through the halls of the high school where I taught English last year: His grandpa bought him the twelve-gauge so they could go hunting together. Joey did it while on the phone with his ex-girlfriend. It sickens me to think of Jesse or his little sister walking in the room afterward. Such a thing you would go on seeing and hearing, in dreams, nightmares—especially in a strange room, on a floor hard and cold as bone.

"He won't be mad," I promise. "Just call him."

In our age of plenty, we have forgotten the terrible things hunger does to our bodies. Auto-cannibalism, a process where your body begins to eat itself from the inside out, sets in after only twelve hours without food. Once your glycogen stores are exhausted, the body, a machine that is always burning, starts to devour fatty tissue and muscle. The side effects are immediate: joints stiffen, spots dance behind your eyes, and pinprick headaches flare and spread within your sinuses. You feel the cold more. This is the body eating itself.

The night the fast begins, we take the kids to the neighboring town of Springfield for disco bowling. Jesse, seated in the passenger seat, seizes control of the radio and puts on a country station. Outside there are black fields creased with furrows and farmsteads in huddles of leafless trees. A starless dark split only by our headlights. The other boys in the back seat josh and jab one another until they can't stop giggling. Then Jesse starts singing along to the radio and they go quiet to listen to him. His voice, hushed and insistent, echoes the crooner on the airwaves. It's the words of the song, though, that catch our attention. "You watch out brother for that long black train," Jesse sings. "The devil's a driving that long black train."

You are Boldkhuyag, a thirteen-year-old child living in Mongolia. Though the sun rose hours before, you have no sense of time down here in the tunnels. Your only possession is a dimming flashlight and the clothes wet against your skin. Late in the morning, you awaken with the taste of metal in your mouth. You lie on a cardboard slab perched on a warm pipe. Steam groans around you and hissing fluids drip in the darkness. You were dreaming of your lost brother, Antayaar, and hearing his laughter as you imagined the room you knew in the daylight world, a pallet near a potbellied stove. You awaken disoriented, lost. The flashlight illuminates your chamber, a cylindrical cavern split with monstrous pipes carrying hot water to the daylight-world above, and sewage pipes humming below. Other children stir around you and the concrete floor pulses with red-eyed rats. Before the batteries can dim, you shut out the light and let your eyes adjust. Your stomach twists within you, a furred thing with claws, and for a moment, your vision blurs with hunger-pangs.

When you can see again, your friends Batbataar and Unganbataar, both dressed in American-style baseball caps, stand waiting. Batbataar carries a kerosene lantern, a treasured possession in the tunnels, blinding as a torch.

"What is it?" you say. "Have the police come again?" Sometimes the authorities descend into the tunnels with dogs to chase out the children who shelter here illegally. It's not the police, Batbataar tells you, there's something else happening: a new shelter has opened that promises to help the children of Mongolia. You can leave the tunnels and go there.

But life is manageable here. You have friends. Before you knew of this place, you once found a girl beneath a stack of newspapers, eyes turned up to show the whites, her tongue pinched between her teeth. You shut her eyes to the falling snow.

There are too many risks to return to the daylight-world. Maybe this program is just another trick of the police to get you out of a place where you are safe. Stay here. You know enough to avoid the pipes that rupture and fill rooms with boiling steam.

Or perhaps you should search for your family. Before your parents got sick and your brother died, you had food and love. Maybe your father has another job and can provide for you now. Perhaps that is the reason for the dream, a message that means it's time to go back home and find your family once again.

I meet Jesse for the first time at our church's annual harvest festival. After we've been introduced, he looks up at me and asks, "You heard about my brother?"

"Yes," I say. It happened only four days before. My wife was called into the school along with the crisis counselor and the town priest, Father Bill.

"I'm sorry. Your family has been in our prayers."

At Joey's funeral, Father Bill does not hide behind euphemisms when he gives the sermon. He has also lost a brother to suicide, and this memory darkens his voice during the eulogy. He speaks the word *suicide* from the pulpit, and there is a sense of relief in the crowded pews, a lifting. By naming the truth aloud in public assembly, he has not made Joey's death any less terrible. Here is the diagnosis. Here is honesty. Now let there be healing.

I don't like sleeping separately from my wife since she had a second grand mal seizure, less than two weeks before we began this fast. The seizures happen only when she sleeps, just past midnight, a mysterious electric storm in her brain. Minutes pass while her body contorts in a struggle to draw a single breath of oxygen. She's just healed from the last one, the sores gone from her tongue and mouth. I check on her and the girls at the parsonage before settling the boys down for bed. In the up-stairs bedroom of the parsonage, I have prepared a secret stash of food to help her anti-seizure meds go down: pretzel sticks and peanut butter, a Powerbar. "Just run the water so the girls can't hear," I advise. My wife isn't the only one to worry about. One girl, a diabetic, must keep a choc-olate bar near because the fast plays havoc with her blood sugar level. I bid my wife goodnight and head back to the boys, only to discover that two of them, Jesse and another boy, have come to the sleepover without blankets, sleeping bags, or changes of clothing. I find blankets for them and put on a movie in the background, so they can pretend it's not really bedtime while falling fast asleep.

This fast will take most of us into unfamiliar territory since we have never known hunger. If this were April of 1877, we would have heard Governor Pillsbury exhorting Minnesotans to pray and fast to avoid another year of the locust scourges that had terrorized farmers on the prairie. Miraculously, a frost would steal over the land four days after the statewide fast and transform the waiting bronze hordes into calcified dust.

Were we Dakota Indians this fast would be part of a four-day vision quest. Deprived of food and water on some high place in the wilderness, we might hope to see terrible and wonderful things, as described by John Lame Deer at the turn of the century:

> Sounds came to me through the darkness: the cries of the wind, the whisper of the trees . . . I heard a voice that said, "You are sacrificing yourself to become a medicine man. In time, you will be one." Slowly fear left me . . . I felt power surge through me like a flood and when old man Chest came for me, he told me I was no longer a boy.

Food blinds. A hungry hunter is more keen-eyed, senses sharpened. Our bellies filled, it is easier to turn away from poverty and suffering, easier to feel self-sufficient, powerful as wolves. Like the Dakota, we have separated ourselves from this ever-ravenous world by choosing not to eat. For twenty-four hours, in this culture of instant gratification, we are adrift on our own journey. While outside the headlines scream that we are eating ourselves to death and the CDC proclaims that obesity will soon surpass smoking as the number one cause of death, we go hungry. And we hope that in this time, the children's world vision will grow larger and less focused on their own inner angst.

But not every fast ends with a vision or salvation. Not every fast ends well, as one of our early Bible studies during the day points out.

The diabetic girl, Kristin, face already paling in the early hours of evening, reads to us from Isaiah, chapter 58, "We have fasted before you, they say. Why aren't you impressed? We have done much—"

"Penance," my wife encourages.

". . . penance, and you don't even notice it! I tell you why! It is because you are living for yourselves even while you are fasting. You keep right on op—"

"Oppressing."

". . . oppressing your workers. What good is fasting when you keep fighting and quarreling? This kind of fasting will never get you anywhere with me."

We're back to morning again, and sunshine, rare for Minnesota in March, coats the room. Jesse's father, a man called Outlaw around town, has arrived with fresh clothes. I greet him at the door and introduce myself. Outlaw wears a wide-brim Stetson and a chambray shirt knotted with a red kerchief. His boots click across the basement tiles. For all his careful appearance, right down to the walrus mustache that shadows his mouth, I can see he just woke up. His light brown eyes are going yellow, one sign of liver failure. His hand is rough within my own.

"Are you the pastor?" he asks.

"Nope. My wife does the pastoring around here."

"Oh. You got one of them lady pastors."

I nod in response. We continue to make small talk. He drives truck for a living and makes his home in the country. Later my wife will tell me part of his backstory, how difficult it was for him to find work when he got out of prison. Only a local farmer and his wife, members of our congregation, provided him with work and kindness. I am curious about this man who wants to look like he stepped out of a Western, a cowboy in black boots.

"Where's Jesse?" he asks at one point, even though the boy is seated right beside us.

"Right here," I say. Outlaw tells Jesse to go to his mother's tonight when all this is done. An awkward moment of silence spans out. I should tell him to look after his son better. I should tell him about driving home last night and the song his boy sang, or what happened when we came back into town, but I don't.

Last night, when we drove past the City & Country Tavern on the way back to church, Jesse turned and looked toward the bar's parking lot. "You see my dad's truck?"

"Always," his friend said.

I picture the boy's father seated at the bar, a cigarette between his yellowing fingers. He's lost in his private grief, his world shrinking with every drink. Meanwhile, his remaining son drives past in the dark, past the tavern and the great hulking shadow of the Harvestland Co-op, brimful with grain. The boy goes quiet in the car.

With only three hours remaining before we "break fast," our energy dwindles to a bare nub. Headaches make it difficult to concentrate, and none of the games last for very long. To pass time we put in another movie, *Edward Scissorhands*, and build a pile of sleeping bags and pillows on the floor. Movie time becomes nap time for most of us, but Jesse clings to a pole that rises up to the sanctuary, his attention fixed on this modern fairy tale with its misanthropic hero.

Beside me on the hard floor, my wife naps. She is so very pale, my arctic flower, the movement of her breath insubstantial. Like teenagers, we hold hands. Her palm is cold and I squeeze it to keep her from sleeping too deeply. I remain frightened of her deep sleeps, her slipping away; the memory of her last seizure is too vivid. She is the one who must lead us out of this fast.

After the movie, adult volunteers arrive and begin heating the ovens. My wife takes us up to the sanctuary to hold one final worship service, a Communion to "break fast." I am certain the children will be too tired to listen to anything she says, but when she speaks of Jesus in the desert fasting for forty days, they are hushed. She tells them about the devil's temptations, about how Jesus is challenged to turn stones into bread. An easy miracle. We can taste that bread in our mouth, a sweet sun-baked dough that melts on our tongue.

Our church stands at the edge of town, at the edge of endless prairie. Soon boys will move through the fields, clearing stones winter forced up from the earth's spine. April rains will moisten the good black ground. After a green summer, the harvest will be rich and plentiful. "Lord, listen to your children praying," we sing during the time of prayer. And we hope that it is true, the old story. That bread can transport us, touch a longing deeper than the one in our bellies. That we will not forget Boldkhuyag or Joey or all those who suffer famine in one form or another. Soon we will go downstairs and eat the pizza waiting for us, and our stomachs will fill. And as we are sated, may we not be blinded, nor turn from those who hunger.

Tuscan Pizza

This recipe comes from the best cook I know, my cousin Nik Fode, a trained chef who makes his home in Anchorage, Alaska. Nik is also a generous teacher as well.

INGREDIENTS

Dough

1/4 cup olive oil

1 ¾ cups warm water

2 tablespoons honey

2 teaspoons salt

4 cups high-gluten flour

1 teaspoon active yeast

1/2 cup semolina flour

2 tablespoons roughly crushed dry rosemary (optional)

Toppings

Marinara sauce (I recommend Newman's Own of the store-bought
   varieties)
Roma tomatoes
3 ounces prosciutto
Kalamata olives (quartered)
Whole-milk mozzarella cheese
Romano and Asiago cheese (light coating)
Chiffonaded basil and diced chives (for garnish)

RECIPE

Dough

Add wet ingredients together along with honey, salt, and yeast in mixing bowl.

Let yeast activate while stirring theses ingredients using a dough hook in an electric mixer (approximately 10 minutes).

Next, add flour slowly, with the mixer on a medium-low setting.

After all the flour has been added, add the rosemary and allow the mixer to knead the dough for approximately 10 minutes until a smooth consistency has been reached and the dough begins to make a slapping noise while spinning. More flour or water may be needed if the dough feels too sticky (add more flour) or too loose (add more liquid), according to the humidity.

When finished, lightly coat the dough in olive oil and divide it into 4 mounds. Leave the mounds out to proof for approximately 45 minutes while covered with plastic wrap. Dough should be pillow-like.

Each mound of risen dough should be about 9 ounces (1 ounce for each inch in diameter for the pizza you desire). Either hand-toss the pizza or roll it out using a rolling pin. When rolled out to the proper diameter (8 to 9 inches), the mounds will be ready to throw into the oven. Each little ball of dough will become an 8-to-9-inch pizza.

Remember to flour the counter and the top of the dough (or even drop it into a flour-filled salad bowl) in order to keep the dough from sticking while working it out. If all the dough is not to be used, it can be frozen in an airtight container or refrigerated. Make sure to use a pizza paddle (that is, one of those long ones used for manipulating pizzas in the oven) dusted with Semolina to get the built (that is, rolled and spread with ingredients) pie into the oven. I even build pies on the paddle to ensure that they keep their shape until hitting the oven.

Preheat the oven to 500° F, with a pizza stone for best results. The pizza stone should be in the 500° oven for at least a half hour to ensure a proper even heating.

Toppings and baking

Use a choice marinara sauce to *lightly* cover the rolled-out pizza, but leave a half-inch margin around the pizza clear of sauce; this will develop into a crust when the pizza bakes.

Toss a light amount of whole-milk mozzarella cheese over the sauced pizza (the sauce should still be visible).

Evenly fan out freshly sliced (1/16 inch) roma tomatoes over the cheese, followed by thinly sliced strips of prosciutto (around 3 ounces), and quartered kalamata olives (1/4 cup). Be careful to not put too many toppings on the pizza (especially in the center), as this will ruin the crust.

Finish with a light coating of grated Romano and Asiago cheese mixture before placing in the oven.

Watch pizza to make sure browning is even while popping any bubbles that might expand. Five minutes should do the trick, but make sure the bottom does not go beyond a golden brown color and that the top does not burn.

Garnish with some freshly chiffonaded basil and diced chives and then cut into six even pieces. Bon appétit!

MARY KENAGY MITCHELL is the managing editor of *Image*, a quarterly that explores the intersection of art and faith. Her short stories have appeared in the *Georgia Review*, *Image*, *Beloit Fiction Journal*, and the anthologies *Not Safe but Good* and *Peculiar Pilgrims: Stories from the Left Hand of God*. Her awards include a grant from the Seattle Arts Commission and a special mention in the Pushcart Prize Anthology. She occasionally teaches a fiction-writing workshop at Seattle Pacific University.

25

Common Elements

We got married just before Lent. I moved into his apartment in Silicon Valley, where every day the UPS man carried up more extravagant wedding presents. Everything was new: sex, sharing a bathroom, eating regular dinners together (we had lived two states apart the whole time we were dating and engaged), and our stainless steel coffee machine, so beloved that it was almost like a household pet to us.

We felt a combination of elation and mild embarrassment over the presents. Two dutiful, first-born, idealistic Presbyterian kids whose first impulse is usually to save rather than to splurge, we saw the deluge of gifts as a sort of spiritual test. Would having such nice things change us? Would we become slaves of our possessions?

And though our cooking skills didn't go much beyond the basics, we wanted to be the kind of couple who has people over a lot. My husband's favorite way to spend a Saturday evening is a dinner party. He told me when we were first in love that his favorite image of heaven is the wedding feast.

Together we worked our way through our new cookbooks and learned to use our kitchen equipment, making rookie mistakes and feeding our friends until some of them hurt. Life was very rich. We said that to each other a lot.

For me, though, one thing was missing. A few months before we met, I had started the process of becoming a Catholic. A year before we were married, I had entered and joined a church in Seattle with the most visually lush environment imaginable. The community, priest, and music of Saint James were all dear to me, but it was the cathedral that swept me away: a soaring neo-Baroque structure, lovingly restored and crowned with wonders, from the bronze doors and white marble altar to the dark gold chapel of Mary that glowed with fragrant beeswax candles.

The parish church I had found in California was a mid-century construction with an oddly Nordic pitched roof, and to me it looked like an International House of Pancakes. The nervous, young priest said Mass in semi-intelligible bursts. We sang songs I had learned in vacation Bible school, accompanied by three guitars, two flutes, and an electronic keyboard.

But I was determined not to be a fair-weather Catholic. Most Catholics don't get to attend Mass in exquisite cathedrals week after week, and I believed that the beauty and power of the liturgy could come through under even humbler circumstances than this.

When Lent came, I started going to mid-morning daily Mass, partly to fulfill a Lenten obligation to pray more and partly to get myself out of the house—I had been working from home since the move, and I was hungry for human contact. Daily masses were celebrated by a different priest, an elderly man who spoke in a voice husky with years and smoke:

> Blessed are you, Lord, God of all creation. Through your goodness we have this bread to offer, which earth has given and human hands have made. It will become for us the bread of life.

These words were new to me. They are said at Saint James on Sundays, too, but quietly, while the choir sings, and you're sitting at a distance. Here in the tiny side chapel, we all sat close together, the priest hardly more than a table's width away. Speaking seemed an immense labor for him, an act he had to put his shoulder to. Sometimes he'd skip over parts of the Mass altogether, as if hurrying toward the climactic moment. In his gallows rasp, everything sounded urgent, as if each word might be his last. Jesus might have sounded like this when he ate for the last time with his disciples, *knowing he was about to die,* as the liturgy I grew up with put it.

Which human hands have made. Those words, spoken in that ruined, emphysemic voice, followed me home, back to our apartment, where we kept our slow cooker, our china from Luxembourg, our salad bowl big enough to bathe triplets in, and our German-made knives. *Through your goodness we have these gifts to offer.*

On some mornings, a different priest would appear, a serene Filipino man who sang the words in a pure, clear tenor and included prayers for the old priest's health during the intercessions. But the old priest's voice stayed with me, even when he wasn't there.

> *Blessed are you, Lord, God of all creation. Through your goodness*
> *we have this wine to offer, fruit of the vine and work of human*
> *hands. It will become our spiritual drink.*

More than a year later, wherever I hear those words, or see them whispered, I hear that voice. They have become my favorite moment of the Mass. The celebration of the Eucharist begins with an acknowledgment of the elements as ordinary food: gift of the earth, fruit of the vine, work of human hands, sign of God's goodness. Ordinary food is the raw material for the event that stands at the foundation of the Christian life.

I had known this before, but that Lent, fasting, even as briefly and haphazardly as I practiced it, cleared a space for me to take this knowledge in more deeply. The absence of the visual beauties of a cathedral worked the same way, making me alive to the beauty of a well-worn human voice and of the bare words of the liturgy itself. Hunger reminded me of the place of ordinary food—bread made by hands, gift of the earth—in the mystical feast. The common elements are folded into the holy drama, but if they didn't also remain food and drink, we couldn't take them into ourselves.

Each time we eat or drink anything at all, we have a chance to remember this. What better lesson to bring to the first pages of a marriage, a long book full of repetitive chapters, many of them having to do with the gifts of the earth and the fruit of the vine: purchasing and washing and chopping and cooking and storing them, and then cleaning up afterward? Every day at churches large and small, glorious and homely, in every neighborhood of every city, these same common elements are raised up and dignified at the center of the Christian feast.

I like to think that from there that holiness radiates out to every cupboard and pantry and produce drawer in every refrigerator in the neighborhood, and that it's our job—especially the job of a couple with so many wedding presents—to notice the traces of this holy offering and to bring it to our friends and family whenever we feed them.

Salad Dressing

My favorite salad dressing is very simple:

INGREDIENTS

3 parts olive oil
1 part champagne vinegar
Salt and pepper to taste

RECIPE

Just before serving, mix vigorously with a fork until emulsified. Drizzle over a chilled salad and toss very well.

A good, serviceable salad dressing, the kind that holds a salad together without making a spectacle of itself, really needs only four ingredients: oil, vinegar, salt, and pepper. Choosing the oil and vinegar is the fun part. You might use a ratio of two parts oil to one part vinegar, if you like a little more bite, like I do. Or if you prefer more smoothness, as my husband does, you might use four parts oil.

Vinegar

I learned to make salad dressing from my mother, who says it's good to have a vinegar "wardrobe"—much better than spending money on pre-made dressings. Standard vinegars are balsamic, red wine, rice, and cider. More luxurious and delicious are champagne and sherry vinegars. Trader Joe's is a great place to buy your wild and crazy vinegars such as "orange muscat champagne." With a vinegar like that, you can add olive oil, salt, and pepper, and just stand back and wait for the compliments to roll in. Other acids, like lemon or lime juice, can also stand in for vinegar and shine in salads that include fruit.

Oils

Olive, sesame, and walnut are flexible performers. With pricey and flavorful oils like sesame and walnut, you might mix in a plain oil like canola so as not to break the bank.

Extras

Even if you live in an apartment, you can grow dill, tarragon, Italian parsley, basil, mint, thyme, and other herbs in pots if you have a sunny sill. Most herbs are remarkably hard to kill and appreciate being pinched back. Cut them up with sharp scissors (leaving out the stems), and add them to the dressing. It is possible to use more unusual or exotic ingredients in salad dressing, such as jam, fish or soy sauce, beer, yogurt, orange juice concentrate, peanut butter, or pureed carrots and ginger (though not all at once). You want a dressing that plays well with the salad, and with the meal, whether it's hearty or summery, Asian or Italian, fruity or heavy on the protein. But a great dressing doesn't really need more than the basic four ingredients. The key to deliciousness is figuring out what oil-to-vinegar ratio pleases your palate.

My husband would like me to add that avocado goes with everything. Don't skimp. A 1/4 per person is about right.

ALEXANDER SCHMEMANN was a protopresbyter and dean of liturgical theology at St. Vladimir's Orthodox Seminary from 1962 until his untimely death in 1983. He is the author of many books, including *Great Lent, Our Father, O Death Where Is Thy Sting?* and *For the Life of the World: Sacraments and Orthodoxy*, from which this excerpt comes.

26

The Eucharist

Bread and wine: to understand their initial and eternal meaning in the Eucharist we must forget for a time the endless controversies which little by little transformed them into "elements" of an almost abstract theological speculation. . . . The Fathers called "eucharist" the bread and wine of the offering, and their offering and consecration, and finally, communion. All this was *Eucharist* and all this could be understood only within the Eucharist.

. . . . The time has come now to offer to God the totality of all our lives, of ourselves, of the world in which we live. This is the first meaning of our bringing to the altar the elements of our food. For we already know that food is life, that it is the very principle of life and that the whole world has been created as food for man. We also know that to offer this food, this world, this life to God is the initial "eucharistic" function of man, his very fulfillment as man. We know that we were created as *celebrants* of the sacrament of life, of its transformation into life in God, communion with God. We know that real life is "eucharist," a movement of love and adoration toward God, the movement in which alone the meaning and the value of all that exists can be revealed and fulfilled. We know that we have lost this eucharistic life, and finally we know that in Christ, the new Adam, the perfect man, this Eucharistic life was restored to man. For he himself was the perfect Eucharist; he offered himself in total obedience, love and thanksgiving to God. God was his very life. And he gave this perfect and eucharistic life to us. In him God became our life.

And thus this offering to God of bread and wine, of the food that we must eat in order to live, is our offering to him of ourselves, of our life and of the whole world. "To take in our hands the whole world as if it were an apple!" said a Russian poet. It is our Eucharist. It is the movement that Adam failed to perform, and that in Christ has become the very life of man: a movement of adoration and praise in which all joy and suffering, all beauty and all frustration, all hunger and all satisfaction are referred to their ultimate End and become finally *meaningful*. Yes, to be sure, it is a *sacrifice*: but sacrifice is the most natural act of man, the very essence of his life.

⤳

. . . . We are at the paschal table of the Kingdom. What we have offered—our food, our life, ourselves, and the whole world—we offered in Christ and as Christ because he himself has assumed our life and is our life. And now all this is given back to us as the gift of new life, and therefore—necessarily—as food.

"This is my body, this is my blood. Take, eat, drink . . . ." And generations upon generations of theologians ask the same questions. How is this possible? How does this happen? And what exactly does happen in this transformation? And when exactly? And what is the cause? No answer seems to be satisfactory. Symbol? But what is a symbol? Substance, accidents? Yet one immediately feels that something is lacking in all these theories, in which the Sacrament is reduced to the categories of time, substance, and causality, the very categories of "this world."

Something is lacking because the theologian thinks of the sacrament and forgets the liturgy. As a good scientist he first isolates the object of his study, reduces it to one moment, to one "phenomenon"—and then, proceeding from the general to the particular, from the known to the unknown, he gives a definition, which in fact raises more questions than it answers. But throughout our study the main point has been that the whole liturgy is *sacramental*, that is, one transforming act and one ascending movement. And the very goal of this movement of ascension is to take us out of "this world" and to make us partakers of the *world to come*. In *this world*—the one that condemned Christ and by doing so has condemned itself—no bread, no wine can become the body and blood of Christ. Nothing which is a part of it can be "sacralized." But the liturgy of the Church is always an *anaphora*, a lifting up, an ascension. The Church fulfills itself in heaven in that *new eon* which Christ has inaugurated in his death, resurrection, and ascension, and which was given to the Church on the day of Pentecost as its life, as the "end" toward which it moves. In this world Christ is crucified, his body broken, and his blood shed. And we must go out of this world, we must ascend to heaven in Christ in order to become partakers of the world to come.

But this is not an "other" world, different from the one God has created and given to us. It is our same world, *already* perfected in Christ, but *not yet* in us. It is our same world, redeemed and restored, in which Christ "fills all things with himself." And since God has created the world as food for us and has given us food as means of communion with him, of life in him, the new food of the new life which we receive from God in his Kingdom is *Christ himself*. He is our bread—because from the very beginning all our hunger was a hunger for him and all our bread was but a symbol of him, a symbol that had to become reality.

He became man and lived in this world. He ate and drank, and this means that that world of which he partook, the very food of our world became his body, his life. But His life was totally, absolutely *Eucharistic*—all of it was transformed into communion with God and all of it as-cended into heaven. And now he shares this glorified life with us. "What I have done alone—I give it now to you: take, eat . . . ."

We offered the bread in remembrance of Christ because we know that Christ is Life, and all food, therefore, must lead us to him. And now when we receive this bread from his hands, we know that he has taken up all life, filled it with himself, made it what it was meant to be: communion with God, sacrament of his presence and love. Only in the Kingdom can we confess with St. Basil that "this bread is in very truth the precious body of our Lord, this wine the precious blood of Christ." What is "supernatural" here, in *this world*, is revealed as "natural" there. And it is always in order to lead us "there" and to make us what we are that the Church fulfills herself in liturgy.

Luci Shaw is a poet, essayist, and writer in residence at Regent College, Vancouver, Canada. In 1972, Luci and her husband Harold Shaw began a publishing house that specialized in "literature for thoughtful Christians." Much of her work involved editing authors such as Madeleine L'Engle. After Harold's death, Luci became president of the company. In 1991, she married John Hoyte and later moved to Bellingham, Washington, where they now live. Luci is the author of widely anthologized poetry and nonfiction prose. Her most recent books are *Accompanied by Angels*, *What the Light Was Like*, and *Breath for the Bones: Art, Imagination & Spirit*. Her most recent release, *Harvesting Fog*, is her thirtieth book. She is an enthusiastic camper, sailor, photographer, and gardener. She has five children and growing numbers of grandchildren and great-grandchildren.

27

Soul Food

My mother was a queen of domesticity. Her cookery was precise and delicious, her kitchen a model of organization. She always set the table with candles, flowers from our garden (she had a vividly green thumb), and white linen table napkins, rolled neatly in silver napkin rings on which each of our initials were inscribed. Beauty and order prevailed; everything bent to her will.

Good table manners were essential to my mother—careless elbows on the table were firmly thumped, bread was to be "broken, not cut." If we felt something in our mouths like fish bones or gristle that was hard to chew, we were to discreetly convey it to the side of the plate. We were expected to finish every crumb of our bread or toast including (of course) the crusts. I loved the soft, wheaty insides of bread lightly buttered, but I despised those bread crusts. Years later, when the house was sold and the oak table disassembled, we found a dusty row of old, dry crusts on a ledge under the edge of the table. I had become skilled in palming them and inconspicuously hiding them from view.

On the sly, I was sometimes able to break free and experiment with my own ideas of food. Under my mom's watchful eye, the kitchen was, like the dinner table, a place of rules and regulations. Recipes were the law of some golden order. But on Saturdays, perhaps in preparation for the iron-clad observance of Sunday, the Lord's Day, when normal activities like reading novels or shopping were banned, Mother's rules were relaxed a bit, and I was free to dream the impossible—could flour, orange juice, and beaten egg whites end up as a dessert soufflé? What would emerge if I combined cheese and grated raw potato with baking powder and seasonings, cooked in an oven at low heat? Sometimes these combinations ended up edible, sometimes not, but the excitement of putting ingredients together *without* a recipe gave me that exhilarating taste that came from freely creating something on my own.

But my secret disposal of the unwanted crusts and these moments of culinary freedom were the exception to my mother's rule. Her weight scale and measuring cups, her unrelenting expectations for perfection— these traits pushed me to seek her specific rubric of approval in every- thing. I remember how one year when she was ill I made her breakfast in bed, and she coldly remarked that the boiled egg was overcooked and the toast not crisp enough.

I learned that it was vital to *earn* approval by pleasing people, to justify my existence by following rules and fulfilling expectations. My perceived inadequacies always rose like brick walls between me and my idea of how to be in the world. I was sent to a prestigious girl's private school, but I had to sit at the side of the gym when the other children learned the waltz in our physical education class—dancing was carnal. And because associating with those who danced was viewed by my fam- ily with suspicion, I was forbidden to attend any parties. My desire to meet my mother's standards made me an outsider. Since then, recogni- tion and approval have become my food and drink.

Though I'd been adequately fed, housed, and educated, I lacked spiritual and emotional nourishment; I longed for unconditional love. Christian duty and obedience were the key words in our family credo, not compassion and forgiveness. I always felt we had a kind of Old Testament, judicial God, on the watch for iniquity.

Growing up, we belonged to a conservative church community modeled on the pattern suggested in the book of Acts. We took the Lord's Supper each Sunday, and we observed Communion as a memorial, not as a sacrament, with the bread and wine representing not only the body and blood of Jesus, but also the essential food and drink of life and faith. My parents had been missionaries, and on the Pacific island chain where they worked, things like wine and bread were usually unobtainable. They used bananas and coconut milk as the elements for the Communion meal in their worship services with the native peoples, substitutes that worked quite well in that context as symbols of divinely given food and drink, pointers to the provision made by a generous God. Communion was meant not only for body, but for soul nourishment.

Somehow, though, this sense of Communion didn't translate to my childhood. I longed for love, mother love, not based on how "good" I was or how well I succeeded, but a tender, loving maternal care. I was often reminded by my mother that it was my duty to love her, that we were to live by fact and faith, not by feelings. This felt arbitrary, abstract, and obligatory. It lacked true embrace or emotional closeness. It lacked skin and heart.

I have a ragged cookbook from my early days as a wife and mother. Between its covers still lie the detailed, yellowed, grease-stained slips of paper with recipes for my mother's favorite dishes. There are the pikelets, small Scottish pancakes that are served cold and spread with jam, honey or butter. There are her Indian curries and green tomato chutneys, for which I now grow my own tomatoes, adding raisins and onions and apple vinegar, extending the short summer life of this luscious fruit into winter in a relish that harkens me back to the Toronto kitchen of my childhood and redeems some of my regrets.

My mother's specialty was a hot-milk sponge cake that required only flour, baking powder, a tablespoon of butter, two eggs, and a cup of scalded milk. Every family birthday, I still make this delicious cake, dressed up with jam and whipped cream between the layers, and on the top, a decoration of frosting sugar lightly shaken through a lace paper doily.

And there is "French steak," a dish that is prepared by cubing beef into a casserole dish and slow-cooking it, covered, in a sauce of brown sugar, ketchup, vinegar, Worcestershire sauce, water, and flour. All my children have versions of this dish, so simple to prepare, and vigorous family discussions occur about proportions of the ingredients.

My children also call me to help with culinary improvisation. When my son John was in England, studying at the London School of Tropical Medicine, he sometimes made transatlantic phone calls to me with questions about the recipes he cooked in his tiny third-floor flat. He had to run down two flights of narrow stairs to the house phone to ask me how long to bake the Yorkshire pudding in the drippings from the roast of beef. Or he'd wonder, "Mom, I'm doing crème brûlée for friends, but I don't have a torch for caramelizing. Any ideas?" Or "How do I keep oyster stuffing from getting slimy?" A fine doctor, a poet, and an imaginative man who still cooks with love in his heart, I am blessed that he and Christa are my neighbors, getting together with us for a meal every week.

I still hunger for emotional and spiritual nourishment, and I occasionally grimace as I think back on my mother's rules and unrealistic expectations. When I take Communion in my Episcopal Church, I go to kneel at the altar like a hungry baby bird, or like the widow in the Jesus story who was willing to eat the crumbs that fell from the table to the floor. I am ravenous for the food dealt out in wafer and wine, in the circle of the loving presence of Christ, with others who are also starving for this inner nourishment, the kind that finally assures me of an unconditional love.

And so each week, as I kneel at the Lord's Table and then I dine with Christa and John, perhaps over my mother's hot-milk sponge cake or her rhubarb pie, I realize that the freedom and love that accompanies our eating is the soul food that God has freely given me, a soul food that I now live to provide for my own children.

Luci's Mother's Hot-Milk Sponge Cake

INGREDIENTS

2 eggs

1 cup sugar

1 teaspoon vanilla

1 cup all-purpose flour

1 teaspoon baking powder

1/4 teaspoon salt

1/2 cup 2-percent milk

1 tablespoon butter or margarine

Serves 9 to 10

RECIPE

Beat the eggs well.

Add the sugar and vanilla.

Beat the mixture until light.

Combine the flour, baking powder, and salt separately.

Fold the dry ingredients into an egg mixture.

Bring to boil the milk and butter.

Slowly add the boiling milk and butter to the batter, stirring gently.

Pour the batter into a greased and floured 9x9-inch pan.

Recipe may be doubled to make a 2-layer cake.

HANNAH FAITH NOTESS is managing editor of Seattle Pacific University's *Response* magazine and the editor of *Jesus Girls: True Tales of Growing Up Female and Evangelical*, a collection of personal essays. Her writing has appeared in publications such as the *Christian Century, Christianity and Literature, Los Angeles Review,* and *Slate*. She lives in Seattle, where she battles garden slugs, covets other people's backyard poultry, and attempts to cook with dark leafy greens.

28

A Blessing for the Rice Cracker

The last time I took Communion with my brother Ben, we walked down the aisle as the worship band played soft praise choruses. We both took a chunk of bread, dipped it in grape juice, and gulped it down before heading back to our seats. This might not sound like an act of teenage rebellion. But for Ben, it was.

Ben was diagnosed with celiac disease when he was eleven; he and my mother both tested positive for celiac disease in a routine screening at the juvenile diabetes clinic he'd been going to since age three. The doctors told him that in the biopsy, his intestines looked stressed-out. And now, in addition to all the potential health risks of diabetes, he was at risk for even more unpleasant diseases, such as colon cancer.

But there was a cure.

The cure, the only known cure, is a gluten-free diet. This means abstinence from the following culinary delights: pizza, spaghetti, chocolate chip cookies, cream puffs, birthday cake, bagels, Twinkies, beer, fried chicken, fish 'n' chips, macaroni and cheese, fettuccine Alfredo, sweet-and-sour pork, couscous, most soy sauce, most canned soups, most gravies, and most breads.

If you are on a gluten-free diet, life is just a little easier if you avoid certain places and activities: Italian restaurants, Chinese restaurants, bakeries, birthday parties, office coffee-and-donut breaks, and Holy Communion.

I was away at college around the time of the celiac diagnosis, but when I came home on break, the kitchen had undergone a transformation. If we were having spaghetti for dinner, two pots of pasta bubbled on the stove. There were two tubs of I Can't Believe It's Not Butter in the fridge and two toasters on the counter. It reminded me of one of those kosher kitchens with two separate ovens so that the meat never touches the milk. My mom observes the gluten-free diet seriously, one might even say religiously.

At times, I feel like a convert. It turns out that rice-flour brownie mix isn't bad. And she's perfected an angel food cake she likes to serve on the Fourth of July, covered with Cool Whip and fresh strawberries and blueberries in an American flag pattern, tasty enough to start any cynic humming "God Bless America."

The next summer, Ben was a camper at the camp where I was working as a volunteer counselor. My mom came too, carting a giant cooler of food. That week, she answered phones in the camp office, so at mealtimes she could run up to the kitchen and make food for herself and Ben. That way he could play capture the flag without worrying that his dinner would turn out to be fried chicken and biscuits, or something else he couldn't eat. It was a lot of work for her, and Ben tells me he appreciates it even more now, since he's moved out and has to cook for himself.

But when he was in high school—well, he was a teenager. He dyed his hair pink and got his forearms tattooed. And he ignored adults' advice, including the advice of his doctors. He cheated on his diet—he cheated a lot. He snuck pizza at the school cafeteria. He never checked labels for "modified food starch" or "hydrolyzed wheat protein." He just wanted to do what normal people did.

Eventually Ben started to feel side effects. He developed a painful rash on his elbows, and when he ate wheat, he began to feel his throat closing up. He's stuck to the diet since then, but that hasn't changed the fact that celiac disease can make him feel like an outsider. When I asked Ben why he used to avoid the rice cracker at Communion, he said he felt uncomfortable stepping out of line. Even though the church was doing its best to be inclusive, it didn't seem to fit the ritual, and he didn't want to feel different.

And despite people's best attempts at gluten-free cooking, despite the church's best intentions, gluten-free substitutes just aren't the same. As Ben says, "It's either an Oreo, or it's not an Oreo. There's no semi-Oreo."

Ben's position on Oreos is not unlike the Catholic Church's position on the eucharistic wafer. In order for the elements to become the *actual* body and blood of Christ, say the Church authorities, they have to start out being *actual* bread and wine. There's no semi-Eucharist.

Some parishioners and priests have petitioned to use a gluten-free substitute, such as the rice cracker, during Mass. But they've been turned down. The church officials who decide about these matters are called the Congregation for the Doctrine of the Faith—back in the day they were called the Inquisition, so yes, they're serious. And to be honest, I admire that seriousness. This is *Christ* we're eating. We've been performing this ritual for nearly two thousand years; we shouldn't mess with it now just because of somebody's allergies.

At the same time, does it really make sense for the Church to deny grace to someone because of a physical condition? If some of the members of Christ's body are fasting, not by their own volition, but because they want to stay alive, how can they be forbidden from taking part in the one true feast, the meal that speaks of eternal life?

Fortunately for Catholics with celiac disease, a low-gluten (less than 0.01 percent), Congregation for the Doctrine of the Faith–approved wafer has been produced by some forward-thinking nuns in Missouri. These Benedictine Sisters cut each wafer by hand and, I imagine, do it with extra tender loving care. My brother could almost surely eat this wafer without his throat closing up. I admire the careful craft of the hand-cut wafers, just as I admire the Congregation for the Doctrine of the Faith's consistency and clarity in saying "we have to do this right."

By contrast, the bread I've partaken over the years in assorted Protestant churches has taken a variety of forms—papier-mâché-flavored squares in a silver tray; stale oyster crackers on a plastic plate; a giant wad of fresh-baked multigrain bread that took ten minutes to chew, even when soaked in juice; and chopped-up matzo crackers that (we were told) were better than everyone else's Communion bread because they were more Jewish and therefore more like what Jesus actually ate on the night he was betrayed. I've waited out an awkward pause in the music while the pianist ducked her head for a wafer. I've listened to a pastor stumble over his explanation of "intinction." I've passed a bottle of hand sanitizer around before passing the loaf and then tasting the sanitizer's chemical tang as I ate the bread.

Communion is messy, awkward, and confusing, but I keep coming back because I need it, even if I can't quite explain why. And though I gaze with awe and respect (and perhaps idealistic longing) upon the constancy and beauty of the Catholic approach, it is Communion that leaves me Protestant. I want to be able to partake of Communion with my Protestant family, even if that Communion is weird-tasting flour-and-water nuggets, and even if I don't always understand what it means.

From what I do understand, Communion symbolizes the church's unity: first, we are united because we all partake together, and second, we are united because we all eat the same substance, the same body of Christ. But celiac disease forces churches to choose between unity and inclusiveness. Either we all partake of the same body, or we invite everyone to the table. We may sing "Let us break bread together on our knees," but we can't actually do it, because Ben's elbows might break out in a painful rash.

What if churches just served rice crackers to everybody? I asked Ben if he thought that would be a good idea, and he said he did: "There's nowhere in the Bible that says 'This needs to be made from wheat flour, thus saith the Lord.'" Those rice crackers may taste like Styrofoam packing peanuts, but I'd consider that Styrofoam taste a blessing if it meant I could share Communion with my brother.

And think about those little thimbles of grape juice. Until Prohibition activists exorcised the demon of drink from American churches, making a fortune for a guy named Welch, Protestants used to drink *actual* wine during Communion. Although many church attitudes toward alcohol have softened since Prohibition, we still use grape juice, in part to avoid pushing recovering alcoholics off the wagon, to avoid making them break the fast they must keep to live a better life. Churches could help people with celiac disease keep their fast in a similar way.

Remember the loaf of bread doused in hand sanitizer? That particular Sunday, we stood in a circle, passing the bread around, and each person said the words of institution—"Body of Christ"—to the person next to them. The bread eventually made its way around the circle to a woman in our church whose lively artist hands have been mostly stilled by multiple sclerosis.

After her neighbor placed the bread in her mouth, the woman wasn't able to take the loaf and offer it to the person next to her, her husband. So the husband gently took the loaf from the person who had just fed his wife. His wife then looked up at him from her wheelchair to say the words of institution—"Body of Christ"—as he broke off a piece of the loaf and put it in his own mouth. He bent over her slightly as he did this, as if to receive a blessing, and then passed the loaf on as if this, feeding himself the bread, was all quite ordinary. He fed himself, but I saw him receive grace.

Perhaps there is no way to smooth over the awkward truth. Our bodies are broken, diseased, and hurting. Some of us have bodies that can't accept the physical substance of Christ's bread of life—in this life. And yet, it is in this human life, among these sick and achy bodies, that Christ came to join us, to eat with us, to break this bread with calloused human hands.

Fourth of July Cake

INGREDIENTS

Cake

7 eggs
1 ½ cups sugar
1 ½ tablespoons lemon juice
1 ½ teaspoons grated lemon zest
3/4 cup potato starch
Dash salt

Topping

1 8-ounce container Cool Whip Lite
1 cup blueberries
2 to 3 cups strawberries, sliced in half (lengthwise)

RECIPE

Separate 6 of the eggs. Beat the 6 yolks and 1 whole egg until frothy. Gradually add the sugar, lemon juice, and lemon rind, beating constantly and thoroughly. Then gradually add potato starch, stirring constantly until blended.

Beat egg whites with salt until stiff but not dry. Fold gently but thoroughly into the egg yolk mixture.

Place in ungreased 9x13-inch glass baking dish. Bake at 350° F about 55 minutes, until the cake springs back after touched gently with fingers.

When cake is completely cool, cover with Cool Whip Lite.

Make an American flag pattern using blueberries in the top left corner to indicate stars, and put strawberries in lines (with Cool Whip showing between the lines) to indicate red and white stripes. Chill until ready to serve.

ANDRE DUBUS is considered by many to be one of the nation's best short story writers, but his essays, many of which openly express his struggles with faith and suffering, are just as powerful. While assisting a stranded motorist in 1986, he was struck by a car, losing one leg and the use of the other. Despite his great loss, and his confinement to a wheelchair, he continued to write. He authored numerous collections of short stories and essays including *Broken Vessels, Dancing after Hours*, and *Meditations from a Moving Chair*. He was awarded a Pen/Malamud award, a Rea Award, and fellowships from the Guggenheim and MacArthur Foundations. He died in 1996 at the age of sixty-one. This is an excerpt from *Broken Vessels*.

29

On Charon's Wharf

Since we are all terminally ill, each breath and step and day is closer to the last, I must consider those sacraments which soothe our passage. I write on a Wednesday morning in December when snow covers the earth, the sky is gray and the evergreens seem alive. This morning I received a sacrament I still believe in: at seven-fifteen the priest elevated the host, then the chalice, and spoke the words of the ritual, and the bread became flesh, the wine became blood, and minutes later I placed on my tongue the taste of forgiveness and love that affirmed, perhaps celebrated, my being alive, my being mortal. This has nothing to do with immortality, with eternity; I love the earth too much to contemplate a life apart from it, although I believe in that life. No, this has to do with mortality and the touch of flesh, and my belief in the sacrament of the Eucharist is simple: without touch, God is a monologue, an idea, a philosophy; he must touch and be touched, the tongue on flesh, and that touch is the result of monologues, the idea, the philosophies which lead to faith; but in the instant of the touch there is no place for thinking, for talking; the silent touch affirms all that, and goes deeper: it affirms the mysteries of love and mortality.

And that is why I am drawn again and again to see Bergman's *The Seventh Seal,* to watch the knight who, because finally he has been told by Death that he is going to die, must now act within that knowledge, and for the rest of the movie he lives in constant touch with his mortality, as we all should every day, with everyone (but we don't, we don't, we are distracted, we run errands . . .); and that is why one of my favorite scenes in the movie is the knight sitting on the earth with the young couple and their child, and the woman offers him a bowl of berries: he reaches out with both hands, receives the bowl from her, and eats, and the scene is invested with his awareness that his time is confused and lonely and fearful and short, but for these moments, with these people, with the gift of food, he has been given an eternal touch: eternal because, although death will destroy him, it cannot obliterate the act between him and the woman. She has given him the food. He has taken it. In the face of time, the act is completed. Death cannot touch it now, can only finally stop the hearts that were united in it.

So many of us fail: we divorce our wives and husbands, we leave the roofs of our lovers, go once again into the lonely march, mustering our courage with work, friends, half pleasures which are not whole because they are not shared. Yet still I believe in love's possibility, in its presence on the earth; as I believe I can approach the altar on any morning on any day which may be the last and receive the touch that dies not, for me, say: There is not death; but does say: In this instant I recognize, with you, that you must die. And I believe I can do this in an ordinary kitchen with an ordinary woman and five eggs. I scramble them in a saucepan, as my now-dead friend taught me; they stand deeper and cook softer, he said. I take our plates, spoon eggs on them, we set and eat. She and I and the kitchen have become extraordinary: we are not simply eating; we are pausing in the march to perform an act together; we are in love; and the meal offered and received is a sacrament which says: I know you will die; I am sharing food with you; it is all I can do, and it is everything.

As lovers we must have these sacraments, these actions which restore our focus, and therefore ourselves. For our lives are hurried and much too distracted, and one of the strangest and most dangerous of all distractions is this lethargy of self we suffer from, this part of ourselves that does not want to get out of bed and once out of bed does not want to dress and once dressed does not want to prepare breakfast and once fed does not want to work. And what does it want? Perhaps it wants nothing at all. It is a mystery, a lovely one because it is human, but it is also dangerous. Some days it does not want to love, and we yield to it, we drop into an abyss whose walls echo with strange dialogues. These dialogues are with the beloved, and at their center is a repetition of the word *I* and sometimes *you*, but neither word now is uttered with a nimbus of blessing. These are the nights when we sit in that kitchen and talk long and too much, so that the words multiply each other, and what they express—pain, doubt, anxiousness, dread—becomes emotions which are not rooted in our true (or better) selves, which exist apart from those two gentle people who shared eggs at this same table which is now soiled with ashes and glass-rings.

~

So what I want and want to give, more than the intimacy of words, is shared ritual, the sacraments. I believe that, without those, all our talking, no matter how enlightened, will finally drain us, divide us into two confused and frustrated people, then destroy us as lovers. We are of the flesh, and we must turn with faith toward that truth. We need the companion on the march, the arms and lips and body against the dark of the night. It is our flesh which lives in time and will die, and it is our love which comforts the flesh. Beneath all the words we must have this daily acknowledgment from the beloved, and we must give it too or pay the lonely price of not living fully in the world: that as lovers we live on Charon's wharf, and he's out there somewhere in that boat of his, and today he may row in to where we sit laughing, and reach out to grasp an ankle, hers or mine.

It would be madness to try to live so intensely as lovers that every word and every gesture between us was a sacrament, a pure sign that our love exists despite and perhaps even because of our mortality. But we can do what the priest does, with his morning consecration before entering the routine of his day; what the communicant does in that instant of touch, that quick song of the flesh, before he goes to work. We can bring our human, distracted love into focus with an act that doesn't need words, an act which dramatizes for us what we are together. The act itself can be anything: five beaten and scrambled eggs, two glasses of wine, running beside each other in rhythm with the pace and breath of the beloved. They are all parts of that loveliest of all sacraments between man and woman, that passionate harmony of flesh whose breath and dance and murmur says: We are, we are, we *are* . . .

Vinita Hampton Wright has been writing—and cooking—for many years. Currently she is senior book editor at Loyola Press in Chicago. Her novels include *Velma Still Cooks in Leeway* (winner of Logos Book Award, Best Fiction of 2000) and *Dwelling Places* (Christianity Today Award for Best Fiction 2007). Her nonfiction titles are *The Soul Tells a Story, Simple Acts of Moving Forward, A Catalogue of Angels, The St. Thérèse of Lisieux Prayer Book,* and *Days of Deepening Friendship.* Vinita and her husband, Jim, reside on Chicago's South Side, where they keep a tiny vegetable-and-herb garden for the purpose of "tasting real tomatoes at least during the summer."

30

Grandma Virgi's Feast

As the holidays approach, my guilt increases. It is not guilt for what I have already done, but for what I plan to do. It is guilt over a sin that I commit boldly and confess only after New Years. With the benefit of up-to-date information on health and diet, and knowing full well the importance of green, leafy vegetables and lots of fiber, I am already overcome by visions of the holiday table. It is a gruesome sight to the health conscious, to the guardians of their bodies, to the well-toned soldiers of the Lord. But it is my cherished vision and I cannot give it up. I always say that I have a good excuse. I am a Sellars.

Sellars is my mother's mother's maiden name. The Sellars family hailed from the hills of Southwest Missouri. Grandma Virgi, my mother's mother, spent her early childhood in a log cabin back in the Ozarks. Whenever I go home, I like to get her and her sisters talking about those years. Their dad and his brothers had a small farm. On the side, they gigged frogs, which they would ship to restaurants in St. Louis. Grandma's father was killed on a Sunday—shot in a saloon over a card game. The men came and got Great-grandma Mamie out of church to tell her.

Mamie took in ironings to feed her six children. Like many folks during the Depression, they barely survived. Eventually Mamie ended up here in Chicago, chief cook for a rich couple who had a home on the north lakefront. When my mother was a little girl, she would come up summers and stay with her Grandma Mamie in her quarters. Mamie would open up the family's refrigerator—which, in my mother's memory, ran the length of an entire wall—and let Mom choose whatever she wanted to eat. Not a bad treat for a little girl whose immediate ancestors had nearly starved to death just a few years earlier. As for Mamie's cooking, the people she worked for insisted that she make her own dishes, not digress to any trendy, city cooking. Oh no, they wanted honest-to-God gravy and pie crusts that flaked into buttery memory if you so much as looked at them with true longing in your heart.

How well I know about this, coming as I do from a string of women in several generations of kitchens in which butter fat meant luxury; sugar cubes spoke civility; second and third helpings were the least of courtesy; and bubbling, meaty gravy was a downright necessity: luxurious eating habits are hard to break. To the women in my family, green, leafy vegetables are something you decorate with, like a leaf of lettuce to lace the plate under a pound or two of lime & pineapple–cream cheese molded salad. Green beans are not something to be sautéed or stir-fried, but boiled for hours with hunks of salty ham and new potatoes. Fiber is provided through baked sweet potatoes, loaded with peaches, brown sugar, and marshmallows. To women for whom cooking is both art and reputation, preparing meals only half fulfills their life purpose. To be validated is to be eaten out of house and home. If you set foot in Grandma Virgi's house, you will eat. She welcomes you as though it were still the turn of the century, when company chugged along by buggy or Model T for near-starvation hours between destinations. Whatever time of day, a new meal begins after the cursory greetings, and if you wish to visit, you may as well scoot your chair to the doorway of the kitchen, where Virgi is melting Crisco into skillets, renovating the leftovers from her last guest dinner (sometime yesterday), and cutting the pecan pie or coconut cake into mile sections, one per guest.

Holiday dinners are her zenith, times meant for hearty meals served to the entire extended family, captives all. Virgi lines up her battle plan while peeling potatoes; by the time the first group has arrived, she knows where each person will be seated and what dishes will be served from which stations. When the food is ready to serve, she begins tugging guests from living rooms and porches and conversations, directing each to his or her place, and the one who hesitates, whether five years old or fifty, receives a verbal box to the ears. Once seated, there is no way out but to tunnel with spoon, fork, and knife, through three kinds of meat, vegetable variations (vegetables are made edible by cream soups, cheeses, and sauces, the way fruits are presented only in the context of pastry or Jell-O), potatoes, homemade noodles, relishes, rolls, dressing, and—never the least—gravy.

She watches us like a foreman overseeing construction of the Hoover Dam, with eyes that can barely make out the newspaper cross-word puzzle without glasses yet somehow latch onto the single hand that passes down the noodle-chicken-and-cheese casserole without ladling some onto the plate. If a dish gets held up in heavy traffic at one end of the table, she's there to rescue it back into service. And all the while, a steady rhythm of orders: *Randy, there's scalloped corn over there. Blanche, aren't you going to try this new broccoli-rice casserole? Jessica, pass the dressing over to Bud, I think he missed it—you didn't? Why don't you want dressing? It's the kind you like. You all don't miss the relish plates over there on the card table. Valerie—what do you need?* This last question is fired at anyone with an inch of white space on her plate or who has been thoughtless enough to stop chewing.

Eventually, in the manner of all older women in farm communities who are used to feeding everyone else first, Virgi does sit down to the table herself, consuming without emotion the cold remains. The flavor is still there, but for her the thrill is gone, unless a latecomer walks in whom she can coax over and feed.

But her day is not over yet. Two hours after dinner, she becomes the Dessert Commando. Wherever you are, reclined and belching help-lessly like a foundered horse because you haven't eaten a meal this size since the last holiday, whatever sofa or floor space upon which you are prostrated, she hunts you down and aims the question right at your pleading eyes: *Which dessert do you want?* She then proceeds down the list of homemade pies and cakes, which are identified by their creators. It's Virginia Lee's pumpkin pie, Veta's pecan pie, Blanche's pineapple cake, Grandma's own Cherrie Delight. There's also Cindy's caramel corn, Lorraine's fudge, and Amy's homemade cherry chocolates. And also nearly three tons of cookies in many styles, but these things do not count as dessert; they are merely snacks.

The correct response to Virgi's question is to name your dessert. This should not at all be related to your hunger or lack thereof. Should you decline, she asks, "You don't want dessert?" in the same tone you would expect to hear her saying, "You'll not mourn me when I'm dead?"

Once you have given your preference, she demands, "What kind of ice cream do you want with that? Or would you rather have whipped cream? I can put on both if you like"—this last offer is in a kinder tone, but don't be fooled; she lets no one off the hook.

The best you can do is ask for "just a sliver, Grandma." This request will bring you an only slightly smaller-than-normal hunk of confection. There is no small size in the Sellars mentality. Virgi can take four pies and divide them among sixty people so that each person gets a fourth of a pie. Jesus could have taken lessons from her.

Which is why I think Jesus understands my holiday failings. Although his Spirit reminds me that my body is a temple, he understands the comfort of abundance—and the nurturing properties of food. When he walked among us, he enjoyed the pungent flavor of roasted fish over a beach fire, the rich offerings of wedding feasts, the breads and sweets and savory meats served up by the hands of Jewish mothers and aunts and grandmothers during celebrations of family or faith. He understands the relief we experience when the harvest has been brought in, safe and sound, to sustain us through another season. He knows the unspoken yet overwhelming sense of thankfulness as we gather around the communal table and see those who have survived the storms and change of one more year, those whose love and—yes, idiosyncrasies—continue to grace our lives.

I, too, enjoy these seasonal, culinary extravagances, not merely for their taste, but as a matter of memory and family connection. Now that I'm a city girl, living not that far from where Great-grandma Mamie served up country delicacies on the North Shore, I am creating recipes and traditions of my own. They tend toward less of the personal and social evils such as fat, sodium, sugar, and cholesterol. But my inspiration is fueled by the Sellars spirit. In my very heart I know that any table handsomely set, steaming, and ready says today as always, "You are welcome here." And—through the Depression or recession, through moments of celebration or painful loss, through the passing of our elders and the birthing of new generations—there will somehow always be room to set one more place at the table.

Pecan Pie

I first wrote "Grandma Virgi's Feast" more than a decade ago and read it to my grandma and other relatives at one of those lovely holiday dinners. Grandma Virgi died a few years ago, and now her daughter (and my mother), Virginia, makes certain that regular feasts continue. Meanwhile, I collect and invent recipes and boss around my dinner guests almost as effectively as Grandma once did.

This recipe was created for my novel, *Velma Still Cooks in Leeway*, in which it first appeared in 2000. Used by permission.

INGREDIENTS

3 eggs
1/3 cup sugar
1/2 teaspoon salt
1/2 teaspoon cinnamon
1/2 teaspoon ground ginger
1/2 teaspoon nutmeg
1 tablespoon cornstarch
1/4 cup butter, melted
2/3 cup light corn syrup
1/3 cup peach preserves
1 cup pecan halves

RECIPE

Prepare a standard piecrust, or buy one ready-made.
Heat oven to 375° F. With a mixer, combine eggs, sugar, salt, cinnamon, ginger, nutmeg, cornstarch, butter, corn syrup, and peach preserves. Stir in pecans. Pour into the piecrust.

Bake until set, 40 to 50 minutes. Let it cool at least half an hour before serving.

Jeremy Clive Huggins is an adjunct everything. In his ample free time, he builds things, fills out the *New York Times* crossword, and plays trains with his toddler. His house in St. Louis, Missouri, features chickens in the backyard and a grill in the front. A brief list of his idols, mentors, and influences includes John McPhee, Thomas Lynch, Natalie Kusz, Wade Bradshaw, Jock McGregor, BBQ (pulled pork with vinegar-based sauce, please), Saturday morning NPR, and the song "Loro" by Pinback.

31

The Church Potluck, Seriously

When choosing between green bean casseroles, I'm faced with a problem: do I go with or without Durkee fried onions? It's not a life-and-death problem, but it matters to me. I usually go with. I need the texture, something to hold the mass together on both the palate and the plate. Perhaps you feel otherwise. Or your feelings are mixed. Not just on the fried onions, but on the whole enterprise, this religious custom of eating together. Behold the church potluck.

Perhaps you are on the church grounds and the weather is lovely. Having filled your plate with an impossible assortment of salads and proteins and pastries, you get comfortable on your quilt. You are with your family or with friends whom you consider family. Having worshipped in creed and Word and hymn, you now give thanks for the gifts of downtime, of laughter, of fellowship. The children are running and playing tag, their mouths crammed with brownies, and you aren't worried. This is no time to be tense. Tell stories. Catch up. Rest. Eat. Be glad.

I, however, am more likely in the church basement. Someone who will not be thanked arrived early and set up a gauntlet of wood-veneer folding tables whose corners have disintegrated. The tables perform architectural miracle by bearing the load of soggy lasagnas, pounds of Pyrexed casseroles, buckets of chicken, a singular serving of twice-baked fish, and baskets of garlic bread, one of which was surely seasoned by someone who mistook "tsp" for "tbsp."

As a rule, I avoid Jell-O containing anything besides more Jell-O. I'm in line, and I can see that the Grant children—bless their greedy little hearts—have pillaged the home-baked lemon squares, leaving unmangled only the store-bought M&M cookies. Honey-baked ham hunks gelatinize. At the end of the tables: a solo pack of cups (thanks, Dave—you *always* bring cups), plastic knives, napkin stack.

I forgot to have Michael save me a seat, so I'm most likely stuck, again, at a table with Elder Maynor, who will ask, again, "Why don't we stop saying 'potluck'?"

His question is both predictable and rhetorical, but he will answer anyway: "We should call it potprovidence!" I stuff my face with meatloaf, heavy on the ketchup.

Our experience at the table differs. Some have tasted glory, some ruin. All of us, though, regardless of denomination or geography, have eaten, have fed and been fed. This tradition, despite the motives by which we enact it and the meanings with which we infuse it, requires food. Despite our differences, it's just food.

But it's never just food.

I joined the church my freshman year of college. My college was located in a very southern town in Mississippi, a state that takes pride in feeding people. This church didn't take me into its fold so much as group-hug me into belonging. They took seriously their call to love people, especially people who weren't eating right. I was one of those people, an undergrad with an underfed bank account and an eager appetite. The day I joined the church, I stood in front of the congregation, recited membership vows, was baptized, was hugged, and was fed. Over the next five years, I would receive their guidance, their encouragement, their BBQ, their crawfish boils, their sun-brewed tea, and their love, sweet in equal measure. I drank and ate it up.

I never brought anything to those potlucks, and no one said a thing. "Just bring yourself," they'd say, "that's enough." I believed them. I went as I was: empty-handed, needy, and willing to receive.

The church potluck as we know it has no direct biblical precedent. Its origins are murky, and no one, it seems, is too concerned. The word itself can be found in manuscripts as early as the sixteenth century, in, as I call them, the olden times, as in "Ye Olde Pot Lucke." Pot Lucke, as I understand the rules, worked like this: someone shows up at your cottage unannounced, and your obligation, whether you're feasting, fasting, praying, or reproducing, is to acknowledge your guest's need and act on it. You welcome him, despite the imposition, and you say, whether your guest is the nephew of the prince or, more likely, the pest of the hamlet, whether your crock is full of pungent dregs or royal stock, "What I have in the pot is yours; yours is the lucke of the pot." What you don't say, though it is nonetheless true, is "Don't you dare complain. Clearly, you're not in a position to make demands, or you wouldn't be showing up all unannounced and needy like this at a time, frankly, that's not really good for me. If you think you can do better elsewhere, by all means, go for it—no one's holding a musket to your head."

Pardon my Early Modern English. When I speculate on the reasons someone might show up unannounced like that, I get annoyed. Not so much because the guest is needy but because he displays his need so nakedly, so directly, so shamelessly, that he's willing both to ask for help and to receive it. The way I used to, when I was willing to identify myself as the guest. I get annoyed because I see myself as I used to be, as I'm not anymore, and I know that I have lost, to a large degree, this willingness to admit my need, to confess it, to act on it, to receive.

Somewhere along the line, I went from gladly identifying myself as guest to thinking it was about time I got to be the host, the one with something to offer. So you will not be surprised when I tell you that I haven't willingly attended a church potluck in a long time, not since my undergraduate years, when I was keenly aware of how much I needed and was willing to admit that need.

I know it's more complicated than that. I know there's no one-to-one correlation between my potluck problems and my personal problems. But I also know that when I have problems with the church, I should always seek to take them seriously. I want to take seriously, then, my problems, perhaps yours, with the church potluck.

Number one: the church potluck is unique in that everyone, regardless of wealth, class, status, or beauty can bring something to the table, has something to offer. Paper-plate dude, award-winning chili-master, body-odor guy, college kid, over-enunciating chorister, grocery-store-cookie buyer, beloved pastor, crooked preacher—all are invited, all are guests. We are in this together, so come, sit, eat.

I don't like that. I don't like being lumped together like that. I don't like how the potluck puts us all at the same table. I don't like that I often have to sit with someone I wouldn't otherwise choose to sit with. When that happens, what I'll say is "How are you doing? Tell me about your job, your dog, your stock portfolio." What I'm thinking is "He is so annoying. When is this going to be over?" What I'm believing is that you have nothing to offer me, that I have no need for you.

Number two: the potluck is a buffet. Whether the food is haute, ho-hum, or hell-no, the selection is limited. You do not get to order what you want. You must make the best of what's available. You are at the mercy of those who contribute to the meal.

I do not like that. I'm a picky eater, I confess, but it's more than that. Should someone remark on how wonderful everything looks, I'll say, "Mmmmm, yes, looks great." But what I'm thinking is "It's the same stuff every time. Can we not improve the menu? If I were in charge, this would be amazing." What I'm believing is that you have nothing to offer me, that I deserve better.

Maybe I'm reading too much into the church potluck, but I don't think so. I would like to justify my attitude toward the potluck as a reasonable critique of a superfluous tradition. But I know that I can find reasons to criticize or reject pretty much everything the church does. In fact, I occasionally catch myself thinking that I don't really need the church, that I can just skip the physical and go straight to the spiritual, push aside the means and deal directly with the ends. I know that's not true. I am no gnostic. But I get so desperate for spiritual communion that I'm terrifyingly ready to resent the people and their food for getting in my way: "I do not need your food," I convince myself, "Quit wasting my time. I deserve better."

I would hate to confess this, except that you are not shocked by my condition. You probably don't know me, but you know yourself. And you struggle with this, too. None of us wants twice-baked fish and over-seasoned loaves. What I want, what we all want, though we express it in different ways, is for God to come to us directly, to walk down from his hill and hold us, to tell us, directly and in his own words, that what we're doing is worthwhile, that we are loved.

That's why I groan, finally, over the church potluck. If anyone is going to feed me, I want Jesus to do it. I want him to be my host. I want to be his guest. In the meantime, I have the casserole queen and the pot-providence elder and the brownie-mouthed children, all of us desperate for the same thing. We are doing, each of us, what we can to host each other and to be each other's guests. At the church potluck, all distinctions between guest and host are gone. We are neither. We are both. We need more than we can say, more than we can give.

The church, I think, is God's way of saying, "What I have in the pot is yours, and what I have is a group of misfits whom you need more than you know and who need you more than they know. Take, and eat," he says, "and take, and eat, until the day, and it is coming, that you knock on my door. I will open it, and you will see me face to face." He is preparing a table. He will welcome us in. Jesus will be there, smiling and holy, holding out a green bean casserole. I will not care about the fried onions. And at that moment, what we say, what we think, and what we believe will be the same: "I didn't know how badly I needed this."

Potluck Drink and Quinoa Salad with Cucumbers and Feta Cheese

Quinoa (pronounced KEEN-wah) is a kind of grain, but not really, that originated in the Andes Mountains. It is high in protein and nutrients and is gluten-free. Quinoa has a mild, nutty flavor, and it is often used as an alternative to rice or couscous. This recipe is courtesy of Margie Haack of the Toad Hall Recipe Vault.

INGREDIENTS

Drink

Cups, preferably paper, at least 12 ounces

Salad

1 ½ cups quinoa

3 cups water

1 large (or two smallish) cucumber(s), peeled, quartered lengthwise, and chopped

1 red bell pepper, chopped

1/4 cup scallions, sliced thin

1/4 cup red onion, finely chopped

1/2 cup finely chopped fresh dill, cilantro, or parsley

1/4 cup kalamata olives, sliced or left whole (optional)

2/3 cup crumbled feta cheese

Dressing:

    1/3 cup olive oil

    1/4 cup balsamic vinegar

    2 ½ tablespoon honey

    1 tablespoon Dijon mustard

    Salt and pepper to taste

RECIPE

Drink

Remove the container or wrapper around the cups.

Find a spot near the end of the table, but before the drinks.

Set the cups down, in stacks of no more than 15, preferably upside-down to avoid tipping.

Watch others fill cups with whatever unnaturally colored beverage is available. Enjoy.

Salad

Rinse quinoa well before cooking to remove slightly bitter coating.

Place quinoa and water in a pan. Bring to a boil. Reduce heat, cover, and simmer for 15 minutes or until liquid is absorbed.

Place in a large bowl and allow to cool to room temperature.

In a large bowl, combine chopped vegetables including chopped herb of your choice.

Add quinoa, olives, and cheese and gently mix.

Add dressing, gently toss again, adding more salt and pepper if needed.

Cover and chill for 1 to 2 hours to allow flavors to blend.

Garnish with fresh herbs or sliced tomatoes and olives.

K. C. Lee grew up in the mountains of Colorado and Ecuador and then moved to the Last Frontier as a teenager, embarking on a life by the sea. Once owned by a sled-dog team, now a stage actor, dramaturg, writer, editor, student of natural health (a couple of doctorates loom), and repository of reams of useless trivia, K.C.'s time is divided between Alaska and Washington . . . and Texas . . . and Colorado . . . and points in between and beyond.

32

A Subsistence Feast

The path leading from the lagoon back to the cabin takes me right through the raspberry bushes. It's late evening, and the area is frequented by black bears, but the dusky aroma is heightened by the rising damp and I can't help but pause and hunt for fruit. Succulent ruby globes dangle in the branches, begging to be plucked and savored. Twirling one on its tenuous hold, I marvel at the symmetry, the plumpness, the appeal of this lovely berry. I fold the front of my faded shirt into a makeshift basket and pick until only a few fuzzy green nubs remain, as humankind has done for ages. The tartness of the first sampling rasps my teeth, but the second is summer in a bite, all juicy sweetness and warmth. I continue on my way up the twilit hill, more grateful than ever to be here.

I have come home to recover. Life has crushed my body and spirit and, like a skittish bride, I have run to the familiar for comfort. In ways everything is simpler here—no deadlines, no traffic, no social demands. Gone are the shows and the shops, the obligations and the oughts. The basics of life here, however, require more of my energies. I have the idea that these two realities will undo my pain and make some sort of sense of things. There is time enough and solitude enough to be intentional, but work enough to spur me out of bed in the morning. The boat must be launched and the running line cleaned and repositioned. Wood must be felled and chopped and managed. Water must be sourced and guided. The generator must be serviced and readied to power the freezer. Hauling takes up great chunks of days—something always needs hauling somewhere. And then there is food. Food here is not just what you consume, it is what you *do*.

I have come home for the rhythms of subsistence. My therapy consists of shuffling, bent, across a vast mountainside, picking blueberries and mulling life's mysteries. It is in the readying of hundreds of salmon to be dried or cured for the long winter, my *ulu* making the same steady cuts over and over again. It is in the raking of rocks and sand in search of rich clams, in the hanging of nets, the casting of lines, the harvesting of greens and ferns. In all of these rhythms I hope, I *expect* to once again recover myself and realign with God. It has always worked in the past.

I arrive during a particularly chilly spring. Too early for devil's club to encroach on the path to the outhouse. Too early for salmon to be in the bay. Too early for mosquitoes to whine elusively in the night. It is never too early, fortunately, to acquire kelp and clams, halibut and dulse, and I dive with gusto into nature's pantry. I have come with staples— brown rice, beans, salt, coffee, vinegar, oil, pasta, spices, lemons, lots of lemons—but with plans to live as much as possible off the land. There is nothing like the first helping of halibut caught just an hour before. Lusciously tender and silky, smothered in lemon butter and jalapeños— it is comfort and lightness in one. Or clams, roasted with garlic and olive oil, poured with their juices over just-done pasta—salty and sweet together.

My cabin snuggles on the lip of a small cove on Kachemak Bay on the lower end of Alaska's Kenai Peninsula. This is an introspective place in the spring. It does not have, even on its sunniest days, the sanguine friendliness of Hawaii, or the laid-back ease of the Rockies. It sits squarely at the melancholic end of the spectrum—breathing quiet awareness that life is tenuous and however glorious and livened the summer may be, lengthy winter darkness looms. Its beauty breaks your heart. Growth and decay are its constants. There is an atmosphere of solitary campfires in mist-filled woods, and the old Native legends seem entirely plausible as I paddle up the coast under low clouds, a chill sprucey breeze rolling down the blue mountainside.

As an antidote to my own sorrows, I have come prepared for a summer of glorious gathering, to feast my way through the days and fill the larder for colder months, but I have no sooner settled in than the word overtakes me.

Fast.

Is this the forest speaking, or God, or my own heart?

Fast.

Leave it all. Just leave it. Leave the forest. Leave the clam beds. Leave the set line and the kelp beds. Step back. Step away.

Were it my own idea, I could imagine it away, but this is divine prompting, an imperative I sense in my core. The timing makes me feel just as I did when as a child I was being scolded, I thought, unfairly. I have suffered loss upon loss already this year. And now, really? I am to fast?

I step back from forest and shore. I step back from food altogether. And I find that I am suddenly a stranger here. I am out of step with the rhythm of the place. The waves roll inexorably over the clam and kelp beds. The halibut rest peacefully on the sea floor. The trout make their way up the bay. The tides come and go and I hardly notice. I stay up late into the night, now never quite getting dark, and sleep late into the day, listless and uncaring that my woodpile is dwindling and my fuel is running low and nothing, nothing is getting hauled.

It has become a fast from subsistence—no harvesting now to enjoy later. No freezing or salting or pickling or drying. It is jarring, this marching off beat. It is walking ghostlike through my own natural home—disconnected from the ring of mountains, the contours of the bay, the towering trees that support my gently swinging hammock. The oneness I normally feel with this place dissolves. I wish I could lay claim to deep conversations with God, but the reality is deep wordless longing.

Inertia takes over my life. This won't do. I think of Thoreau's words: "To affect the quality of the day, that is the highest of arts. Every man is tasked to make his life, even in its details, worthy of the contemplation of his most elevated and critical hour." Convicted, I am propelled off the deck and take a long hike down the coast. A campfire, I think. Once warm, I walk to the water's edge. The volcanoes are out. Two of them are smoking. The earth is breathing. I begin to breathe. At my feet, wrack is swaying to the pulse of the sea.

It is OK, I am told. Surely this can't be right. What, after all, has changed?

Hesitantly, I pull a bunch and pop a few bladders between my teeth, filling my mouth with unmistakable, mucilaginous *ocean*. I listen for reassurance. The tide is receding, leaving pools that teem with sea urchins, crab, eels, limpets, snails, shrimp, fingerlings, mussels. Later the shoreline will be rich with beach peas, sea chickweed, lovage, and sea blite. The abundance is almost obscene.

It is OK. Dive in.

Inner guidance, that Quaker sensibility above conscience or moral values, has directed much of my journey, but the startling abruptness of this detour leaves me dazed, at a loss. Did I simply underappreciate the table spread before me? Did I need even this comfort stripped from me to learn deep thanksgiving?

I don't exactly dive in, but ease back into rhythm, so shaken with gratitude that I suddenly tear up as I rinse the day's clam take and snip the first young lettuces and set the salmon net, and take the first bite of the first meal, hardly able to eat. In fact, I am tearing most of the time, not entirely sure why. I am one small child, surrounded by riches beyond what I could ever use up. I will likely never know why I was placed here and not in the slums of Mumbai, Soweto, Rio, nor in the barrenness of the Gobi, the Sahara, the Atacama. I only know that I feel awe.

When I first arrived, my mind was like a mangled net washed ashore, knotted and useless. From the center out, my tensions are beginning to loosen and straighten and take on purpose. All of the overwhelming whys have fallen hush. In thankfulness there is some peace.

A fortnight later and I am realigned with the flow. Morning low tides find me out with my bucket—butter clams and cockles, razors and geoducks slowly but steadily coming to the surface. Standing in the flats, below sea level as it were, I feel I'm part of the clam bed, so very short and solidly in the mud. Afternoon high tides cut off beach access but free the boat for laying nets and trolling. This is also the time for foraging, drying plants, gathering wood, and the endless hauling hauling hauling of water, fuel, rocks. And always there is something needing repair—a hose, an eave, a front step, a motor. Mornings are cold and the fire must be stoked, water heated, weather assessed. Evenings are cold and the fire must be stoked, equipment stowed, everything bear-proofed. Only the most extreme conditions prevent the day's planned activities—rain or wind, cold or waves, subsistence gathering goes on.

The herring make their brief run through the bay and I have mere days to complete the time-consuming chore of filleting and salting the slender fish, and harvesting the roe-laden kelp. Kings will be running soon, and I will do still more cutting, this time in long strips for drying and smoking. This quiet, steady work affords hours to watch the loons and coyotes, the squirrels and sea otters. I throw scraps to the Steller's jays and magpies, the larger piles of guts becoming the spoils of epic battles between warring eagles and thieving ravens. Under vast skies I anticipate the bounty yet to come—blueberry pies and crowberry jam; grilled reds, their crispy skin crackling with a few flakes of sea salt; pickled kelp bulbs; baby octopus sautéed with coarse pepper; salmonberry *agutaq*; and *uuraq* cooked over a campfire with *sura* and wild celery.

Earlier in the year I cut ferns back extensively to force a new crop of fiddleheads. The tightly wound curls are perfect now and there are several patches close enough to the cabin that I needn't worry much about surprising a bear, though I'll take a whistle along anyway. Pocketknife and stainless bowl in hand, I kneel into the springy earth. I have been waiting for this day. Some of the fiddleheads I will sauté right away— olive oil, a spritz of lemon and sea salt. Others I will parboil and freeze, and the rest I will pickle for a few days to add to salads.

But my salads are not all wild. I spent many months on the road before arriving in Alaska, indulging the restlessness I always feel away from this place. One of my stops was Virginia, and I have come home with seeds from the garden at Monticello. Salty soil and salty air don't allow for the sort of extensive gardening I have enjoyed in other parts of the state, but containers protected from stormy sprays adequately provide me with strawberries, herbs, and greens—including, this year, brown Dutch lettuce and dill bred by Mr. Jefferson. The earthiness of these inland plants plays well against the saline subtleness of many of my local foods. Daily watering and weeding, pruning and harvesting, all become part of my routine. And overarching the entire summer—the fasting and the feeding, the cultivating and the foraging—pulses *joy*. This becomes the new rhythm of the place.

It is a glorious fall, with warm days and cold nights. The shorter hours of sunlight mean more candlelit evenings and more blankets on the bed. There are still a few berries that have not been eaten by bears or gone mushy. Most of the salmon are *maluqsuq*, their post-spawning, decayed bodies providing pre-winter bounty for eagle and bear alike, but a few viable specimens show up in the net. The clams are ever available. The kelp is always there. The dulse tastes just as sweet. The halibut can be found. I feel it is time for my own pre-winter feast.

An earlier visit from a friend who lives in the Interior is prompted by a subsistence swap—buffalo and caribou from his groaning freezer for halibut and salmon from mine. Ribs and steak sizzle on the grill alongside clams, mussels, and a marinated slab of halibut. White fish *agutaq*, pickled herring, and smoked salmon strips are on the table, along with a salad of second-crop lettuce, sea vegetables, beach peas, and pickled fiddleheads.

I enjoy my feast on the deck, bundled against the chill. The mergansers paddle slowly along the shoreline, their babies long gone. The bay is glassy, reflecting the mountains, now dusted with snow. Winter is coming, but the wealth of summer has left me well-provisioned, with more than enough to share. I am flush with joy. Time for a walk along the lagoon.

Uuraq

As I first learned it on Norton Sound:

Fill a pot with water from the river, and set the pot over campfire. Cast a couple of times until you pull in a nice, female humpy. Gut it, leaving the roe intact, and cut it into two or three pieces. Toss them into the pot. Add cut up onion, if you have one. Throw in a handful of *sura* (diamond-leaf willow leaves). Add salt and pepper. Boil a few minutes until the eyes and roe are opaque and the flesh is flaking off the bones. Ladle into bowls and drizzle with good, clear seal oil.

As you might make it at home:

INGREDIENTS

1 white onion, medium-chopped
2 celery sticks
Olive oil

2 quarts fish stock, preferably homemade

1 pound salmon steaks (or skinless fillets, if you prefer, although the result
   is less rich)

1 tablespoon fish sauce

1 jar salmon caviar

1 cup coarsely chopped bok choy

Coarse black pepper to taste

Sea salt (optional)

Sesame oil (optional)

2 tablespoons butter (optional)

RECIPE

In a stock pot, sauté the onion and celery sticks in a small amount of olive
oil just until soft.

Add the fish stock, salmon steaks, fish sauce, salmon caviar, and chopped
bok choy. Then add pepper to taste; the fish sauce and caviar are salty, so
taste before adding sea salt.

Bring to a boil and cook just until fish flakes apart

Drizzle the top with more olive oil. For a more smoky flavor, drizzle with
sesame oil instead. For a richer taste, use butter.

Laura Bramon Good lives in Washington, DC, with her husband Ben, where she works on human trafficking issues and blogs about life in an urban family commune. Her childhood culinary exploits revolved around church potlucks and family fish frys. Laura has contributed production and research to documentaries and educational television shows, and she has worked with international aid initiatives serving sexually exploited persons in Bolivia, Thailand, Nepal, and India. A former Milton Fellow and a Pushcart Prize nominee, her fiction and nonfiction have been published by *Image* and *Featherproof Books*, and she writes for *Image*'s Good Letters arts and faith omniblog. She received her masters in fiction writing from the Johns Hopkins University Writing Seminars.

33

Banqueting Table

There are two tables: the table of home and the table of far away. The table of home wears a soft white cloth; it bears a grid of bowls and scents, food piled high on crazed white china platters that Aunt Ida left in her farmhouse, beautiful things that her son has since given away. The table is so crowded with food that we only fill our plates here. We will sit in the small living room on straight-backed chairs and stiff couch pillows. We walk around the table: child, child, mother, father, stepping slowly, side to side, the closest that we ever come to dancing. Someday at my wedding, two friends will pull my grandpa up onto the makeshift dance floor, each of them taking one of his red, rough hands. Even then he steps in an uncertain circle, slow and careful, as if skirting that table. His hips barely move, his arms bow out. I see him dance, but even in the music and the laughter of the wedding feast, it is as if he stands before the table, the food, and all the people that, in childhood, I ever knew to

242

love. I hear him say the words of the prayer he has prayed at every meal I have eaten with him. I could recite that prayer, but I never will. We know, at that table, that every believer is a priest, but he is our priest and it is his prayer. It makes the table holy and steady; it binds us to each other.

The table of far away is in a yellow room where windows move. Sometimes light comes from the east, sometimes the south. There are bottles of wine and crates of beer and tureens of strange, spiced foods; there is the recklessness of wondering if I will fall in love. There are boys in shirtsleeves on the front porch, and tossed on the crumbling steps, there are red packs of clove cigarettes that girls will tap open when the party dwindles down. Faces shift, no one stays. This will not sadden me until all of it is gone. In memories, the faces run together, as if one feast leads to another. When the food is eaten, we sit on the steps in the dark, passing the same cigarettes back and forth, barely breathing in the sweet smoke. We stretch our sweaters around each other's shoulders as the stars come out, and when it is all over, we will remember the taste of each other's mouths, the wine and garlic and ginger that each pair of pink lips pursed around those cigarettes. We will marry the boys on the porch behind us, pipes tipped in their hands, the glow and steam of tobacco rising up around their faces. We will scatter from this table. We will never come back, because the table will disappear.

⤳

When I was eighteen, I met a boy I thought I could marry. I asked my father again and again: how do you know? He wrote me a letter naming all the things that would change with time: bodies, love, hopes, even faith, sometimes. Everything changes, he said. You will bind yourself to someone who will change, and in very dark moments, you will not know who he is. The letter silenced me; I was afraid. I could feel everyone I loved hanging like soft fruits of a tree, and the tree was made of human bones and words that do not change—promises, vows and creeds, and all the habits they require. It would be so easy for that tree to break, for a bough to crack and fall.

I was twenty before I sipped real wine from a Communion cup. By that time, the boy I thought I could marry was long gone. I knew the Revelation stories of the beasts and wars, but I barely knew the promise of the banquet. I was in another country where a woman held a chalice out to me; the table of home was far away. *The Word was God, and the Word was with God*; the Word kept human time together. But when I sipped that gold wine I saw, too, that God was a man who walked from table to table, crowd to crowd, always drinking, always eating, always seeking a lonely place. The hot taste on my lips and down my throat, a cord cut through the softness of my body. It was evensong, and walking home in the dark, I could feel each brick of the street beneath my feet. I could feel how strange it all was: to grow up, to grow away, to believe God was my bridegroom, and that time would end in a feast.

↭

I loved one of those boys on the front porch, and I brought him home to marry me. The women that I loved made all the food. Laid out on long tables, it was a known feast: bread, meat, flowers, cake. The church hall's round tables bore white tablecloths and candles; the room was full of family, the faces that stay, and up on the old stage, behind the black, pulled-back curtains, the friends from the disappeared table. The room was hot; the wood floor sweated. Beneath the food and perfumes you could smell its old pine musk. Someone threw the doors open to the night and snow was cold on the air. I wanted to press my face and hands to that cool glass, but my husband drew me to the dance floor. Held to his body, he kissed me, sealing me between those two lives: old and new, waning and gone. He was that tree, those words and promises; was I the fruit, a bough? There was no wine at that meal. There was water and punch, the kind that made me laugh, with its pink ring of ice and frozen strawberry studs. I knew that it would be there, a forgotten mark of feasting, and I was glad to taste it, to imagine it as something sacred, to drink it and remember the past and what was to come.

Brownies of Love

Because these brownies played an important role in my parents' courtship, they are sometimes called the brownies of love—and thought to be a home-grown aphrodisiac. You'll have to try them for yourself.

INGREDIENTS

3/4 cup cocoa
1/4 cup Crisco
(These two ingredients = 4 ounces of unsweetened chocolate)

2/3 cup Crisco
2 cups sugar
4 eggs
1 teaspoon vanilla
1 ¼ cups flour
1 teaspoon baking powder
1 teaspoon salt

RECIPE

Melt Crisco (*all*) and cocoa in a saucepan on medium heat.

Remove pan from heat and let it cool a bit.

Mix in the sugar and then mix in the eggs and vanilla.

In a separate mixing bowl, mix all the dry ingredients together. Add them to the chocolate mixture.

Spread in greased 4x13-inch pan. Bake at 350° F for 20 minutes.

From the kitchen of Becky Bramon

LESLIE LEYLAND FIELDS lives on Kodiak Island, Alaska, where she works with her husband and six children in commercial salmon fishing and cooks on an old Olympia oil stove. She used to carry her own water, milk goats, make yogurt, chop wood, and other delightful earthy activities but spends more of her time now writing, teaching, and speaking. She teaches in Seattle Pacific University's MFA program and is the author of seven books, including *Surviving the Island of Grace: Life on the Wild Edge of America* and *Parenting Is Your Highest Calling . . . and 8 Other Myths*. She believes in progress but doesn't believe in bread machines and will never stop kneading bread.

34

Making the Perfect Loaf of Bread

. . . you gave them bread from heaven for their hunger.
—Nehemiah 9:15

It's just after dinner. I know I should be working, but a recipe burns in my pocket. My eyes lock on the kitchen counter, my breadboard, on the tins of flour on the baker's hutch—and just three feet from there, my office door, behind which sits a deadline. An essay is due in six days, as many days as I have been carrying the recipe in my back pocket. I've known about this bread for months. Cooks I knew were giving up their traditional bread-making for this new method. I found it online, printed it, and have warmed it ever since with my body and my hope. I pull it out now. "Baking the Perfect Loaf of Bread," it reads in bold caps.[1] "Bread" alone would be enough to snag me.

1. The recipe in this essay is adapted from Jim Lahey, owner of Sullivan St. Bakery, http://www.sullivanstreetbakery.com/recipes.

Equipment:

  2 mixing bowls
  6-to-8–quart pot with lid
  Wooden spoon or spatula (optional)
  Plastic wrap
  Cotton dish towels (not terrycloth)

Is it this simple, then, assemble these few everyday materials from my cupboards and I will create perfection? I have been after it for years. For more than thirty summers on this Alaskan island where we commercial fish, I have baked all my family's bread, ten to fifteen loaves a week, sometimes by recipe but often not: pumpernickel, whole wheat, honey-oatmeal, buckwheat-sunflower, barley, baguettes, sourdough, flatbreads. The goods are served with every meal and quickly consumed, but I am often disappointed with my efforts. Sometimes the bread is too dry, the crust too soft, the crumb too dense; I've baked it too long, added too many whole grains—I know what I'm after: a thick outside crust that flakes like a wafer, a light inside with pockets of air, a crumb that stretches when you pull it apart and smells slightly sweet—heaven, perfection. My deadline can wait. I have another chance.

Formula:

  3 cups flour
  1 ½ cups water
  1/4 teaspoon yeast
  1 ¼ teaspoon salt
  Olive oil
  Extra flour, wheat bran, or cornmeal (for dusting)

I've never made just a single loaf of bread. Nor from so few ingredients. And no sugar for the yeast? It seems more like a recipe for unleavened bread, the kind the ancient Hebrew people made the night before they fled their captors. I think of them sometimes when I make bread—their story so improbable, sometimes like my own. I decide to suspend my disbelief and gather the simple ingredients on the countertop.

I have been making bread most of my life. I grew up making twenty-one loaves a week in a steel milking pail. There was no recipe but only a kind of order. It started with the pot of leftover seven-grain cereal that we were served every morning for most of our childhood. The leftovers were stashed in the refrigerator, in the pressure cooker the cereal was first made in. The next morning, the pot emerged, the potato masher came out to break up the globs of cereal, water and new grains were added to the old, and so it went on through the week, the same pot of gruel greeting us every morning. The six of us, my brothers and sisters and I, became adept at slipping out of the house without eating—but our hunger only fed the pot for the next morning. It all ended on Saturday when the pot was upended and its glutinous contents were pried out of the pressure cooker and plopped into the bottom of the pail. The quivering mass was soon met with whole-wheat flour, blackstrap molasses, sea salt, kelp powder, milk powder, and yeast, nothing measured.

Twenty-one loaves meant we could eat three a day. It took two loaves to make lunch for six kids. The extra loaf was our snack after we walked home from school—our only food between meals. We carried our sandwich to school down a mountain road in a brown paper bag, running the one-mile hill, the bread rattling in the bag like a snake. We didn't want it. It was all we had. My family had no income; my father seldom worked, but even necessity could not sweeten or lighten its weight.

⤶

Process:

Mix all the dry ingredients in a bowl. Add the water and blend with a wooden spoon or spatula for 30 seconds to 1 minute.

I try to follow the instructions exactly, but I am too good at disbelieving. I think of recipes as suggestions. The flour and water—blend for thirty seconds? It does not look like bread dough. It is shaggy and too soft. I trust my body, my eyes, my hands on a whisk, the feel of the thickness of a batter more than I trust a page with someone else's formulations. I trust the years of making bread and all I've learned from the bowls, the kneading board. Now, this is it? There's so little dough, it could fit in my hands, but I'm not to knead it or to touch it in any way. Even the Hebrews kneaded their flat bread, without even hoping it would rise.

I know what comes from not kneading. I barely kneaded those twenty-one loaves either, but I more than touched them. The pail was too deep and the contents too dense for a spoon. Two or three of us sisters, with long black hair and homemade clothes, between ten and fourteen years old when we began, rolled up our sleeves and took turns plunging our arms, mashing and squeezing the cereal, flour, and molasses into a homogenous mass before tilting the pail and easing it out onto the kitchen table. Our arms were gunked to the elbows—we gave it what we could. We scraped the slurry off, then floured the dough to keep our hands from sticking to it as we moved it about the table, folding and pushing apathetically. Kneading was hopeless—the bread always turned out the same no matter how long we worked the dough. We didn't know there wasn't enough gluten to inspire its weight. We didn't know it needed white flour, which my mother did not buy. We knew our mother was trying to feed us well, but we knew, too, this would never make good bread. When we pulled the pans from the oven, tipped them onto the kitchen table, the bread landed with a thud—dark brown, the size and weight of a brick. It was meant to nourish us, but we were still hungry. We stole candy from the store whenever we could.

We stopped taking the bread to school, eventually, each of us, on our own. For me, it was seventh grade, when a boy saw my same everyday sandwich as if for the first time. "Yuck! What *is* that?" he cried, scrunching his face in distaste. Others looked and chorused in. I never ate my lunch in school again.

In the desert, they said the same words when they saw the morning ground dusted in frost. *Man ha? What is it?* they asked each other, perhaps disgusted. They were hungry. They wanted bread, not frost or dust. Their own bread was gone, the dough they carried out of Egypt in kneading troughs swaddled in clothes and hoisted on their shoulders, and this was now their bread.

Their process was simple. Gather the *man ha* every morning, enough for the day, knead it, flatten, bake—it was white like coriander and honey-sweet, like wafers, light on the tongue. For forty years, their daily bread, fed from the clouds. They did not even have to ask for it and they always had enough. But they were not satisfied.

↩

With one eye on every word of the recipe, I am done with the measurements and mixing.

> Coat the inside of a second bowl with oil and set the dough in the bowl. Cover with plastic wrap and let the dough rest for 12 hours at room temperature.

Waiting is the hardest part of making bread for me. I will walk by the oil stove five times each rising and lift the cloth on the bowl set on the warming shelf to check the dough's growth. Most doughs need three hours for two risings. This requires twelve. What will I do in those hours the bread is making but I am not making it? I will go to bed. Does it require my inattention, then, to succeed?

Kneading is the secret to good bread, I learned after I left home. That and the right blend of flours. The loaves that crumble under a slicing hand, the stiff crumb, the bread that is airy and dense in the wrong places—I didn't use the enough white flour, or I didn't knead long or hard enough.

This is how you knead. You pull the dough from the bowl onto the breadboard, a board that should cover half the table. You need lots of room. Flour your hands, and flour the spill that breathes now, relaxing outward. It's still ragged, not yet formed, its surface cratered and still new. Lift beneath and pull the edges inward, halfway in. Press it into the middle. Pull the new outer edge on another side of the dough and press it in. Lean, use your whole body, fold and press, shape. Keep flouring if it sticks. The loaves you are making, whether it is two or ten, should feel like a single loaf right now, the surface soft as skin, the body elastic, both yielding and resisting. Under your hands, stroking with new flour, you are making a body. Look, feel it, how soft it is, how supple. You do not need a timer or directions. See, when you press it, it dimples and returns, alive.

∽

It is morning. I rush to the kitchen, to the glass bowl over the oil stove where it is warm. The dough has risen more than I expected. I pull the wrap off.

> Take the dough out of the bowl and fold once or twice. Leave it to
> rest 15 minutes in the bowl or on the work surface.

I lift the dough, glad for its weight in my hands at last. It is loose, like skin. Fold once or twice? The moment of handling is over.

It takes a body to make bread, I told Hannah that first summer she came to live with us, to help with a house and six children. She arrived at our island tight, angry, thin as a wire, at war with herself. I had been through that war, my siblings too. After our lost meals, the lunches hidden in our dresser drawers, the small, bitter food on our plates, when we left our house, we did not know how to live where meat and casseroles and pie rain on every table, where, without even asking, and without stealing, the ground is littered with bread. Do we eat for this day only or for all the days we missed and might miss ahead? When a hunger is long and deep, how do we measure "enough"? Surfeit could not answer, I found. Too much food sickened and addled. *If I cannot eat it all, then I will eat none*, but it was not long before absence consumed me.

Who would deliver me from this death? The babies. I ate to grow their bodies within me. I ate to fill my milk. My body was not mine to keep or starve. I entered the kitchen and cooked to grow us all whole and well.

I brought Hannah to the kitchen, and we stayed there that summer and the next. We stood before two cavernous bowls and table-sized kneading boards, pouring flour, proofing yeast, spilling golden olive oil, tossing in flax, bran, millet, both of us floured and pasty. We leaned over mounds of dough, pushing, folding, our bodies finding their own rhythm while I narrated the life and breath of yeast, the gluten's catch of air to raise the dough, how much extra gluten to add for the whole grains. We watched the whole-wheat bread together, all the way until we tipped the browned loaves onto racks, releasing a yeasty cloud, then thumping their base for the hollow echo back. We cut the first loaf still hot and ate, a cloud of steam from our mouths. *This is how you make bread.*

Seeded bread came next, then bagels, and then we did not bother with recipes, every batch a new creation. The best of our twinned efforts was a marbled bread, chocolate and egg bread rolled into a swirl, the two colors and flavors a nearly perfect spiral of rich sweetness we named "tiger bread."

Hannah gained ten pounds those summers. The second year she left our island, her face soft, she was going to work for a caterer; she was going to cooking school.

～

The dough has rested from its quiet work, relaxing into the counter where I have laid it. I watch it doubtfully and read on:

> Shape the dough into a ball. Generously coat a cotton towel with flour, wheat bran, or cornmeal; place the dough seam side down on the towel and dust with flour. Cover the dough with a cotton towel and let rise 1 to 2 hours at room temperature, until more than doubled in size.

I follow instructions, leaving the dough on the counter again under the towel. This bread will double again from a pinch of yeast? Every leavened bread that I know of takes four times as much for a single loaf. I think now of the meal that is coming next, what all of this is for. I will be setting this bread on the table for ten of us in a few hours. I am not sure even double this amount will be enough for everyone. Especially if it is good, as good as its name promises. If this bread is even close to perfect, I will need much more of it, not less. I should have doubled the recipe. My children won't have enough. Will I ever get it right?

Isn't it always this way? The crowds on the hillside that late afternoon, they didn't get enough, though they were filled past eating. He tore the bread, piece after piece, passed from one hand to another hand to a mouth and another, a banquet for thousands rising from a single lunch basket. They all ate until they stopped wanting to eat. Bread so good, so worth saving, the leftovers were gathered for another meal. But they wanted more. *A miracle!* they cried. *Give us a miracle! Give us man ha like our fathers ate!*

I know what he tells them. That he already has. That bread was him, that bread that fell like dust from the clouds—it was him, feeding them, feeding the world. And he's just done it again from the basket.

They are so sated, they have no hunger to hear. The question, *what is it?* asked for all those generations is answered. But it's not the answer or the kind of bread they want. It's not good enough. They are not satisfied.

Not even when he breaks his body and passes it to their plates, the best bread they will ever eat.

⌐

The dough has not risen double, but it is close and dinner is less than an hour away. I read the last steps:

> Preheat the oven to 450 to 500° F. Heat the pot in the oven for 30 minutes before baking. When the dough has risen double, remove the heated pot from the oven and set the dough in the pot, placing the seam side on top. Cover with the lid and bake 30 minutes.

Dinner will be late, then, by at least thirty minutes. I am using a cast-iron Dutch oven for my lidded pot. I heat the pot until it nearly smokes, slide my hands beneath the dough I have barely stirred, drop it into the heated pot, clap the lid on. I have not set the timer—this propane oven is old and the temperature gauge doesn't work. I remove the lid on my own guess, then watch the crust. I have never baked in such heat before.

I peer at it anxiously through the oven door while finishing the rest of the meal: venison stroganoff over egg noodles, a green salad with lettuce and radishes from our garden in my own balsamic dressing, a fruit salad, and this bread. I would have made the noodles myself, but I didn't have time, and most of the fruit in the salad is from cans. The lettuce from the garden is limp, the radishes wormy. I want better. I want this meal, every meal, to be bountiful and bright with color and health, grown and made by my own hands. I don't want my children to grow up as I did. I want them to sit at a table where the needy are filled and all wanting ended, a feast every day.

Hannah wanted the same those summers, for us and for her. Her bread was soon joined by flowery soups, marinated salmon, delicate cakes and pastries, all created by her hands, her art. She fed us and herself; we all ate well. But halfway through the second summer, her anger and intensity returned. She would not look at us, rarely spoke, wanted nothing else but the cooking. I let her take the kitchen, the bread pans, the table—I gave it over. She was cooking for reasons so much more desperate than mine, though I did not know them then. I did not know that, surrounded by a family and by food she now loved, she felt healed, so healed she stopped her medications.

Eight months later, the phone rang early Saturday morning, before breakfast. It was Hannah's mother. Hannah had refused to take her medications. She drifted away from her family and friends. They found her in her room; she had taken her life.

My daughter put a cross up on the hill; I named our bread, "Hannah's Tiger Bread."

It could not save her, then, my kitchen, our table. It wasn't enough.

⤙

> Take off the lid and bake 15 to 30 minutes uncovered, until the loaf is gently browned.

I open the oven finally, the heat a furnace on my face, pull the pot out by its iron hoop handle, set it on the stove. Is it finished? More than finished—I have baked it too long. The dinner is late and everyone is waiting for me. I look at them, children, husband, crewmen, all here from working on the water. They watch me struggle with the heavy pot. "What is it?" they call from their benches, not knowing bread can come from such a pot. I tip it, the bread falls, a thick wedge of steaming crust. There is not enough for all of us, I fear. The crust is too hard and dark. It should cool before we eat it, but we are hungry and its breath rises, fills the room. I hold it in one hand, slice it, wrap its heat into a cloth basket, and set it on the table.

We join hands around the table, pray thanks. The bowls are lifted, the basket is handed down, followed by the butter. Flatware clinks against the stoneware plates; one pours iced tea for another. There is talk about the tide rips, the nets filled with kelp, each one's work on the salmon nets that morning. Stroganoff and questions and jokes are exchanged, answered with fruit, noodles, stories, bread. I watch and hear it all from my end of the long, full table, passing the food by me as it comes, not even needing to eat. "This is really good," I hear. "What kind of bread is this?" another asks. "This is the best bread you've ever made," from a son who seldom compliments. The basket passes again to eager hands, comes to me. I reach, butter, bite. The crust is thick, the crumb is soft and moist. I close my eyes and chew. It is not perfect. It should be lighter, a little less chewy, but it is good, maybe the best bread I have served all year, closer to my ideal than I have come before.

I am saddened. Will I give up kneading, then?

"How did you make this?" my daughter asks. How do I tell her? I didn't, really. This is not mine; this is like my childhood bread: so little of this is the doing of my hands. I was told what to use. I followed someone else's formula. I didn't lean my own body into it. I didn't press and shape it into life. It is not my work but the patient work of hours I spent sleeping, while the yeast exhaled gasses, caught by the gluten, then transformed in the magic of heat and steam—none of this mine, all borrowed. How can I rightly claim it? I look around the table. How little of this is mine: the fruit from a can, the noodles from a bag, the plates from a cannery across the bay, the deer from the hillside, the money to buy the flour, the sun that grew the wheat . . . even these children, not mine. I bore them and fed them but I did not make them: all borrowed, all given, not the work of my hands. Suddenly I know it *is* the perfect loaf of bread.

Perfect, I remember, means finished, complete.

Like the bread I ate with my siblings this winter, white bread from cellophane made by a machine. We tossed it in a microwave and dropped it in a cloth on a plate for our first shared meal in sixteen years. We had gathered from across the country to see our dying father, who neither loved nor fed us. The last night before we scattered to our homes again, we bought a meal from the store and set it on the table in our rented house: shrimp and steak, green salad, baked potatoes with sour cream, and chocolate cake, most of it already made. The platters kept circling, the store-bought bread kept passing, until our plates spilled over and the hungry brothers were filled, the hidden lunches forgotten, the sisters satisfied. We sat for a long time after the food was gone, joining our distant lives, needing each other again, and we *knew*—everything was *perfect*.

I look around this table now, the stroganoff and salads soon gone, the breadbasket already empty, and still we sit. I know we will need to eat again, all of us, that nothing I can make or buy will cure the body's wants for long, but look how filled we are! It is not my making that fills us. The work of my hands is undone without the sun on the wheat, the ones I love who come to eat, the one who fed us his body, his life.

Even the Maker of the world did not make the bread he broke that final night: the grain was grown by a farmer down the road, the bread was made by someone he did not know, bought and carried by another up to a borrowed room. He laid his hands on someone else's bread, blessed it, and claimed it—*this is my body*—and passed it to waiting hands, to every hungry soul. And it was done. Their bread became his bread became ours—so many hands upon the bread until it was finished: the bread of his body for the hunger of the world.

Our dinner is almost done. "Is the bread all gone? Someone asks. I rummage in the cloth, "Yes, sorry there wasn't enough. I'll double it next time."

I know now how to make the best bread. I know what to claim. The bread I make, kneaded or not, isn't mine—it is ours. We pass our work from hand to hand like a breadbasket down a clamoring, joyful table. As we reach into the warm cloth, take and butter and eat—bread that is dry or crusty, crumbling, brick-heavy or wafer-light—we look around the crowded table at one another and say, "Isn't it *perfect*?"

Hannah's Tiger Bread

INGREDIENTS

3 packages active dry yeast

3/4 cup warm water (body temperature)

1 ½ cups warm buttermilk

1 cup sugar

2 teaspoons salt

3 eggs

2/3 cup melted butter or margarine

1 tablespoon vanilla

1/2 cup cocoa

2/3 cup chocolate chips or to taste

7 ½ to 8 cups flour (white or a blend of whole wheat and white)

1/2 cup flax

Cornmeal

Makes 2 loaves

RECIPE

Dissolve the yeast in the warm water.

Stir in the buttermilk, sugar, salt, eggs, vanilla, and butter, and mix these ingredients together until they are blended.

Add the flax and 4 cups of flour. Beat until smooth. It should be the consistency of cake batter.

Divide the dough in half by pouring it into 2 mixing bowls. The bowls will have about 2 ½ cups of "batter" each. The vanilla and chocolate dough will be kept separate until the bread is shaped for its final rise.

Add the cocoa to one batch. Blend until smooth. Add the chocolate chips.

Mix in the remaining flour to each batch, between 2 and 2 ½ cups each, until the dough is soft, but not sticky, and easy to handle.

Turn each batch of dough onto a lightly floured board and knead each one until it is smooth and elastic, at least 5 minutes.

Place each batch in a greased bowl. Rub butter or oil over the top so the dough does not dry while rising.

Cover with a cloth. Let it rise in a warm place until it doubles in size (1 ½ to 2 hours).

Punch down the dough. Divide each batch of dough in half, so you have even pieces of dough: 2 chocolate, 2 vanilla.

Begin with a piece of vanilla dough. Roll it out in a rectangle to about 1/4-inch thick.

Take one of the chocolate dough pieces and roll it out to roughly the same size. Place the chocolate dough on top of the vanilla dough. Roll the dough pieces up and place them seam side down onto an ungreased cookie sheet sprinkled with cornmeal. Do this again with the other pieces of dough. Cover and let rise until double, about 1 hour.

Heat oven to 350° F. Bake 35 to 40 minutes, until browned.

Set immediately on wire rack to cool.

Wait at least 20 minutes before the first slice—you can't taste the flavors when it's too hot!